THE BOOK OF
BROADWAY MUSICAL DEBATES,
DISPUTES, AND DISAGREEMENTS

THE BOOK OF
BROADWAY MUSICAL DEBATES, DISPUTES, AND DISAGREEMENTS

BY PETER FILICHIA

APPLAUSE
THEATRE & CINEMA BOOKS
Essex, Connecticut

APPLAUSE
THEATRE & CINEMA BOOKS
An imprint of Globe Pequot, the trade division of
The Rowman & Littlefield Publishing Group, Inc.
4501 Forbes Blvd., Ste. 200
Lanham, MD 20706
www.rowman.com

Distributed by NATIONAL BOOK NETWORK

Library of Congress Cataloging-in-Publication Data

Names: Filichia, Peter, author.
Title: The book of Broadway musical debates, disputes, and disagreements / Peter Filichia.
Description: Essex, Connecticut : Applause Theatre & Cinema, 2022. | Includes index. |
    Summary: "Peter Filichia has written six books on theater and has written for Playbill,
    Theatermania, Broadway Select, Encore, and more. He serves on the nominating committee for
    Lucille Lortel Awards, Theater World Awards, and Drama Desk Awards, the latter of which
    he was president for four terms. He's been a National Endowment for the Arts assessor and
    Cincinnati Conservatory of Music critic-in-residence. Currently, he is the musical theater judge
    for ASCAP's awards and a Broadway Radio commentator" —Provided by publisher.
Identifiers: LCCN 2022006619 (print) | LCCN 2022006620 (ebook) | ISBN 9781493067947
    (paperback) | ISBN 9781493067954 (epub)
Subjects: LCSH: Musicals—New York (State)—New York—Miscellanea.
Classification: LCC ML1711.8.N3 F52 2022 (print) | LCC ML1711.8.N3 (ebook) | DDC
    782.1/4097471—dc23
LC record available at https://lccn.loc.gov/2022006619
LC ebook record available at https://lccn.loc.gov/2022006620

CONTENTS

The author would like to thank David Benkof, Aubrey Berg, Bari Biern, Ken Bloom, Wayne Bryan, Jay Clark, Jason Cocovinis, Drew Cohen, Dan Dietz, Josh Ellis, Scott Farthing, Don Gagnon, Ed Gaynes, Freddie Gershon, Alan Gomberg, Erik Haagensen, John Harrison, Kenneth Kantor, Charles Kirsch, Skip Koenig, James Marino, Kevin McAnarney, Ethan Mordden, Richard C. Norton, Andrew Parks, Michael Portantiere, Lee Roy Reams, Paul Roberts, Howard Rogut, David Schmittou, Steven Suskin, Robert Viagas, and the late, great David Wolf.

Last but hardly least, Linda Konner, my agent in literature and in love.

INTRODUCTION

This book is for completely dedicated musical theater fans.

And how are such people defined?

You're a completely dedicated musical theater fan if you can remember where you were standing and what you were doing when you heard that Patti LuPone was having her hips replaced.

You're also qualified if you believe that those who don't like musicals are Children of a Lesser God.

In addition, you hate at least one musical that most everyone else loves *and* you love at least one musical that most everyone else hates. You can also give scores of reasons why you don't like certain scores.

And just let anyone try to convince you otherwise.

Musical theater enthusiasts learn early on that we can't agree on everything. When a bunch of us get together and start trading opinions, if we occasionally see eye to eye, that counts as one of the hundred million miracles that happens every day.

But far more often than not, civilized discussions turn to heated arguments and opinions are stated as incontrovertible facts.

So here's a book to make your blood boil—well, I should say! As Passionella sings in *The Apple Tree*, "That's what I'm here for"—dispensing one man's opinions on many musical theater matters.

You're well within your rights to respond:

"What?! How could he possibly think that!"

"Huh?! How could he leave out (fill-in-the-blank)?!"

"Did he simply ignore (fill-in-the-blank?!) or just forget?"

"Is he kidding!?"

"Is he *crazy?!*"

On the other hand, maybe every now and then you'll find yourself nodding your head in agreement when you see the conclusions that your author has reached.

In terms of structure, we're taking a leaf out of the Tony Awards playbook. Most of the time, a Tony category has five nominees and an eventual winner. As a result, far more often than not, we'll have five "nominees" in each category, one of which will be an "Author's Choice" that names the "winner."

Sometimes there'll be fewer nominees, just as the Tonys have had. In 1995, the nation heard "The nominees for Best Musical are *Smokey Joe's Café . . . Sunset Boulevard . . .* and the Tony goes to—."

And then there was Aaron Tveit's uncontested win for *Moulin Rouge.*

Conversely, there will on occasion be six, which has been known to happen in certain Tony categories, too.

Theater, as we know, is ephemeral. A case can even be made that these days, the only time we even *hear* the word "ephemeral" occurs when someone talks about theater.

Granted, this isn't as true as it used to be. Videos, be they professionally or surreptitiously shot, have captured many shows and performances in the last four decades.

But alas, comparatively few alive today saw *Gypsy* with Ethel Merman, Angela Lansbury, Tyne Daly, Linda Lavin, Bernadette Peters, *and* Patti LuPone to say with any authority which one was the definitive Broadway Rose.

Fewer still are alive today who saw the original *Oklahoma!* even toward the end of its then-mammoth run. Happily, since 1943, when the cast of *Oklahoma!* went into a Decca studio and made the original cast album, a legitimate part of theater and recording history, generations have had some idea of which Broadway personalities were wonderful and which ones weren't.

Thus, most choices will be selected from *Oklahoma!* and beyond.

Don't look for detailed plot synopses for the hits; those will be few, for summations of those musicals can be found in dozens of other tomes.

However, you will find synopses for lesser-known musicals just in case you missed these short-running shows.

All set? To quote the name of a 1943 Rodgers and Hammerstein musical that played New Haven and Boston (before its title was changed for Broadway), *Away We Go!*

CHAPTER ONE

Debating the Musicals

WHEN A TIME MACHINE IS INVENTED, WHAT MUSICAL WOULD YOU FIRST RETURN TO SEE?

Girl Crazy (1930). When Ethel Merman hit that high-C for sixteen bars in "I Got Rhythm," did the first-nighters scream halfway through as they would today? At the end, did anyone go "Whooo!" Or did applauding in awe suffice?

Another Evening with Harry Stoones (1961). Barbra Streisand's one and only off-Broadway show opened on October 21, 1961, and closed on—yes—October 21, 1961.

Diana Sands, the original Beneatha in *A Raisin in the Sun*, was in it, too; so was ever-so-delightfully silly comedian Dom DeLuise.

With those three on board, could it really have been that bad? We'll never know.

Yet here's the real question: Had we been there, would we have said "Gee, that young woman whose first name was misspelled in the program is really something"?

(Probably.)

1776 (1970). Stuart Ostrow produced the Tony-winning musical on Broadway but decided not to bring a company to London. So Alexander H. Cohen, the Broadway producer who had little luck or wisdom with musicals, did the honors.

Ostrow must have inferred that The West End wouldn't welcome a show with such lines as "The king is a tyrant" and such lyrics as "We say to hell with Great Britain!"

1776 closed after 168 performances, less than a tenth of the Broadway run. Cohen, not Ostrow, suffered the slings and arrows while losing an outrageous fortune.

***South Pacific* (1984).** No, not a business-as-usual production with Mary Martin or someone like her. Director Anne Bogart offered quite the rethinking at New York University.

More than three dozen actors played war-scarred World War II veterans who'd be introduced to the Rodgers and Hammerstein musical. Their caretakers hoped that its optimism, be it cockeyed or grounded, would help them return to a happier civilian life.

A doctor simply watched and said not a word. The nurses and interns were played by the five musicians. (Did John Doyle see this production on a trip to New York?)

Sounds crazy, no? Don Shewey in *The Village Voice* would later write that "this *South Pacific* was hilarious and sexy. What made it chilling was the way it captured today's yuppie conformism to a tee."

As Jerry Herman's big uptown hit was then asking "Who knows? Who knows? Who knows?"

Author's Choice: *The Cradle Will Rock* (1937). Take me back to Manhattan on June 17, 1937, to the Maxine Elliot's Theatre at 109 West 39th Street. Let me join six hundred audience members who are arriving to see the opening of bookwriter-composer-lyricist Marc Blitzstein's *The Cradle Will Rock*.

What we find is that the Works Progress Administration Federal Theatre Project has been shut down and shot down by the Feds. They've literally padlocked the theater's doors.

Apparently some of their powers-that-be have seen a rehearsal or a run-through. They've found the show too anti-government, anti-capitalistic, anti-religion, et cetera, et cetera, et cetera. The Feds have forbidden the show to open.

The government agents also frowned on the implication that the steel industry wasn't fair to its employees. Only three weeks earlier, eighty thousand steel workers had gone on strike and would be out for four months more. Although the forges weren't burning, this show could fan the flames.

Under these dire circumstances, most producers and directors would say "The padlocks are on our wrists as well as the doors." That's not the style of two future legends: John Houseman, *Cradle*'s producer, and Orson Welles, its director. They'll just find another theater, that's all.

But even if they do, how can the show go on? The fifty-nine-member cast consists of those who are in actuality government employees, and thus aren't allowed to perform on stage. Actors' Equity president Frank Gilmore agrees.

Houseman and Welles circumvent that dictate with an ingenious loophole. If the actors are merely seated in the audience and stand when each is scheduled to speak or sing, they won't "perform on stage." Abe Feder, now in the fourth year of what would be a nearly half-century Broadway career in lighting design, will shine a spotlight on each individual when he or she starts a line or dialogue or a song.

Now Gilmore points out that any cast members who aren't Equity members may not perform in a commercial enterprise in a commercial house . . . unless they join his union. That'll be fifty-nine dollars for the first year's dues, please.

In today's money, that's $1,185. And the Great Depression still isn't over.

Press agent Helen Deutsch has money, and she'll pony up. (Luckily, in the years to come, Deutsch will make that back and more for writing a short story on which the 1961 hit musical *Carnival* is based.)

What of the musicians? The twenty-six-piece orchestra consists of government employees, too. They too would have to be paid rates commensurate to Broadway. Deutsch's pockets aren't that deep, so Blitzstein will accompany the performers on a piano. But what if the theater they find doesn't have one?

So while Houseman searches for a house, Jean Rosenthal—the future acclaimed lighting designer but at the time a production manager—is sent to find a piano. She eventually does and even resourcefully hails a truck whose bribed driver gets the upright into his trailer.

Now they must ride around the block and stop whenever she spots a pay phone. Rosenthal hopes to discover where to deliver the instrument, but where she'll stop, nobody knows.

Finally, after more than an hour, Rosenthal learns The Venice Theatre on Seventh Avenue and West 58th Street has been engaged. The house will be hastily put into service at the cost of one hundred dollars ($1,896 in today's dollars). The real surprise is that the reporters who were covering this story put up most of the money.

Oh, to be one of the one hundred or so game theatergoers who form a veritable parade as they walk twenty blocks uptown to see this new work. Passersby ask what they're doing, are told, and join the march. Their numbers swell to about twenty-five hundred by the time everyone reaches the Venice. There's not an empty seat and plenty of standees.

Blitzstein begins playing and singing. Imagine the pressure on Olive Stanton, who has the show's first words. Will she stand and sing them? Actresses with lesser fortitude wouldn't have had the courage to rise on cue, for they'd be fearful that the law would arrest them and arrest their careers as well.

Stanton stood, sang, and set the tone for all to follow suit, each standing when the time came to perform. The result was a unique night in musical theater history.

What Were the Best Musicals of Each Decade?

Musicals with original scores will be the only ones eligible here. Jukebox musicals belong in a separate category, and will get their due after we examine the musicals of the last eight decades.

We'll go along merrily as *Merrily We Roll Along* rolled along: backwards in time from the most recent decade back to the 1940s.

The 2010s?

The Book of Mormon (2011). When the creators of *South Park* collaborate with the composer of *Avenue Q*, you can expect naughtiness that's on a much higher level than *Naughty Marietta*.

Matt Stone, Robert Lopez, and Trey Parker took plenty of risks with this one. They spoofed a religion that's dear to more than sixteen million, dealt with female circumcision, and used a vulgarism for vagina that had made many women slap the faces of those who dared to use it in their presence.

At *The Book of Mormon*, some of those same women were using their hands to applaud wildly.

Elf **(2012).** Who'd expect that this Christmas musical would contain such a significant piece of dialogue?

North Pole resident Buddy the Elf has learned that he's really Buddy the Human. He comes to New York City to find his actual father and winds up in the man's office. Buddy's the type of guy who finds childish delight in everything and is naturally affectionate—so exuberant, in fact, that he runs over to Jim, one of his father's employees, hugs him tight and lifts him high off the ground.

To which Jim says, "I already have a boyfriend!"

Many of us remember a time when Jim would have reacted in horror. He would have given Buddy a startled look that said "You're crazy!" or a disgusted one that said "You're queer!" before he'd have run off in horror.

Such a situation would have passed for humor; indeed, the audience would have laughed at the plight of a heterosexual man enduring an ostensibly gay man.

That bookwriters Thomas Meehan and Bob Martin even dared to insert the line in a "family musical" show, and they had confidence that today's parents wouldn't hear the quip, wince, screech, and put their hands over the children's ears.

God bless us, everyone.

Matilda **(2013).** Although the Dennis Kelly–Tim Minchin musical had a fine 1,554-performance run, its London edition, which opened in 2011, has played nearly three times as long and is still on the boards as of this writing. So why didn't *Matilda* run longer and win the Best Musical Tony that went to *Kinky Boots*?

An oft-heard complaint during intermission was "I can't understand a word those kids are saying!"

The four West End actresses who alternated as Matilda were all nominated and won the Olivier Award (London's Tony).

The four Broadway actresses received no Tony nominations, let alone the award.

This doesn't mean that there are more talented moppets in London than in New York. No, British kids were delivering dialogue and songs in their "native language"; American child performers had to adopt British accents that were unnatural to them.

When Roald Dahl's novel *Matilda* was turned into a 1996 non-musical film, it was Americanized; so should have this musical. Note that the 2000 Broadway musical version of the 1997 film *The Full Monty* (2000) changed its locale from a northern England town to Buffalo and thus avoided the language issue.

Granted, *The Full Monty* only ran half as long as *Matilda*, but it didn't have the youth appeal so vital to today's success on Broadway. But it did run almost two years, which it might not have accomplished had the audience been expected to decipher thick accents for two-plus hours.

A Gentleman's Guide to Love & Murder (2013). How could Robert L. Freedman and Steven Lutvak make murders be funny?

A prologue "A Warning to the Audience" ameliorated: "Those of you who may be faint of heart ... before we start you'd best depart ... an usher fainted in the aisle, a nun from Leicester lost her wits."

Set designer Alexander Dodge immeasurably helped by placing another stage atop the actual one at The Walter Kerr Theatre. This smaller version of an English music hall sported six very old-fashioned gold scalloped footlights. Two fanciful pillars, each of which had a bas-relief bust of some prominent Roman, supported an elegant proscenium arch with statues of little cherubic angels atop it.

The set almost resembled a dollhouse, which one doesn't associate with murders. With its set within a set, *Gentleman's Guide* could read as a musical within a musical. It took the show one step further away from reality so that we weren't appalled by all the blood-letting.

Dear Evan Hansen (2016). Some dislike this musical because Evan tells one lie after another. Yes, but consider his motivation.

After Connor Murphy's suicide, Evan sees how the boy's parents are grieving. He wants to alleviate their pain, so he tells them what they want and need to hear, and is nervous throughout.

When Connor's sister takes a romantic interest in him, he's grateful to finally have a girlfriend but is never cocky about all the good things that are happening to him.

Evan's lies come from a noble place. He has a heart, which is why he wants to help the Murphys heal their broken ones.

The message that one lie leads to another and then another has been a topic in many stories. The point was made stronger by the presence of social media that bookwriter Steven Levenson as well as songwriters Benj Pasek and Justin Paul well established.

In an earlier era, Evan's lies wouldn't have been able to go viral. But this electronic virus turns out to be just another malady that the unfortunate Evan must encounter. Let's feel sorry for him rather than blame him.

Author's Choice: *Hamilton* (2015). Lin-Manuel Miranda is one of those rare musical theater writers who was able to follow his freshman Best Musical Tony winner (*In the Heights*) with an even greater success.

Alexander Hamilton was one of the country's many immigrants who reminds us that "we get the job done." Although Hamilton recognizes that "New York City is insidious," he also sees possibilities and proclaims "I am not throwing away my shot!"

This line is repeated so much that it's a wonder that Aaron Burr didn't sing it before shooting Hamilton dead. (We're glad that he didn't.)

Miranda quickly establishes each man's character. After Burr advises "Don't let them know what you're against or for," Hamilton says "You can't be serious!"

Burr's oh-so-careful, oh-so-planned, oh-so-political machinations don't yield what he'd expected. He's so jealous of Hamilton's rise that gives rise to the first conservative versus liberal battle in American history.

As for Miranda's music, rap certainly wasn't heard in the late eighteenth century. Although anachronistic, its inherently angry and agitated sound works for this period of intense tumult.

Hamilton offers the grandchild of Sondheim's "Someone in a Tree" as the uninvited Burr wonders what Hamilton, Jefferson, and Madison are deciding in their closed-door meeting. "The room where it happened," he snarls. Beneath the red, white, and blue bunting is a green-eyed monster.

Meanwhile, Hamilton's wife Eliza loves him very much, but his infidelity makes her snarl "I hope that you die!" She'll get her wish before wishing that she could take it back.

Miranda doesn't forget George III. "You'll Be Back," the king inaccurately predicts to his previous subjects. The confident melody could just as easily serve a spurned lover who staunchly believes that the person who did the dumping will soon be sorry.

If God is in the details, the Supreme Being has blessed Miranda. What a powerful line is "Your perfume tells me your father has money." Musical theater writers are urged not to write "on the nose," meaning to say things in the most obvious way. Miranda abides.

Considering that the term "ground-breaking" has been so often used when describing *Hamilton*, its line "A revolution is happening in New York" turned out to be an inadvertent comment about the show.

Miranda described his title character as "young, scrappy, and hungry." The first two still apply to his own life, but he'll never be hungry again.

The First Decade of the Twenty-First Century?

Hairspray (2002). Twenty-five years after *Annie* had opened at the Alvin, we had another fairy tale at the same (albeit renamed) theater.

Tracy Turnblad's winding up with Link Larkin is as unlikely as Annie's getting the world's richest man to adopt her. As for Tracy's mother, we'd like to think that a wife that ample would still have a husband that was desperately in love with her. However, if you can't have fairytales in musical comedy, where can you have them?

But why was a great line dropped in "Mama, I'm a Big Girl Now"? The B-section once had "Mom, you're always telling me to act my age! Well, that's just what I'm trying to do!"

Don't we all wish that we'd had the presence of mind when we were teens to say that to our mothers when they levied that charge against us? Indeed, we were *acting* our age; what they wanted was for us to act *their* age.

***Avenue Q* (2003).** The time-honored policy for puppeteers is that they'd be masked in black from head to shoes. That way, no one would be distracted from the puppets who'd create their own little world.

Avenue Q unapologetically showed the performers in street clothes. Songwriters Robert Lopez and Jeff Marx didn't plan it that way. They were writing a musical that they hoped would wind up on television, where only puppets would be seen.

For a reading at the York Theatre Company, *Sesame Street*'s puppeteers John Tartaglia, Stephanie D'Abruzzo, Rick Lyon, and Lara MacLean were in full view. After the presentation, so many attendees not only told Lopez and Marx that the show should be a stage musical, but also that the facial expressions from the puppeteers were such fun that they should be seen and not just heard.

The two writers took both pieces of advice and saw *Avenue Q* run six years on Broadway and nearly ten more off-Broadway. I wonder how many professional puppeteers have since come out of their closets with their best clothes on?

***Urinetown* (2001).** Has any musical ever triumphed over so terrible a title? As daring as it was, more daring still was killing off the hero—one we'd come to love—midway through the second act.

The creators set the anything-can-happen tone even before we heard a word or note. A no-nonsense policeman brought a distraught looking man on stage. We wondered what the poor guy did.

Practiced his piano, no doubt, for the cop took him to an upright, sat him down, and had him play the Overture. From its first notes, it sounded very Kurt Weill-ian—fitting, for *Urinetown* is the grandchild of *The Threepenny Opera*.

In the Heights **(2007).** *Bubbling Brown Sugar,* a 1975 revue, did it first. It took us to Harlem and showed theatergoers that it was more of a fun part of the world than a dangerous place.

Lin-Manuel Miranda's first Tony-winning musical did the same for Washington Heights. He showed us a community of people who cared about each other. Some say that the friends you make become your real family; here, real families and honorary ones merged nicely.

Wicked **(2003).** Ben Brantley of the *New York Times*—the critic who most counted—called Stephen Schwartz and Winnie Holzman's show a "sermon of a musical," a "bloated production that might otherwise spend close to three hours flapping its oversized wings without taking off." He felt it was an "indignant deconstruction of L. Frank Baum's *Oz*" and that "its swirling pop-eretta score sheds any glimmer of originality."

Brantley wasn't finished. *Wicked,* he thought, "so overplays its hand that it seriously dilutes its power" and "wears its political heart as if it were a slogan button." Peppered throughout were such words as *colorless, plainness,* and *loses* before Brantley concluded that "*Wicked* does not, alas, speak hopefully for the future of the Broadway musical."

For most of the twentieth century, such a review from the *Times* would have meant that ads in that very paper would soon scream "Last four performances!" Instead, *Wicked* showed that it was the *New York Times* that no longer spoke for the American musical.

Longtime Broadway observers often say that *Seussical* (2000) was the first musical victimized by internet chatters. Conversely, *Wicked* was the first musical saved by reviews written by many an amateur (a term meant affectionately; after all, the word does mean "one who loves").

Those posting on the internet—especially teenage girls who could identify with outsider Elphaba—helped *Wicked* to run cumulatively longer than all of Stephen Schwartz's five other Broadway musicals—and that even includes the revivals of his *Godspell* and *Pippin.*

Elphaba continues to defy gravity just as *Wicked* continues to defy the *New York Times.*

Author's Choice: *Caroline, or Change* **(2004).** Young Noah is always leaving his change in his pockets when he leaves his pants to be cleaned by maid Caroline. Mrs. Gellman, in order to teach her stepson a lesson, tells Caroline that she can keep any change she finds.

Noah doesn't mind, for he heroine-worships Caroline. ("The president of the United States . . . stronger than my dad!")

Caroline sees herself quite differently. "Thirty-nine and still a maid. I thought for sure by now that I'd be better off than this." Noah will purposely leave a few shekels for her, although Caroline tells both him and his stepmother that she doesn't want the coins that she finds.

Yet she does find herself taking them so that she can give her three young children *lagniappes*. (The show takes place in Louisiana.) This scene, an hour into the musical, is the first time we ever see Caroline smile.

She can't afford to dispense little gifts very often, for she only makes thirty dollars a week. This is more telling when one realizes that *Caroline, or Change* takes place in 1963—literally thirty years after Flora Meszaros (*Flora, the Red Menace*) was making that precise salary—and during the Great Depression, yet.

What Caroline wants is a completely different kind of change. But life is "same as yesterday; same as tomorrow."

Then Noah inadvertently leaves in his pants the twenty dollar bill that his grandfather gave him. This Caroline will take. When Noah realizes his mistake, he demands to have it back.

Caroline at first refuses, but she eventually gives in.

What a great metaphor to suggest that yes, the white privileged want to be accommodating to Blacks—but only to a point. Moreover, Blacks in that pre–Civil Rights era were often forced to pass up opportunities because whites simply didn't want them to have them.

The 1990s?
Assassins (1990). "They're making a musical out of *that*?!?"

That was the response of many when they heard that *Lolita* and *Kiss of the Spider Woman* were headed for the musical stage.

Never did eyebrows raise higher than with *Assassins*.

However, Musical Theater Rule Number One says that people in musicals sing when passions take over and speech will no longer do.

Do they ever in *Assassins*. Stephen Sondheim and John Weidman brilliantly revealed the minds of those crazies who were greatly influenced by John Wilkes Booth's action on April 14, 1865.

It didn't open to particularly good reviews. Yet a lyric that Sondheim wrote for Booth turned out to apply to the show: "They will understand it later."

(Incidentally, Booth's only Broadway appearance was in *Julius Caesar*, in which he played Marc Antony—one of the few men in Shakespeare's play who *isn't* an assassin.)

***Once on This Island* (1990).** Blacks have been known to have their prejudices, too. Even in the French Antilles, light-skinned Blacks, such as the Beauxhommes, are rich and famous, while dark-skinned Blacks, such as Ti Moune and her family, are not. There may be many factors for that, but skin tones are a contributing one.

When Daniel Beauxhommes is injured in a car accident and Ti Moune nurses him back to health, the playing fields are leveled and both fall in love—for a while. On Daniel's wedding day to another light-skinned Black, Daniel follows the custom of throwing change to the poor people assembled outside his sumptuous home. How heartbreaking when he throws coins at Ti Moune.

She wants to die—and does. That she's reincarnated as a tree can't be anyone's idea of a happy ending, but Lynn Ahrens' lyrics and Stephen Flaherty's music is so joyous that we conveniently overlook the bizarre conclusion.

***Titanic* (1997).** In the 1972 film *Avanti*, Juliet Mills' character says that her rock musician beau is working on a musical that deals with the sinking of the *Titanic*—"called *Splash!*"

It's an all-too-obvious gag from director and co-writer Billy Wilder.

A quarter century later, the subject wasn't a joke to bookwriter Peter Stone or songwriter Maury Yeston. Their approach and talent yielded a musical about the *Titanic* that was a Tony-winning artistic achievement.

Two details are worth noting. As the mammoth ship was ready to launch, a little boy who's been holding a toy sailboat raises it high in tribute.

Soon after the iceberg is hit, no one is yet certain how bad the damage is ... until a liquor cart slowly but all too surely rolls across the stage, letting us see the boat is listing.

HMS *Titanic* should have used as much attention to detail before it set out on the Atlantic on that April night in 1912.

A New Brain (1998). Here's another "Are you kidding me?" musical. Granted, literally hundreds of words rhyme with "ation," but that doesn't mean that you write a musical about an arteriovenous malformation.

This brain aneurysm felled William Finn shortly after he'd won the Best Score Tony for *Falsettos*. Nevertheless, he eventually recovered enough to write about his decline, fall, and renaissance.

This musical suggested that Richard Adler and Jerry Ross only told half the story when they wrote "You gotta have heart." Finn expanded it to "You gotta have heart and music."

He's right.

Author's Choice: *Ragtime* (1998). Harry Thaw's 1906 murder of Stanford White was called "The Crime of the Century," although Emma Goldman wisely pointed out that ninety-four years would have to pass before anyone could be sure.

Many musical theater enthusiasts thought *Ragtime*'s losing the Best Musical Tony to *The Lion King* (1997) was The Crime of the Century.

Creating any musical is always difficult, but padding the eighty-eight-minute *Lion King* film to two-and-a-half hours is easier than reducing a 271-page novel to the same 150 minutes.

How bookwriter Terrence McNally and lyricist Lynn Ahrens managed to achieve this is utterly remarkable. Stephen Flaherty certainly honored E. L. Doctorow's characters, providing appropriately Semitic-tinged melodies for the Jews, four-square melodies for the WASPs, and no less than real-sounding ragtime for the Blacks.

Harold Hill maintained that ragtime was "shameless music." Not in this case.

The 1980s?

Sunday in the Park with George (1984). Of all the musicals that have had a "What the hell is happening?" moment, here's the best.

Audiences should have inferred that after Seurat finished his painting at the end of Act One; Act Two would be required to go in a different direction.

Yet after the curtain rose and the Island of La Grande Jatte went disappearing, audiences were either scratching their heads or delving into their *Playbills* to find out where and when they were going next. Matters became even stranger when a machine came on looking like R2D2 on steroids.

But here was another Sondheim musical where we had to catch up with him (this time with James Lapine). Many theatergoers since have, while being reminded of the values of both children and art.

Les Miserables (1987). And to think that the reviews in London were putrid.

We have *Oliver!* to thank for this musical. Alain Boublil saw Lionel Bart's hit in a 1978 London revival. When he saw the Artful Dodger cavorting, he was reminded of Gavroche, a character from his favorite Victor Hugo novel.

That revival of *Oliver!* was produced by Cameron Mackintosh, who would do substantially better with *Les Miz*.

The Phantom of the Opera (1988). Oh, come on, admit it! It belongs on this list.

So many dislike it simply because it's been the longest-running show in Broadway history, and will be for at least eight more years. Even if it has closed by the time you read this, its nearest competitor will need a full fifty-six months to surpass it. And who says that *that* show will still be running?

To assess its longevity in another way, some of the performers who are now appearing in London, Broadway, and touring productions weren't yet born when the show opened.

However, considering that *Phantom* takes place between 1881 to 1911, it shouldn't have a song entitled "The Point of No Return." The term only came into being in 1941 through air travel; it refers to a plane having enough fuel to reach to its destination but not enough to turn back.

Such an oversight certainly hasn't kept *POTO*, as it's chummily known, from flying high.

***City of Angels* (1989).** The always witty Larry Gelbart (*A Funny Thing Happened on the Way to the Forum*; *M*A*S*H*) started out writing a film noir spoof named *Death Is for Suckers*.

"But every morning as I read what I'd written the night before," he reported, "I saw that it wasn't even holding me."

So Gelbart came up with the idea of a Hollywood screenwriter who not only has trouble with his studio boss ("Flashbacks are a thing of the past") but also with his main character, who takes on a life of his own.

With a hard-hitting jazz score needed, the only composer working on Broadway who could do it justice would be Cy Coleman. He came through mightily, and Tonys went to him and David Zippel, a rookie who certainly didn't write like one.

Author's Choice: *Grand Hotel* (1989). In another musical with that adjective—*The Grand Tour* (1979)—Jacobowsky (Joel Grey) said that first class on a train isn't determined by the elegance of the car itself "but the quality of the passengers inside."

Using that as a barometer, the Grand Hotel in Berlin was an Econo Lodge.

Having severe money problems was General Director Preysing, who was cornered into telling a blatant lie to save himself from financial ruin. His stern expression softened into a smile only twice: once when he spoke to his children on the phone, and once when he met Flaemmchen, the type of typist who does make men smile.

Beauty and youth, to paraphrase Shakespeare, are two stuffs that will not endure. "I Want to Go to Hollywood," Flaemmchen decreed. To get the money to travel fifty-eight hundred miles caused her to go to Presying's room. After he made her remove her panties, she longingly looked at them on the floor as if she were genuinely seeing her lost virtue there.

That a Baron was on the premises sounds impressive, and Felix Amadeus Benvenuto von Gaigern certainly had a fine aristocratic bearing. If he only weren't penniless. If only he didn't break into other guests' rooms to steal belongings.

One victim was fading ballerina Grushinskaya, who returns unexpectedly after not finishing a performance for lack of audience response. The Baron attempted to convince her that he was there to meet her and love her; the aging dancer needed to believe this younger man. That was made easier when he sang Maury Yeston's bolt-of-lightning ballad "Love Can't Happen."

The Baron did show nobility when helping Jewish bookkeeper Kringelein secure a room at the "grand" hotel. He was terminally ill and wanted one last fling before he died. Taking a stock tip made him suddenly wealthy, which resulted in "We'll Take a Glass Together," only one of several stunning production numbers devised by Tommy Tune who indeed made *Grand Hotel* grand.

The 1970s?

Company (1970). Examine these previous musicals: *Annie Get Your Gun*; *Allegro*; *Guys and Dolls*; *Bye Bye Birdie*; *How to Succeed*; *Hello, Dolly!*; *Golden Boy*; *Sweet Charity*; and *Zorba*.

Each had a woman who very much wanted marriage while the man in her life wasn't as enthusiastic.

Company showed a man hot to wed while his fiancée was afraid of "Getting Married Today." It was just one of many innovations that George Furth and Stephen Sondheim brought to Broadway's table.

Follies (1971). Audiences had a hard time dealing with the decades-long marital problems of the Stones and the Plummers. Believing that this one night will fix everything was harder to swallow.

Everything else on stage, however, was more than any musical theater enthusiast could have ever imagined.

So was the artwork. Of all the opinions dispensed here, this is the one on which most readers will agree: *Follies* has the best-ever logo.

The face of a Follies Girl as a statue with cracks in it from age and wear was a good metaphor for what James Goldman and Stephen Sondheim had to say about marriage, the country, and entertainment.

Even Frank Verlizzo, the acclaimed artist who drew the logo for *Follies'* 2001 Broadway revival, admits that no one could possibly top what David Edward Byrd did for the original Broadway production.

Then-gofer Ted Chapin's meticulous diary *Everything Was Possible* gave so many details about the lavish costumes and scenery that we see where the money went. Thirty years before "premium" seats were invented, sitting in a first-row-center orchestra seat for *Follies* would set a theatergoer back twelve dollars. That translates to less than eighty dollars today. In retrospect, they were giving it away.

A Little Night Music **(1973).** Whenever Stephen Sondheim appeared at a seminar, during the Q-and-A session afterward, someone inevitably asked "Mr. Sondheim, of all your musicals, which is your favorite?"

Sondheim always answered "I don't have a favorite; I have a *least* favorite: *Do I Hear a Waltz?*"

Ironic, isn't it, that eight years after that 1965 musical, he wrote a score that let us hear many a waltz?

After the Broadway run, subsequent productions advertised the show as "The 'Send in the Clowns' musical." It was proof that having one song from Broadway become popular was so rare that a musical would make it a selling point.

Sweeney Todd **(1979).** A musical about murder and cannibalism that even shows the needless killing of an innocent bird? Here was proof positive that, as the song goes, "It ain't what you do; it's the way that you do it."

And, oh, did Sondheim, Hugh Wheeler, and Harold Prince ever do it.

There was some disagreement over Judge Turpin's "Johanna," in which he flagellates himself because he's ashamed of his lust. It was dropped after a few previews when Prince feared that the audience was enduring enough horrors without having to suffer through this one.

Sondheim ensured that it would make the recording, though. Its inclusion allowed listeners to become inured to it; now it's a rare production of the show that doesn't include it.

Have you noticed a pattern with these 1970s musicals? Yes, they all had scores by Sondheim during his breakout decade.

(But then ...)

Author's Choice: *A Chorus Line* **(1975).** Broadway pros staunchly believed that audiences couldn't relate to show business people or their problems.

Conceiver-director-choreographer Michael Bennett knew that if John Q. and Jane Q. Public could see dancers desperate to get jobs that they truly needed, they'd be reminded of all those interviews and disappointments that they'd endured time and time again in front of would-be employers.

Let's add some information to an oft-told tale: Val's song of rejection was originally titled "Tits and Ass," referring to three reasons why she wasn't landing jobs.

The song wasn't getting laughs at early previews because theatergoers had seen the title in the program. So it became "Dance: Ten; Looks: Three"—representing the point score that one director gave her after her audition.

What's less known is that for a few performances at The Public Theatre prior to Broadway the song was titled "Dance: Ten; Looks: *One.*" The authors mercifully decided that they needn't make Val *that* unattractive.

The 1960s?
How to Succeed in Business Without Really Trying **(1961).** Jack Weinstock, who co-penned the early drafts, was in the medical profession when he wasn't writing. However, his daughter Ethel Weinstock Kaiden frankly admitted that her daddy's claim that he was a neurosurgeon was an aggrandizement.

"He was a surgeon," she's conceded, "but in urology not neurology." Seems that the good doctor felt some people might find the idea of an urologist a little grisly. Hence, the more upmarket specialty.

Alas, Abe Burrows had to come in and do surgery on the book that Weinstock wrote with Willie Gilbert. If Burrows hadn't, *How to Succeed* probably wouldn't have succeeded with not only a Best Musical Tony, but also a Pulitzer Prize.

A Funny Thing Happened on the Way to the Forum **(1962).** One surefire laugh after another followed by a chase scene that somehow seemed funnier on stage than it did in the film.

There were also plenty of laughs in Stephen Sondheim's first Broadway score. Funniest of all was "Impossible," in which an aging father and budding son compare notes on a possible romance with a sweet young woman.

Little did we know that this title was indicative of what was to follow with Sondheim, who often tackled the impossible and conquered it.

Cabaret **(1966).** Only twenty-one years after the fall of Nazi Germany, a musical dared to revisit the era and anticipate the Holocaust. To succeed, it would need great talents. But all the creatives associated with it have only had flops: the lyricist, one; the bookwriter, composer, and choreographer, two; the director, *four*.

The composer was John Kander, the lyricist Fred Ebb, the choreographer Ron Field, and the director was also the producer: Harold Prince. *Willkommen* to another successful career, Mr. Prince.

1776 **(1969).** This Tony winner would be an Author's Choice if its score were better. Sherman Edwards' lyrics often disregarded rhymes and scansion, and his music, while adequate to good, sounded better thanks to orchestrator Eddie Sauter.

Moreover, *1776* only sports a dozen songs, far fewer than the average Broadway musical offers. Many have said that it would have worked just as well as a play, and while its own bookwriter Peter Stone often went on record to disagree, he's the one who made it great.

Author's Choice: *Fiddler on the Roof* **(1964).** In the match between two 1964 musicals that each has a matchmaker, this one wins over *Hello, Dolly!*

Sheldon Harnick's lyrics in his most famous song with Jerry Bock—"Sunrise, Sunset"—describes the entire musical in five words: "Laden with happiness and tears."

As Joseph Stein and Harnick adapted Sholem Aleichem's stories, they found the perfect balance between the show's comedy and tragedy. We grinned, chuckled, and laughed shortly before we turned grim-faced at a serious and often life-altering moment. Only minutes later, we returned to belly laughs only to tear up seconds later.

Just like life.

The 1950s?

Guys and Dolls **(1950).** In an era where musicals had us follow the fates of two couples, one was usually serious and received more time than the frivolous duo.

It was pretty much a tie in this Abe Burrows libretto.

Jo Swerling is credited as well, but co-producer Cy Feuer went to his death swearing that nothing of what Swerling wrote was retained.

This came up in Feuer's autobiography, where he took his title from the opening line of this smash hit: "I've got the horse right here" became *I've Got the Show Right Here.*

(Wouldn't a more arresting title have been *Cy's Matters?*)

The show has a delightful ending, which impresses because it doesn't happen through a song or even a line of dialogue. For after we've spent the show watching Adelaide develop a cold, now that Nathan's married her, *he's* the one who sneezes.

God bless you, Nathan (in more ways than one).

My Fair Lady **(1956).** "*One* man in a million *may* shout *a bit. Now and then* there's *one* with *slight* defects. *One, perhaps,* whose truthfulness you doubt *a bit.*"

Henry Higgins doesn't concede very much, does he? Alan Jay Lerner certainly knew how to write for this character.

The Most Happy Fella (1956). In *Mack & Mabel*, Mack Sennett, when auditioning potential bathing beauties, sees two he likes and says "Let's take 'em both!" Then he notices the others and says "Ah, the hell with it! Let's take 'em all!"

Goddard Lieberson, Columbia Records' cast album guru, did much the same with Frank Loesser's ambitious, forty-three-song, four-reprise score. When he saw that it would require not one long-playing record, but two, he could have released it as a double album.

Instead, he went the distance and released "The Complete Broadway Performance as Presented on Stage" on three records—three times as many as the 1955–1956 season's biggest hit: *My Fair Lady*.

West Side Story (1957). Most musicals end Act One with a big production number. This one concluded with a police siren blaring as two warring gangs run off and leave a pair of dead bodies.

Bookwriter Arthur Laurents also upped the ante on Shakespeare's *Romeo and Juliet* by having the young lover kill his girlfriend's brother, and not "just" her cousin.

Director-choreographer Jerome Robbins conceived the triple threat by abandoning the time-honored practice of a singing chorus and a dancing chorus. He demanded performers who could effectively sing, dance, and act—and got them.

Most every musical since, for better or worse, has tried to do the same.

Author's Choice: *Gypsy* (1959). We have Oscar Hammerstein to thank for one of this show's greatest achievements: the lyrics.

Stephen Sondheim wanted to write the entire score, but Ethel Merman, who'd star, wanted a more seasoned composer. Sondheim was ready to resign until his mentor talked him out of it.

We must be glad Merman didn't demand a more seasoned lyricist, too.

When Rose sings "There I was, in Mr. Orpheum's office," we see a bit of her naiveté. The Orpheum Circuit never had a Mr. Orpheum. In fact, Martin Beck—who built a New York theater in 1924 that he named for himself—was the head of the Orpheum Circuit during the years when Rose was trying to get vaudeville to notice June (and to a much lesser extent, Louise).

Of course, Rose doesn't need to be accurate. After all, she dreamed this situation.

Or at least she said she did . . .

The 1940s?

Oklahoma! (1943). This hasn't been chosen because no author dealing with musicals would dare omit it. The revolutionary "Laurey Makes up Her Mind" dream ballet is potent enough to warrant inclusion.

What follows is even stronger. Laurey's playing Curly versus Jud has been great fun—until Jud arrives to take her to the picnic. His face and clothes are clean, but what's going on in his head may not be.

Those who think this musical is just about a box social should remember how genuinely frightened Laurey is at this moment and how she fears for her immediate future.

As if that weren't enough, who expected that such a life-affirming musical to include a cold-blooded murder? *Oklahoma!* showed that musical comedy and musical play, like the farmer and the cowman, could be friends.

Annie Get Your Gun (1946). No, we don't like that Annie Oakley throws the shooting match just to stroke Frank Butler's ego. That the big guy doesn't care that he wins that way is unsatisfactory, too.

It makes the list, though, because of Irving Berlin's hit-filled score. Witness what the *Billboard* reported in its roundup of 1946 recordings.

"They Say It's Wonderful" was number three in sheet music sales but in first place for radio play. Record sales revealed that "I Got the Sun in the Morning" ranked thirteenth while "Doin' What Comes Naturally" finished in sixteenth and eighteenth place by virtue of *two* different recordings. "The Girl That I Marry" and "Anything You Can Do" showed up in plenty of radio shows, too.

And we haven't even mentioned "There's No Business Like Show Business."

Finian's Rainbow (1947). This one takes white-hot heat from those who believe it mocks Blacks. No, the purpose of turning uber-prejudiced lily-white Senator Billboard Rawkins black is to show that a man doesn't know another man until he walks in his skin.

If you can agree, delight in the Burton Lane–E. Y. Harburg score during this time of the year or any other. The book that Harburg and Fred Saidy wrote offers many a witty exchange, including one between Og, a dyed-in-the-green-wool leprechaun, and our title character.

"You can't be a leprechaun," says Finian. "You're too tall."

To which an anguished and frustrated Og answers, "Yes! And I'm getting taller!"—as if growing means that he's disgracing his people.

David Wayne, who originated the role, was five-foot-seven—not tall, to be sure, but taller than a leprechaun was thought to be. However, Saidy and Harburg were wise to write a line that would allow any actor of any size to play Og.

Gentlemen Prefer Blondes (1949). Music by Jule Styne, lyrics by Leo Robin. And while the former had the much brighter Broadway career—and composed splendid music here—the lyricist's work in this Anita Loos tale is even better.

This becomes apparent as early as the opening number "It's High Time," which everyone in those days of Prohibition is thrilled to be aboard the *Ile de France*; once it's sailed far enough from the U.S. shore, drinking genuine alcohol can commence.

So "It's High Time" doesn't only mean that it's time to get high on liquor; it also says that an event that's been much too long in coming will finally happen.

Author's Choice: *Carousel* (1945). Yes, yes, we all hate that Billy Bigelow hits Julie Jordan and that striking a woman can never, *ever* be condoned on any level. On that plot point alone, many will understandably be aghast at this choice.

That said, throughout the show when people accuse Billy of *beating* Julie, he hotly rebuts that he *hit* her.

Again: Billy can't be let off the hook for what he did. It's horrible. But there is a profound difference between hitting and beating. Hitting implies once and "only" once; beating means a continuous barrage of abuse.

We get the impression that Billy stopped after that first blow, ashamed of what he did and will never forgive himself.

Still, if you can temper your temper and forgive *Carousel*, you'll find that it's the best musical to warn of the dangers of so-called Love at First Sight. You may also be as thrilled with Richard Rodgers' music as he was; he named this his favorite score of the dozens he composed. As for Oscar Hammerstein, his conception and delivery of "Soliloquy" remains the highest achievement in any musical.

WHAT'S THE MOST UNDERRATED MUSICAL OF EACH DECADE?

Author's Choice for 2010–2019: *Rocky* (2014). Thomas Meehan, who co-wrote the book with original auteur Sylvester Stallone, and in conjunction with lyricist Lynn Ahrens, actually improved the Oscar-winning film.

It still told of Rocky Balboa, the aging journeyman boxer struggling to get by. When he isn't a sparring partner for up-and-coming boxers, he strong-arms for a loan shark.

He's to pummel deadbeats, but Rocky doesn't have the heart to break the thumbs that his boss wants fractured. When one debtor can only offer his mackinaw as partial payment, Rocky says a revealing line not in the film: "You'll need that coat for the winter."

Rocky risks losing his job before he experiences a genuine loss. Gym manager has given his locker to the new kid in the ring. "Learn yourself a useful trade," the man advises.

Rocky doesn't feel he's all done, as he expresses in Ahrens' fine lyric "My Nose Ain't Broken." It's part rationalization, part badge of honor, and part ray of hope. "Some guys get to be champs at 29," Rocky muses as he approaches thirty—the first round-numbered birthday most people aren't happy to reach. He looks at the poster of Rocky Marciano he has prominently displayed on his wall. "He and I share a name," he says.

Yes, but Marciano never lost a fight; Rocky's already lost twenty. And when he attempts a chin-up, he's clearly in pain. He wants "to get a second chance and get my life replayed."

Rocky is its own *42nd Street*. Here, instead of the understudy subbing for the injured star, a nobody gets the chance to fight champion Apollo Creed after his much-heralded challenger gets hurt.

The musical has its love story. Adrian works in the pet shop where Rocky buys turtle food. Both are drawn to animals and have withdrawn from people; creatures are, after all, superior in dispensing unconditional love.

Rocky got none from his father, who encouraged him to box because he believed his son was stupid. Actually, the father was deficient in not being able to see Rocky's innate intelligence. "We've been told we're nothing," Rocky and Adrian eventually sing, "but together maybe we can be something." This is the fight we want Rocky and Adrian to win.

The film set one scene at Thanksgiving, but then made little mention of Christmas and none of New Year's. Meehan and Ahrens wisely made more of the holidays. Rocky and Adrian sang about "decorating the Christmas tree like we're a real couple" and experiencing "something like happiness" which, by song's end, turned into their admitting that they'd found *actual* happiness. "The Flip Side" reiterated that each wants to show "the good side of me," which they found in each other and in themselves.

Then came the smartest change. In the film, Adrian's brother Paulie returned to the home that he and she have shared all their lives. He'd expected that Rocky would have recommended him for a loan collecting job; because Rocky hadn't, Paulie went out of control and began destroying his house with a baseball bat.

As dramatic as that is, Meehan and Ahrens instead had Paulie come to Rocky's apartment and swing that bat. Attacking someone else's house is a far greater offense than destroying one's own. To see the decimation of the tree that Rocky and Adrian had so lovingly decorated as the symbol of their love added to their devastation (and ours).

The film didn't establish when the fight would take place; the musical specifically scheduled it for New Year's Day. That ruins New Year's Eve.

(When training, fighters are forbidden to have sex, which both have come to enjoy.) What's more, the two aren't just worried that Rocky will lose the bout; "A vegetable in a wheelchair" and "You wanna end up blind?" are soon said, leading them to mutter "Some New Year's Eve!" Indeed, while everyone else was out celebrating, these two must endure the most difficult night of their lives.

As in the film, Rocky's goal was modest. He doesn't expect to win, but insists "I gotta go the distance." He achieves that victory. Would that *Rocky: The Musical* could have been seen as a winner, too.

Author's Choice for 2000–2009: *Sweet Smell of Success* **(2002).** Ernest Lehman's seventy-two-page novella and the 1957 film told of all-powerful gossip columnist J. J. Hunsecker, who had aberrant love for his sister Susan, and his taunting and enjoying hungry publicist Sidney Falco.

And "How did you get to be you, Sidney Falco?" John Guare's libretto is the only one of the three properties to answer that question. He named the man Sidney Falcone but had J. J. tell him to change his name to the more pungent Falco. It has that nice "o" sound that well served Harlow, Garbo, and Monroe.

That Sidney agrees is a powerful way of showing us J. J.'s all-encompassing influence. Nothing in the novella or film more strongly suggests that Falco would do a-n-y-t-h-i-n-g to please J. J.

Those earlier iterations don't put J. J. in St. Patrick's Cathedral after hours, where in the musical he offhandedly tells Sidney that Cardinal Spellman lets him drop in whenever he wants. Even a man who could be a heartbeat away from the papacy is in J. J.'s thrall.

Now Sidney will officially be, too. J. J. makes him swear (to Marvin Hamlisch's religious-tinted music) to keep his eyes on Susan and ensure that she does nothing to displease her step-brother.

There's another smart complication. Originally, J. J.'s sister was his parents' late baby; in the musical, she's his half-sister from his father's second marriage. Not that lusting for one's half-sister instead of his full-blooded sister is only half as bad, but the choice to make the two characters half-siblings will intrigue many of today's theatergoers. Children of

parents who've had multiple marriages may now have complicated feelings about their half-siblings. This musical dared to address the subject.

All three properties show that J. J. is much too enraptured with
Susan, but the musical offers another improvement: J. J. doesn't solely
try to keep her for himself, but tries to get her to become Mrs. John F.
Kennedy. This makes J. J. a bit better, for he wants the best man for her,
not himself.

What an irony in J. J.'s thinking that JFK would be a sterling husband, now that we've since learned about his many dalliances. The musical reminds us in an oblique way that J. J. is not always accurate.

In the film, Susan is shy and retiring. That's valid, for many people
with powerful siblings often become shrinking violets. She's stronger
in the novella and enacts revenge on Falco in a very creative way. But
she's stronger still in the musical, where she brings down her brother.
So while the film pits strong versus weak and the novella offers strong
versus stronger, the musical goes for strong versus strongest, which always
presents the best dramatic possibilities.

The musical's collaborators give us good reason why Susan is strong,
thanks to "For Susan." The song has J. J. showing Sidney the many letters,
postcards, and souvenirs from Gary Cooper, Humphrey Bogart, and others who have paid her great attention over the years. Yes, a young woman
who's beloved by J. J. will get rapt and fawning attention from many. That
could make a girl feel good about herself.

So Guare, Marvin Hamlisch, and lyricist Craig Carnelia made *Sweet
Smell of Success* their very own. They didn't just turn dialogue into song,
as so many writers of dull movies-to-musicals have. Just as importantly,
Guare and Carnelia had the same voice so both dialogue and lyrics
seemed to be from one bookwriter-lyricist. Their language was in keeping
with the harsh nightlife world of New York in the 1950s.

The 1957 film of *Sweet Smell of Success* opened to dismissive reviews
and public apathy. Only after many years did it become highly respected.
Perhaps that fate awaits the musical.

Author's Choice for 1990–1999: *Fields of Ambrosia* (1993). After a
successful run at the George Street Playhouse in New Brunswick, New

Jersey, the show moved to London where it received poisonous pans. It then made the desperate gesture of saying that those who bought tickets could receive a refund if they didn't like the show.

Apparently many didn't, or didn't take the offer, for twenty-three performances were all the musical could muster. It has never played Broadway.

Based on the 1970 film *The Traveling Executioner*, the musical also had Jonas Candide driving through the southern states with his electric chair in tow—a state-of-the-art invention for 1918. Jonas visits prisons, and, for ready money, will save the state the trouble and higher expense of putting to death any condemned criminal.

Granted, that sounds grisly. What saved the situation was Jonas' very different worldview. Any condemned man would assume that his executioner would be the most severe person he'd yet meet in the entire judicial system. Not at all; Jonas is most loving and tells the victim that one of the men he'd electrocuted returned to him through a medium and said that the afterlife took place in the Fields of Ambrosia where wine, women, song, and good times awaited.

Jonas is undoubtedly lying. But why not give a condemned man a ray of hope about the future when his present has none?

Then Jonas is assigned to electrocute Gretchen, a fetching young woman. You can guess what happens—but you probably can't guess correctly.

Joel Higgins, who wrote the book and lyrics and played Jonas, attempted something daringly different. Martin Silvestri provided music that ranged from a majestic title song to a charming ballad about the "Vieux Carre" that Jonas and Gretchen imagine they would visit if life gave them the opportunity.

Here's hoping that *Fields of Ambrosia* gets another opportunity or two.

Author's Choice for 1980–1989: *Rags* **(1986).** Impoverished immigrants disembarked at Ellis Island after weeks in steerage.

Moments later, some were sent back to the boat and must be returned to Europe.

This wasn't their decision; the poor souls couldn't pass the health test. Imagine spending all that time, energy, money, and oppressive conditions only to see the Statue of Liberty for a few minutes and then enjoy no further liberty.

As for the immigrants who were allowed to stay, librettist Joseph Stein and lyricist Stephen Schwartz showed how much we all owe our forebears, for awful ship conditions weren't all these people endured. Now they'd have to fend for themselves in a land where they didn't know the language and had no immediate opportunities.

And yet, the vast majority of them made a go of it so their children, grandchildren, and great-grandchildren—meaning *us*—could have better lives. Seeing and appreciating *Rags* was a way to honor these pioneers.

Not enough did.

This was the second show about immigrants that composer Charles Strouse set to music. In 1962, he did *All-American*; there, the new arrivals deplaned from, at the worst, economy class. They were more optimistic and perky than their counterparts in *Rags* for some progress had been made since the turn of the century. That was gratifying as well.

Author's Choice for 1970–1979: *Inner City* **(1971).** This virtually unknown masterpiece was based on Eve Merriam's ninety-five-page picture book *Inner City Mother Goose*. She applied to city life famous nursery rhymes: "Mary, Mary, urban Mary; how does your sidewalk grow? With chewing gum wads and cigarette butts and popsicle sticks and potato chip bags."

Merriam also adapted children's poems: "Now I lay me down to sleep. I pray the double lock will keep. May no brick through a window break. And no one rob me till I wake."

If Bertolt Brecht had been living in the 1970s and collaborating with a rock composer, one of their songs might well have been "Hushabye, Baby" in which a single mother bravely promises her child a better life than she's had. Merriam's collaborator, composer Helen Miller, delivered dynamic music here and throughout.

It didn't run because the writers never made clear through an opening number that the songs were riffs on classic children's fare. The audience, confused for too many minutes, got lost.

What Merriam and Miller did do right, however, was end on a positive note. Despite the grim outlook that New York City had in the 1970s, the show had its characters sing that they would stay and make it better. Many did.

Author's Choice for 1960–1969: *Do I Hear a Waltz?* **(1965).** No, Leona Samish doesn't find True Love in Venice. But as a result of her making some big mistakes and learning from them, Leona will return home a better person than she was when she left it. That makes for a more worthwhile vacation than just taking gondolas, sending postcards, and buying vases.

And no matter what Sondheim had always maintained, the score for which he provided lyrics to Richard Rodgers' music is an excellent one.

Author's Choice for 1950–1959: *A Tree Grows in Brooklyn* **(1951).** Everybody adored Shirley Booth.

"To hear Miss Booth sing 'Love Is the Reason' in a sort of comic fugue arrangement is to enjoy musical comedy at its best" (Atkinson, *New York Times*). "Shirley Booth is truly something . . . she had me weeping with laughter" (Chapman, *Daily News*). "The jewel of the evening" (Hawkins, *New York World–Telegram and Sun*). "A grand performance" (Guernsey, *New York Herald–Tribune*). "One of the wonders of the American stage, a superb actress, a magnificent comedienne, and an all-around performer of seemingly endless versatility" (Watts, *New York Post*).

It's said that every great musical must have a great star performance, and *A Tree Grows in Brooklyn* obviously had it. How could it close so relatively quickly after 267 performances?

Because Booth wasn't the show's star; at least, she wasn't supposed to be. What she had, though, was the fun character to play: Cissy, who's been repeatedly married, but has never got over her first love, Harry; she even called all her subsequent husbands Harry in his honor (and to their fury).

In reminiscing about the first Harry, Booth sang musical theater's funniest-ever song: "He Had Refinement." Exhibit A: "He undressed with all the lights off till we was wed."

Booth also had the charming "Love Is the Reason," and shared a delightful romp via "Look Who's Dancing" and a comic duet "Is That My Prince?" when that first idealized Harry turns up years later not remotely resembling the handsome hunk he once was.

Yet the bulk of the evening went to Katie and Johnny. She's a hard worker; he's semi-shiftless. He pawns his watch each Monday morning to have money for the week, and then, after payday on Saturday, retrieves it. "You're mine till Monday," he sings, in a joyous up-tempo song that gets the show off to a good start.

Katie is nevertheless so smitten with him that she decides she must "Make the Man Love Me." Johnny wants to: "I'm Like a New Broom," he tells his friends in a promise to straighten out.

Easier said than done. When they shop for bedroom furniture, he has no money. "Somebody must-a-picked your pocket," says one of his friends, most helpfully. Katie pays; a year later, daughter Francie has arrived. Money is tight, for Johnny's job as a singing waiter is an on-again, off-again proposition. Eventually Katie loses faith and says she'll leave him, but Johnny delivers the glorious "I'll Buy You a Star" that's so convincing that Katie decides to stay.

Act Two begins twelve years later, when the pre-adolescent Francie must hear her schoolmates taunt her because her father's "rum-dumb." She defends him, because to her, he's both sensitive ("Growing Pains") and supportive ("Don't Be Afraid"). Eventually, he's so desperate for money that he takes a dangerous job in helping to excavate the tunnels for subways, but he's killed on the job—and on the day that Francie was to be graduated.

A wastrel husband, a too-devoted wife, difficulties with money, a daughter who defends her dad to her peers, and a father's death and a graduation ceremony must have sounded familiar to musical theater fans who could have seen *Carousel* as recently as four years earlier.

Composer Arthur Schwartz and lyricist Dorothy Fields wrote an extraordinary score, but not quite on the level of the Rodgers and Hammerstein masterpiece. Even without that point of reference and comparison, *Tree* would have had a hard time of it, for *Carousel* was the shortest-running of the famous R&H "Big Five" musicals. It was too bitter a pill for most audiences to swallow, and *A Tree Grows in Brooklyn* was as well.

Author's Choice for 1940–1949: *The Day Before Spring* **(1945).** Lerner and Loewe's second collaboration saw classmates Katherine and Alex at Harrison University. Then they became lovers, and on the day that they'd decided to elope, their car broke down. Along came Peter to give them a ride.

Katherine *really* went along for the ride, for she wound up marrying Peter instead of Alex. Ten years later, their marriage is no longer exciting.

However, Alex's life is. He's written a bestseller called *The Day Before Spring* which tells of his on-again, off-forever relationship with Katherine.

Now comes their tenth reunion. Alex will attend; successful people always do, so they can preen. Peter wants to be there, but Katherine, aware that Alex wrote about her, fears what might happen. And yet, once she's there, she can't wait to see him.

When they finally do meet, Alex sings to Katherine what everyone at a reunion wants to hear: "You Haven't Changed at All."

Meanwhile, Peter, whom Katherine now regards as boring, is chased by a young woman named Christopher (yes, a *woman*) who finds this new man exciting. Lerner makes the point that when you're just meeting someone, that person can seem thrilling. Only after the passage of time can you really know for sure.

With whom do Katherine and Peter wind up? When *Company* was trying out in Boston, Bobby came to the conclusion that being married was essentially living "Happily ever after . . . in hell." That was changed by the time the show reached Broadway.

So if a damnation of marriage was too red-hot for 1970, it was obviously too white-hot for 1945. Still, in an era where musicals concluded with marriage and avoided the point when its participants questioned their decisions, *The Day Before Spring* at least dared to raise the question.

WHAT'S BROADWAY'S BEST JUKEBOX MUSICAL?

When Walter Kerr reviewed *Jamaica* in 1957, he questioned the worth of the score by saying "Can you make a whole show out of sheet music?"

For the last few decades, the answer has essentially been yes. Aside from revues, we've seen librettists take songs both famous and obscure and put them in a new book. The results are usually terrible, but not always.

***Jersey Boys* (2005).** Early on, we see our protagonists antagonize. One winds up in jail. Those who rob a church will never be confused with choir boys, either.

What followed may well have been an utter whitewash, but because bookwriters Marshall Brickman and Rick Elice showed us some unsavory incidents early on, we at least were led to believe that they were telling us *some* truths. We then gave them our forbearance and our hearty applause.

***Beautiful* (2014).** A woman who meets unlikely professional success loses her man. That was old when *Funny Girl* did it literally a half century earlier, but Doug McGrath made the story seem as if this scenario had never happened before while adding many good jokes along the way. McGrath also ensured that Carole King never lost the common touch so that we could continually care for her.

Beautiful would have been a stronger musical if, like *Funny Girl*, it hadn't been a jukebox musical. When Carole and her husband-lyricist Gerry Goffin are starting to succeed, she tells him that she's glad that songwriting is now his day job. Now *that's* a good subject for a song, but we don't hear it because Carole King never wrote anything like it.

She did write a lot of bubble-gum rock with even gummier lyrics, such as those found in "The Loco-motion": "Everybody's doin' a brand new dance now . . . I know you'd get to like it if you give it a chance now."

Oh, you've got to give it a chance? You mean, it isn't inherently appealing?

***Girl from the North Country* (2018).** Or *Not-So-Grand Hotel*—a boarding house in Duluth during the Great Depression.

Actually, this is an ideal setting for a jukebox musical. People from all walks of life can walk into Nick Laine's bed and breakfast and tell stories that the songwriters penned for other situations but can be tailored to the new characters. The tail still wags the dog, but the result doesn't seem as blatant or desperate.

Here were the songs that Bob Dylan had written between 1963 (the title song) and 2012 ("Duquesne Whistle"). Conor McPherson wrote mesmerizing characters to match: Laine has been committing adultery with guest Mrs. Neilsen ("True Love Tends to Forget"); he isn't fooling his wife Elizabeth, addle-brained though she may be (or, as she sees it, "Forever Young").

They have two children: Gene, a budding writer who's taken with Kate ("I Want You"), and Marianne, an adopted Black daughter who's now pregnant by a man who's taken his leave ("Tight Connection to My Heart"). Now she's attracted to Joe Scott, a tortured prizefighter who's one of their transients; "Hurricane" is an apt song to express who he is.

Other occupants include a preacher who plans to blackmail Mr. Burke. His wife knows what's going on ("Is Your Love in Vain?") but is more concerned with their disturbed grown son Elias. There won't be any more of a happy ending for him as anyone else.

McPherson also directed and kept it speeding and accelerating, like, well, like a rolling stone.

Jagged Little Pill (2019). It's a family musical in that it concerns a family. Unfortunately, it's a woefully unhappy one.

Father's overworked. Mother's a pill addict, who does get our sympathy because she endured a serious car accident that's left her with substantial pain.

(However, was it her fault or someone else's? We never know.)

Son is headed for Harvard but suspects that his parents would have stopped loving him had he not been accepted. Jackie is the adopted daughter who believes that her parents chose her so that everyone in this tony Connecticut town would say "Oh, aren't the Healys wonderful for adopting a Black girl!?"

Diablo Cody's Tony-winning book reiterates that the meaning of "*sub*urban" can mean *below* urban. Sidi Larbi Cherkaqui provided the choreography, but director Diane Paulus made the scenery dance to Alanis Morissette and Glen Ballard's strong songs. The ending was as realistically happy as it could be for the Healys, who started on the long road to healing.

Author's Choice: *A Class Act* **(2000).** The biomusical about Edward Kleban who'll always—and only—be known as the lyricist for *A Chorus Line*.

Some people have "fear of success"; Kleban had fear of not having another success. After his landmark triumph, he wound up with many spurts, starts, and unfinished shows.

Lonny Price and Linda Kline—the latter was Kleban's longtime lover—took songs from those would-be musicals and inserted them into his life story. The show's remarkable facet is that you'd swear the songs were written specifically for the script; not a one seemed shoehorned in.

We've heard the cliché that people in show business are crazy to begin with, but Kleban actually did time in a mental institution. Despite his years-long romance with Kline, he had gone through women the way most of us go through tissues. His intransigent nature resulted in his professional setbacks, especially when he was hired to work on the 1973 revival of *Irene* and was summarily fired.

That was the end of Act One, but the start of Act Two showed Kleban in much better spirits. He and his friends and colleagues sang about how things were getting "Better." Exclaimed an enthralled Kleban, "Barbra Streisand is recording one of my songs!"

Indeed she did—and that song was, in fact, "Better." But it wasn't released for decades. Kleban, who died at a mere forty-eight in 1987, didn't live to see it happen.

WHAT'S THE BEST GAY MUSICAL?

Boy Meets Boy **(1975).** Six years after Stonewall, the first gay musical of note was produced. There would have been a time when no one would have anticipated that such a show could have a fourteen-month off-Broadway run.

Granted, it was at a 170-seat theater, but 483 performances are still 483 performances.

Homophobes who insist that gays want to convert the world to homosexuality should see the scene set in a swank nightclub. One man is fox-trotting with a man; one woman is doing the same with a woman—and in between them is a good, ol' fashioned man and woman enjoying their dance.

Donald Ward and Bill Solly wanted to make known that gays aren't out to blatantly or covertly convert heterosexuals into their lifestyle. All they want is peaceful coexistence.

When Pigs Fly (1996). The highlight of this revue was called "A Patriotic Finale" that ended Act One.

What joy lyricist Mark Waldrop must have experienced when he got the idea: American states and cities contain a syllable or two that could be extracted to represent gays.

Hence, "You can't take the 'color' out of Colorado; you can't take the 'Mary' out of Maryland"—pronounced the way the delegates in *1776* say it. "Chicago with no 'chic' would be boring in a week . . . You can't subtract the ten percent from Tennessee."

Waldrop took a few liberties. "You can't take the 'sissi' out of Mississippi . . . Who will never be passé in old El Paso? . . . You can't run the homos out of Oklahoma." These were small prices to pay for the capper: "You need us to make the U.S.A."—which gives us an extra joke because you do indeed need the letters "U" and "S" to create that three-letter abbreviation "U.S.A." And just as those two letters are essential to the three-letter abbreviation for the United States, gays are essential for all that they've brought to the country.

Dick Gallagher composed a most felicitous march-tempo melody that was as delightful as the lyric. And while there were many terrific songs in this revue, this one was great enough to earn the title "The Gay National Anthem."

Zanna, Don't! (2002). Tim Acito's book, music, and lyrics had Steve, the captain of the football team, in love with Mike, the captain of the chess team. Steve's very mighty grateful for the attention, for at this school, chess is much more popular than football.

Mike says he admires Steve when the jock says he's going out for the school musical. Steve shrugs and says in a case-closed voice, "What kind of high school would this be if the captain of the football team didn't?"

Mike plans to try out. Not only do the two expect to land fat parts, but they also anticipate that they'll be elected King and King of the prom.

Meanwhile, cute-as-a-cute-button Kate is the trainer for the school's mechanical bull-riding team. As she tells a young woman named Roberta, "When I see you straddling that bull, I feel a spiritual connection." Soon, these two are a blissfully happy couple. They expect to be elected Queen and Queen of the prom after they also audition for the school musical, a new and original work that wonders whether heterosexuals should be allowed into the army.

Isn't it nice that *Zanna, Don't!* does think they should?

Zanna, meanwhile, is a mythical creature who helps them all. When they see him, Mike says "Ho, Zanna! Hey, Zanna!" Steve adds, "Zanna, Zanna." Roberta and then Kate each contributes "Ho, Zanna!"

Bare **(2012).** Here's a tale of two classmates: Peter, who comes across as gay, and Jason, who doesn't, down to his playing an important role on the school's sports teams.

Under those circumstances, pretty, sweet, and hot Ivy chases Jason like crazy. But he's attracted to Peter.

In this musical at least, high school has progressed to the point where Peter isn't harassed for being gay; everyone assumes he is and leaves him alone. But what's it like for Jason who's butch *and* gay? Coming out would shock friends and family.

John Hartmere's book and lyrics tackled this issue head-on, providing the happiest of endings.

Fun Home **(2015).** Lehman Engel, when helming the BMI Musical Theatre Workshop, encouraged his students to "look for humor in dark places."

A funeral home qualifies.

So an undertaker's children enjoy creating a mock commercial jingle for their father. ("We take dead bodies every day of the week!")

However, Alison Bechdel called her memoir by this name "A Family Tragicomic." The "comic" resulted from her drawing the tale as a comic strip; the "tragi" was her father's feeling the need to marry and have children while wishing that a pre-Stonewall society would just accept him as gay.

Lisa Kron and Jeanine Tesori's potent musical gave us hope through Alison, who, in more enlightened times, was able to live a gay life without the burdens that overwhelmed her father.

It all took place in a funeral home, which wasn't a fun home with a husband who'd "go out for a while" and a wife who strongly suspected why he was making the trip. In the end, it was the father's funeral.

Author's Choice: *Falsettos* **(1992).** Homosexuals, women with children, short insomniacs, and a teeny tiny band made for one riveting show.

Or two, depending on your outlook. *March of the Falsettos* (1981) merged with *Falsettoland* (1990) to make for a very full evening. Long before *Fun Home*, we had Marvin, a husband and father, too, but one who wouldn't accept what society wanted from him; he admitted his mistake in marrying and began living the life he wanted.

Nevertheless, he was not ready to give up his responsibilities as a parent and wanted "a tight knit family." Marvin and everyone else in the show wound up becoming one. Even his son Jason came to like his father's lover.

James Lapine won for Best Book and William Finn won for Best Score. Those two prizes weren't enough to win Best Musical; *Crazy for You* did, in another of those crazy Tony decisions.

WHAT MUSICAL HAS HAD THE BEST REVIVAL?

Chicago's not on this list, despite its becoming the longest-running revival in Broadway history (which it probably always will be) and the longest-running American musical of all time (a title it may not retain, if *The Lion King*, *Wicked*, *The Book of Mormon*, and *Hamilton* have anything to say about it).

No, this *Chicago* can't compare to the original 1975 production, which was comparatively lavish to this stripped-down glorified concert. We're looking for revivals that improved on the originals.

No, No, Nanette **(1971).** In a twenty-year-span, Harry Rigby had only produced three musicals on Broadway. All failed. Now he was reviving a forty-five-year-old show in the 1970s, when Broadway audiences still wanted new musicals? If they wanted an old show, they'd go to their local summer stock tent.

Rigby wanted Ruby Keeler as his star and Busby Berkeley as his director-choreographer. The two old pros had dazzled Hollywood with *Dames, Footlight Parade, Gold Diggers of 1933*, and, of course, *42nd Street*. But Keeler hadn't thought of performing in decades. Berkeley's most recent Broadway credit had been forty years earlier—and that only when he show-doctored someone else's choreography.

Would audiences even recognize these long-retired names? They may have even forgotten the more recent if seldom-now-seen Bobby Van.

Keeler would play Sue, the well-to-do wife of Jimmy (Hiram Sherman), who was suspected of philandering—although he was actually innocent. Sue's friend Lucille (Helen Gallagher) made certain that the wife wasn't the last to know; soon she was suspecting that her own husband Billy (Van) was cheating—although he wasn't.

How would a divorce between Jimmy and Sue affect their ward Nanette (Carole Demas)? Frankly, she was now more interested in new beau Tom (Roger Rathburn). Although they'd have many lovers' quarrels before the end of Act Three (yes, *Three*), they and everyone else would reconcile.

David Merrick, who could then boast of producing Broadway's longest-running musical (*Hello, Dolly!*), predicted a three-week run. He was off by 101 weeks, for *Nanette* would play 861 performances after Shevelove dropped five of the original songs and placed some of the remaining nine in different spots.

So this *No, No, Nanette* was really a revisal. Considering, though, that the term really wasn't yet coined, we can grandfather clause this production as a revival.

And, for better or worse, it was a very influential one. After this, many money-men started looking to the past instead of the present for their next productions.

Carousel (1994). Because Richard Rodgers had decided that "The Carousel Waltz" should start "adagio"—meaning slowly—innovative director Nicholas Hytner took his cue from that.

He didn't begin with Julie Jordan, best friend Carrie Pipperidge, and everyone else enjoying themselves at the amusement park, as *Carousel* had always started. Hytner put us in a workroom in Mr. Bascombe's mill where Julie, Carrie, and other workers were mournfully doing their all-too-boring and repetitive tasks.

Above them was an enormous clock. It was a few minutes before six p.m. when work would finally end. Watching these unhappy workers reminded us that time doesn't always fly. Witnessing that clock making oh-so-slow progress was agonizing—and we were just watching.

Finally, the clock struck six, and all heaven broke loose. All the young ladies rushed to the amusement park. Thanks to Hytner, we realized how much, much more the place meant to them as an escape from their dreary lives.

The show benefited from the non-traditional casting of Audra *Ann* McDonald, as she then called herself. As she was exhibiting a glorious soprano in "Mister Snow," she reached the section where she imagined her wedding night. Suddenly she leaned backwards, fell to the ground flat on her back, spread her arms and legs as wide as any starfish could, and exclaimed "Well, Mr. Snow—here I am!"

(Yes, she was—and not for the last time on Broadway.)

Carousel is famous for its lengthy "Bench Scene." Julie and carnival barker Billy Bigelow flirt before committing to each other. Sally Murphy and Michael Hayden did splendidly by it, but even here Hytner insisted on being different.

No bench.

You're a Good Man, Charlie Brown (1999). If this choice makes you slam the book shut, do come back, will you?

Some people like no scenery and minimal props. Some directors urge the audience to "bring something" to such productions.

(Jean Kerr's response: "When I'm asked to 'bring something to a production,' I bring a book.")

Still, for the small Theatre 80 St. Marks and its 160 seats, the few stylized blocks that were seen most of the night served well enough. When the production moved to The Golden Theatre in 1971, those blocks now looked woebegone even on one of Broadway's smallest stages.

For the show's 1999 Broadway revival, the five producers, director Michael Mayer, and set designer David Gallo had a better plan. Let's spend the money, fill the stage, and have the show resemble a Sunday color *Peanuts* comic strip.

Kristin Chenoweth got her Tony-winning breakout role as Sally, a character that didn't even exist in the original and a strong Andrew Lippa song. You're a good show, *Charlie Brown*.

Hello, Dolly! (2019). In a way, this shouldn't make the list, for Bette Midler was playing Bette Midler more than Dolly Levi, which original Dolly, Carol Channing, didn't.

But in the previous thirty years or so, virtually every Broadway revival had been watered down. What made this one notable is that it wanted to show as much as possible what audiences had seen and loved from early 1964 through late 1970.

True, the cast of forty-five had been whittled to thirty-three, but otherwise, the show's sets, costumes, and lighting looked as grand as they originally did. Say what you will about producer Scott Rudin (and who hasn't?), he spent the money and upped theatergoers' perception of a first-class production. And on Tuesdays when Donna Murphy played Dolly—and Bernadette Peters took over, it was hello, greatness.

Author's Choice: *Porgy and Bess* (1976). The Metropolitan Opera once again blew it with the Gershwins-Heyward masterpiece. In the 1930s, the organization said it would do it with white singers in blackface. George Gershwin decidedly rejected that offer.

Now, for the nation's upcoming bicentennial, The Met would produce America's greatest opera—until the powers-that-be decided that they wouldn't.

Sherwin W. Goldman, a budding producer, was devastated, for he had been yearning to see a first-class production of the opera.

As they say, if you want something done, do it yourself.

Almost, but not quite. Goldman had to get help from Houston Grand Opera, which truly earned the word "grand" in its name. Today, some Broadway musicals *may* reach a total of twenty-four in their casts; this production had twenty-four principals alone and an ensemble of thirty-two.

Some Broadway pit orchestras don't have ten pieces; this production had ten violins as well as four violas, four cellos, and twenty-five other musicians. The pit at the theater brings up the word "grand" once more, for it must have resembled the Grand Canyon.

How fitting, too, that the Uris Theater in which it played would seven years later be renamed the Gershwin. This production could have been one reason why.

WHAT'S THE BEST REVISAL OF A MUSICAL?

A musical that's revived but revised is a revisal. Such efforts have become common in the last fifty years or so, as new directors and writers insist they'll rescue the show and "bring it into the (name of the current decade)."

Sometimes it's been known to work . . .

Candide (1974). Those who missed the short-lived 1956 original production but heard the cast album yearned to see it on stage. They were optimistic about a 1972 production that was aiming for Broadway.

Alas, it died in Washington, DC.

Just when it seemed that no one would ever see *Candide*, Harold Prince made the show come alive in Brooklyn and on Broadway; soon it entered the regional theater repertoire.

Prince's environmental staging, Hugh Wheeler's rewrite of Lillian Hellman's absurdist book, and, last but hardly least, Stephen Sondheim's new lyrics made the difference.

Sondheim's major contribution came in a rewrite of "Venice Gavotte." Dorothy Parker's "Lady frilly, lady silly, pretty lady, willy-nilly, lady lightly, lady brightly, charming lady, fly-by-nightly" might make some believe that she owned stock in a company that sold headache remedies.

Sondheim turned those lines (and Richard Wilbur's section that preceded it) into "Life is Happiness Indeed" in which Candide, his beloved Cunegonde, her brother Maximilian, and their serving girl Paquette all gave their worldviews.

Next Sondheim replaced Wilbur's excellent lyrics with equally excellent ones in "The Best of All Possible Worlds," Professor Pangloss' assertion that everything always works out. Voltaire, who wrote his satire approximately two hundred years before the musical's debut, even then took issue with that; he had his characters endure war, rape, murder, and destruction.

Human beings are resilient, though, especially in musical comedies. So at show's end, everyone sang the optimistic "Make Our Garden Grow." Just as they finished, the cow they were depending on for milk dropped dead.

We had to laugh, though, for Pangloss (Lewis J. Stadlen) gave a disgusted look and dismissive hand gesture that said, "It's always something!" (And we nodded in sad agreement.)

Anything Goes (1987). Patti LuPone gave Reno Sweeney arms-akimbo confidence; Howard McGillin was her suave leading man; Anthony Heald was wisely directed by Jerry Zaks to be a true human being; until then, Sir Evelyn Oakleigh had always been played as one of those stiff-upper-lipped, emotionally constipated parodies of a British man.

"So why would Reno be interested in him?" Zaks asked in a question that no one could satisfactorily answer.

This Tony winner actually revised a revival. An off-Broadway *Anything Goes* in 1962 retained eight songs heard at the 1934 premiere, dropped five and added six from other Cole Porter musicals. It made a terrific cast album that has always been in print lo these sixty years. That in turn brought the show back into consciousness; it's a rare community theater and high school that hasn't done it.

That 1962 production isn't among our list of Best Revisals because of a flaw that isn't apparent from simply listening to Eileen Rodgers' Reno expertly essaying the interpolated "Take Me back to Manhattan" on the cast album.

The revised script reveals that Reno sings the song as the ship on which she's been sailing has *just* reached England. And Reno wants to be taken back to Manhattan and endure another long crossing *now*? Why would she when she's so close to London's West End and its many great plays and musicals?

So the 1987 revisal reigns supreme. It retained ten songs heard at the 1934 premiere, two from the 1962 production, and five from other Porter shows, while only excising two from the original production.

The songs that made all three iterations were "I Get a Kick out of You," "Bon Voyage," "All through the Night," "You're the Top," "Public Enemy Number One," "Be Like the Bluebird," "Blow, Gabriel, Blow," and, need we add, "Anything Goes."

No reviser would dump any of those, even in an era where anything goes.

Big River (2003). When Jeff Calhoun was engaged to direct and choreograph Deaf West's revival of this 1985 Tony winner, he decided not to engage the business-as-usual American Sign Language interpreter on the side of the stage.

That, he felt, pulled focus; moreover, it kept those who couldn't hear from seeing everything on stage at every moment.

Instead, his entire cast would be signing so the deaf wouldn't miss his stage pictures. Nine actors were deaf and silently mouthed Roger Miller's lyrics; nine hearing actors sang and employed the signing skills they'd specifically learned for this production.

The most galvanic moment came in the second act during the reprise of the foot-stomping "Waiting for the Light to Shine." After the hearing actors stopped singing, the hearing audience heard for the last fifteen seconds of the song what the deaf actors heard.

Nothing. It was a potent reminder to those who can hear how fortunate they are.

Merrily We Roll Along (Encores! 2012). Lyrics from two new songs stand out. "Growing Up" has Franklin wonder "Why is it old friends don't want old friends to change?" (He has a point.)

In "That Frank," guests at his party detail his many successes. They include that Frank "has a wife who is gorgeous and a son who's straight."

Leave it to a show biz crowd to never take heterosexuality for granted.

Rodgers + Hammerstein's Cinderella (2013). Douglas Carter Beane so radically reconfigured the story that it should have been retitled *Ella and Topher*.

Our heroine is much more often called Ella than Cinderella. Of course: Cinderella is the derisive nickname that her stepmother bestowed on her, but the lass obviously wasn't named that at birth.

More significantly, Beane fleshed out Prince Chris*topher* Rupert (and his other ten names) and made his story and journey as significant as Ella's. He became a down to earth guy, which is why both the program and script didn't call him "The Prince."

Topher was drawn as insecure because his parents died when he was a boy. That necessitated a regent, Sebastian, who quickly became accustomed to running the kingdom. Now that Topher is of age, Sebastian will do all he can to maintain power and continue his corruption of overtaxing peasants and foreclosing on their homes.

Ella gave thirsty, passing-by Topher a drink of water. He didn't treat her with condescension or made her feel irrelevant, as many a prince would. Ella was right to infer that "he appears to have a heart, mind and a soul."

Jean-Michel disagreed. He was a revolutionary whom Sebastian regarded as a minor annoyance. Jean-Michel wouldn't be swayed, and he offered Ella a book that showed a better life in such countries as Norway, Italy, and Japan. That was smart of Beane, for it explained how, in "In My Own Little Corner," the homebound, small-town Ella could fantasize about being a young Norwegian princess, a prima donna in Milan, or a Japanese heiress.

Sebastian, meanwhile, fearing for his job and power, suggested to Topher "a royal wedding" that would provide "a distraction" to the masses.

THE BOOK OF BROADWAY MUSICAL DEBATES, DISPUTES, AND DISAGREEMENTS

He was right; although the populace had been listening to Jean-Michel's call to arms, they easily and immediately lost interest when they heard that "The Prince Is Giving a Ball."

Beane fleshed out the Fairy Godmother, too, by first showing her in the guise "Crazy Marie," her secret identity, just to see how people treat a demented person; those who acted charitably would be amply rewarded.

Ella did. Thus she received her glorious outfit and transportation to the ball. The Fairy Godmother was glad to see Ella give Topher "charity, generosity and kindness" and would help him to cease being regent-whipped. Thus, Beane gave us more than a man and woman who were merely attracted to each other; each could do the other plenty of good, which is what ideally happens in the best relationships.

Beane's *Rodgers + Hammerstein's Cinderella* also suggested that royalty is interested in doing some good for the common man. And if that isn't fairytale material, what is?

Author's Choice: *Cabaret* **(1998).** For decades Joel Grey had owned the role of the Emcee. No one had ever touched his Tony- and Oscar-winning performance.

Then Alan Cumming came along. Where Grey amused, Cumming alarmed. Grey seemed asexual, Cumming pansexual. A *Jesus Christ Superstar* lyric would apply here: "He is dangerous."

In the original 1966 production, the aging and proper Herr Schultz was about to knock on the proper Fraulein Schneider's door for some premarital intercourse. Before he could do that, prostitute Fraulein Kost entered. Herr Schultz didn't want her to know what he and her landlady were about to do, so he told her he was trying to find a coin that he'd dropped.

"You're looking for a groschen?" Kost asked. "I'm looking for two marks."

It's a good joke and a fine exit line, which is how original director Hal Prince staged it. Director Sam Mendes instead had Kost say it while looking Shultz directly in the eyes and making clear she was looking for business. How embarrassed he was that she even asked; how embarrassed the audience was for him.

Mendes saved the chilliest for last. The Emcee removed his coat to reveal that he was wearing a concentration camp uniform with both the yellow star and the pink triangle that respectively broadcast that he was Jewish and gay. Life isn't always a cabaret, old chums.

WHAT MUSICAL HAD THE WORST TROUBLE EN ROUTE TO BROADWAY?

No, No, Nanette **(1971)** had birthing pains that were worse than The Octomom's. Don Dunn's amazing 1973 *The Making of "No, No, Nanette"* tells of thirty-five firings in at 350 pages—one for every ten pages.

Harry Rigby's production wouldn't have happened without Cyma Rubin; her husband Sam was the Faberge and Revlon magnate who put up the money.

Alas, when aging director-choreographer Busby Berkeley deplaned, he immediately fell; weeks later at a dinner party, he fainted. Rubin decreed that a new director and choreographer had to be found and that Berkeley's percentage would be halved from 2 percent to 1 percent.

Bert Shevelove was better known as the co-librettist of *A Funny Thing Happened on the Way to the Forum* than director of *Hallelujah, Baby!* and Lionel Bart's disastrous *Twang!!* (yes, with two exclamation points). Yet he was hired to stage the show, unaware that he'd soon have to rewrite Charles Gaynor's recent rewrite.

Donald Saddler became the new choreographer, although he would pretend to seek Berkeley's okay after he conceived a number. Berkeley always said yes before dozing off.

One general manager quit, and the one who succeeded him did the same. Saddler's assistant was fired. No wonder that star Ruby Keeler told a radio interviewer that "I'm not excited about the show."

When the mother of Carol Demas—the show's Nanette—visited a rehearsal, Shevelove grandly and warmly introduced her to the cast less than a day before he fired the actress. Demas felt terrible even with a financial settlement. When she phoned Roger Rathburn for sympathy, he told her to spend the money on acting lessons.

Rubin suggested that her daughter Loni Ackerman play Nanette, but Shevelove chose Susan Watson, best known as *Bye Bye Birdie*'s pre–Ann

Margret Kim. Watson had nine days to learn seven songs and the "Tea for Two" dance. Thus the first Boston preview was canceled, but when early performances turned out triumphantly, Rubin soon pointed out to Rigby that the contract she'd had him sign essentially made him a mere employee of her new corporation. So she fired the employee—on Christmas Day, yet.

Hiram Sherman became too ill to continue, so Frank McHugh was hired. He played three performances and then was fired in favor of Jack Gilford. A dancer was canned just as she was boarding the flight from Boston to Toronto. Rathburn quit, but returned. Meanwhile, Berkeley was given the task of punching the holes in new pages so they could be accommodated into three-ring binders.

After all this, how could Van tell an interviewer "There have been no fights in this whole show of 50 people and nobody's had any misunderstandings since we started"?

My One and Only (1983). Many directors of musicals have been fired during the Boston tryout. Here Peter Sellars was canned five days *before* the Boston opening.

Soon bookwriter Timothy S. Mayer as well as the set designer and musical director were heading home earlier than they'd expected.

On opening night, Tommy Tune, who was starring as well as co-choreographing with Thommie Walsh, was so embarrassed by what Bostonians saw that he spent part of his curtain call apologizing for it. Tune announced that he and Walsh would now take over the direction.

They'd accept the little help from their friends Mike Nichols and Michael Bennett. Peter Stone massaged the book, too.

As Frank Rich would later write in the *New York Times*, "seemingly half of show business pitched in to offer anonymous help."

And yet, on opening night on Broadway, the show played as if it had never had a care in the world.

Author's Choice: *Kwamina* (1961). Richard Adler wrote this musical for his wife, Sally Ann Howes, who had proven herself worthy as Julie Andrews' replacement in *My Fair Lady*.

However, during the Toronto tryout, Howes replaced Adler as her sex partner with her leading man. Talk about trouble out-of-town!

WHAT ELEMENT OF A BROADWAY MUSICAL HAS BECOME KNOWN EVEN TO PEOPLE WHO KNOW NOTHING ABOUT BROADWAY?

"Just One of Those Things." Betty Kirkpatrick, in her *Clichés: Over 1,500 Phrases Explored and Explained*, says this phrase has been used "since the middle 1930s, being popularized by a Cole Porter song."

We can assume that Kirkpatrick means "Just One of Those Things" from *Jubilee* in 1935 and not a completely different Porter song with the same title that was cut from *The New Yorkers* in 1930.

"Everything's Coming Up Roses," *Gypsy.* Sondheim took great (and justifiable) pride in originating this phrase. The populace apparently hasn't had the problem that Jerome Robbins had when expecting a direct object. He asked, "Everything's coming up Rose's *what?*"

"Proud of Your Boy," *Aladdin* (2014). Hard as it is to believe, this song has been said to have given The Proud Boys, the far-right-wing organization of Western chauvinists (their term), its name.

At first, we might assume that one of their members had a child who'd incessantly watched the movie on DVD; that in turn made the father enough aware of the phrase to suggest it at the next meeting.

No. "Proud of Your Boy," which composer Alan Menken and lyricist Howard Ashman wrote for the 1992 film, was cut before its release. Only when the stage musical was being readied was it reinstated.

So did the person overhear it when his son or daughter played the original cast album? Or did one Proud Boy actually see the show?

Could there be a Show Queen among The Proud Boys?

"The Room Where It Happens," *Hamilton.* Would John Bolton, the Republican consultant and political commentator, have called his White House memoir *The Room Where It Happened* if Lin-Manuel Miranda hadn't coined the phrase?

Would the writers of *Grey's Anatomy* have titled the eighth episode of its thirteenth season by that name if *Hamilton* hadn't opened the year before?

As of this writing, the phrase has been referenced more than a half-million times on Google. If that doesn't qualify it as a genuine idiom, what would?

Author's Choice: *Camelot* (1960). We've since learned that Jacqueline Kennedy's interview with Theodore H. White in the November 29, 1963, issue of *Life* magazine wasn't as spontaneous as he led readers to believe.

Mrs. Kennedy allegedly told White that her slain husband President John F. Kennedy "loved *Camelot*. It was the song he loved most at the end: 'Camelot . . . don't let it be forgot that for one brief shining moment there was Camelot.'"

Alan Jay Lerner, the musical's librettist-lyricist, told in his 1978 memoir *On the Street Where I Live* what had happened at a subsequent performance: King Arthur "came to those lines (and) there was a sudden wail from the audience. It was not a muffled sob; it was a loud, almost primitive cry of pain. The play stopped, and for almost five minutes, everyone in the theatre—on the stage, in the wings, in the pit and in the audience—wept without restraint."

However how true or manufactured these stories are, the Kennedy administration has since been dubbed Camelot—a lovely tribute to a lovely musical.

WHAT MUSICAL HAS THE BEST COMEBACK LINE?

***Damn Yankees* (1955).** Lola, once the "ugliest woman in Providence, Rhode Island," has sold her soul to the devil to become a beauty. The trade-off is that she must seduce any man that her boss puts before her.

In order to vamp the former Joe Boyd whom the devil has turned into baseball superstar Joe Hardy, Lola adopts the guise and accent of Señorita Lolita Rodriguez Hernando. Here she insists that "Whatever Lola Wants, Lola Gets," which she expects will make Shoeless Joe from Hannibal, Missouri, shirtless, pantsless, and briefless in a brief time.

After Lola completes the number, Joe—who yearns to be home with his wife—earnestly says "But if it was you I promised to come home to, you'd want me to, wouldn't you?"

What can Lola say? Nothing more than "Oh, I see," and not in her Spanish accent, either. She's been that startled to find a man who's totally devoted to his wife.

West Side Story. After Bernardo's murder, Maria begs Anita to go to the drugstore to tell Tony that she'll meet him later. It's a great deal to ask, for Anita will be helping the man who'd killed her beloved Bernardo. Maria prevails, however, and Anita goes to honor the request.

She encounters the Jets, who taunt, humiliate, and virtually rape her. When she cries out "I want to help!" honorary Jet Anybodys sneers, "Bernardo's girl wants to help!"

In fact, she does. But how can Anita convincingly recount the conversation she'd just had with Maria? Anybodys and the Jets are well within their rights to assume that she has a nefarious plan for revenge.

The Music Man **(1957).** Marian confronts Harold head-on about the previous girlfriends that she's sure he's had.

"One hears rumors of traveling salesmen," she says flatly, certain that she's incontrovertibly trapped him.

When Harold responds, "Now, Miss Marian, you mustn't believe everything you hear," she probably thinks he'll try to sweet-talk his way out of the indictment.

No. What he adds is, "After all, one even hears rumors about librarians."

What can Marian say? She knows she's been picked apart more than a little by River City's gossips who swear that she had an illicit relationship with the richest man in town. Marian must concede that the bad press that Harold has received could be as inaccurate as what's been said against her.

Gypsy. Louise, like so many grown children who've endured too-interested mothers, now wants to break free and live her own life. She isn't ungrateful for Rose's guidance; she even offers to fund a school that her mother can run. But all Rose wants to run is Louise.

Rose details all the working, pushing, finagling, scheming, scrimping, and lying awake nights. "So now tell me," she snarls. "What'd I do it for?" Louise simply says, "I thought you did it for me, Momma."

What can Rose say? Parents are *expected* to make sacrifices for their children; it's in the job description. Rose, you were just doing what you were supposed to do (although how and why you did it is up for debate).

The Little Mermaid (2008). After Ariel has fallen in love with a human, she meets her Aunt Ursula, from whom the family has been estranged.

"Father says you're wicked and hateful," says Ariel—to which Ursula blithely says, "Yes! But he says the same thing of humans, doesn't he, snookums? And we both know that's not true, don't we?"

Checkmate! Ariel is convinced her father can't be right about handsome Eric, so she must at least entertain the possibility that her father isn't right about everything. He may not be, but he certainly is about the wicked and hateful Ursula.

Author's Choice: *Curtains* (2007). Frank Cioffi is investigating the murder of Jessica Cranshaw, star of *Robbin' Hood*, the musical that's trying out at the Colonial Theatre in Boston.

There he meets theater critic Darryl Grady and tells him that "your review of *Robbin' Hood* was needlessly cruel and way off the mark."

Grady smugly responds, "Well, I'm not sure you know how to judge acting, Lieutenant."

Cioffi must concede, "Well, you're the expert. However, I regret to inform you that I'm now placing you under arrest for the crime of murder."

Rupert Holmes' stage direction states "All react in shock." Grady says, "What?! Have you lost your mind?! What in God's name are you saying?"

Cioffi, a community theater star during his vacation, responds, "I'm saying my best lines from Agatha Christie's *Murder at the Vicarage*. I played Chief Inspector Slack for the Natick Town Players two summers ago," before he adds in mock surprise, "Oh, did you think I was saying that for real? Gosh, I'm not sure you know how to judge acting."

WHAT MUSICAL IMPROVED ITS SOURCE MATERIAL?

The Secret Life of Walter Mitty **(1964).** Why does James Thurber's pussy-lacerated husband, both in his 1939 short story and the 1947 film version, stay in his horrible marriage?

In musicalizing the property, bookwriter Joe Manchester, composer Leon Carr, and lyricist Earl Shuman gave the couple a teenage daughter. Penninah adores her father, who in turn adores her.

Many miserable husbands and wives stay together "for the children." Walter only has one child, but we're convinced that their mutual admiration is enough to keep him home.

Sweet Charity **(1966).** She was an out-and-out prostitute in Fellini's *Le Notti di Cabiria* (*The Nights of Cabiria*, 1957). Bob Fosse, when conceiving the musical, was wise to change her to a taxi-dancer. Granted, these women, who charged men who wanted to rub their bodies against theirs, weren't paragons of virtue. Still, few prostituted themselves.

In the musical, movie star Vittorio Vidal has just been dumped by his girlfriend when Charity just happens to bump into him; she accompanies him home. In the original film, after Alberto Lazzari is abandoned by *his* girlfriend, he happens to look across the street and sees Cabiria street-walking. That would make his picking her up and taking her home far less likely than the chance meeting that Vittorio and Charity had.

(Not that Fosse and eventual bookwriter Neil Simon solved all the musical's problems. More on that later.)

King of Hearts **(1978).** No, the musical version of the cult film suffered from not-quite-right ersatz French music from rock-centric Peter Link as well as atrocious lyrics from Jacob Brackman.

("It's simply scandalous how they've abandoned us" doesn't quite rhyme. Didn't anyone through rehearsals or the Boston tryout, seeing the show night after night, think to suggest "It's simply *scandalous* the way they *handle us*"?)

And yet, either original bookwriter Steve Tesich or reliever Joseph Stein found a way to avoid the criticism that had plagued the original 1966 film. Daniel Boulanger's screenplay showed us lovable lunatics who seemed well adjusted. Well, then, why were they institutionalized? The musical gave each significant character a monologue that explained how.

Frankly, though, had a more talented and experienced composer and lyricist done the musical, each explanation would have been a most moving song.

Author's Choice: *Thoroughly Modern Millie* **(2002).** One of bookwriter Dick Scanlan's first stage directions stated that his Millie would have "verve and confidence."

In the film, Julie Andrews' Millie was a nice enough young miss who let a number of adventures happen to her. Although she had a goal of marrying her wealthy boss (whomever he might be), she didn't pursue it with the vigor that Scanlan's Millie showed in the first song that he and composer Jeanine Tesori had her sing: "Not for the Life of Me." Here she told why she moved to the Big City from "a one-light town where the light is always red."

Andrews had no analogous song or even a line of dialogue that showed such passion. She also wasn't mugged as Scanlan's Millie was on her first day in the city. Many young women who endured that would take the next bus home. Millie, however, was even more determined to conquer New York.

After Millie moved into the Hotel Priscilla and met the obviously rich Miss Dorothy Brown, she took umbrage when her new friend accused her of being "poor"; Millie preferred "broke."

"'Poor' sounds permanent," Millie said. "'Broke' can be fixed."

The film never gave a clue to the nefarious Mrs. Meers' past. Scanlan made her a former actress whose failure on stage resulted in her getting into the business of kidnapping women and delivering them into white slavery. Could it be that she was jealous of young women who might have the career that had been denied her?

In the film, her two helpers were simply named Oriental #1 and #2. Scanlan not only gave them names—Bun Foo and Ching Ho—but also enhanced the plot by having the latter greatly taken with Miss Dorothy. As a result, he made certain that she wasn't harmed; in the film, her fate is left to fate.

While no one can condone kidnapping and white slavery, at least these men were given a seemingly worthy cause that made their crimes a tiny bit easier to bear: the money that they earned would help them get their beloved mother to America. In the film, they simply seemed like bad guys out solely out to make a buck.

In the office, Andrews' Millie seemed genuinely afraid of longtime receptionist Miss Flannery. Foster's Millie was written to stand up for what she saw as her rights.

That Sheryl Lee Ralph, Terry Burrell, and Leslie Uggams portrayed Muzzy Van Hossmere—played by Oscar-nominated Carol Channing in the film—was not a case of non-traditional casting. Scanlan stated in his stage directions that the character was "a glamorous and wise African-American." (The decision to make her Black also resulted in an added benefit near show's end.)

In the film, Jimmy Smith, who'd been pursuing Millie, took her to Muzzy's party where she ruined a guest's dress by dousing it with soy sauce. In the stage musical, that happened as well—but Scanlan made the victim no less than celebrated author Dorothy Parker. Thus the gaffe was far more embarrassing and serious.

Later Millie saw Jimmy and Miss Dorothy come out of the same hotel room. Although Millie had set her sights for her rich boss Trevor Graydon, she was nevertheless fast falling for Jimmy, despite his being impoverished and lackadaisical. She felt devastated that he and her new best friend were apparently dallying together.

This happened in both properties—but Scanlan and Tesori know that musicals make characters sing when they reach emotional peaks. So they didn't just leave the plot at that; they created "Forget about the Boy," giving Millie a far more forceful view of matters.

Millie eventually gleaned what Mrs. Meers was doing, but in order to prove it, a new hotel guest needed to be set up as a plant. The film put Jimmy in drag; actor James Fox was unconvincing in look and speech. Far smarter were Scanlan and Tesori, who had Muzzy—totally unknown to Mrs. Meers—perpetrate the ruse.

Or so they thought. As it turned out, Muzzy and Mrs. Meers previously knew each other when *both* were actresses.

Ching Ho wasn't a mere stereotype who couldn't possibly capture a white woman's love; he won Miss Dorothy to the delight of Muzzy, who was her stepmother, and Jimmy's too.

Yes, that plot twist came from Richard Morris' screenplay, but the resolution was so much more meaningful here. Not unlike *Ragtime*, where a Jewish man marries a WASP woman and both adopt a Black child, *Thoroughly Modern Millie* showed an African American woman delighted that her white stepdaughter was giving her an Asian son-in-law *and* that her wealthy stepson was marrying a lovely lass who's worthy despite her poor—nay, broke—status.

As a little lagniappe, the curtain call showed Bun Foo and Ching Ho's mother arriving in America at last. On stage, *Thoroughly Modern Millie* became a thoroughly successful improvement.

WHAT CHARACTER IN A MUSICAL HAS THE MOST INTERESTING NAME?

Jack S. Farnsworth (*Li'l Abner*, 1956). To get the joke, quickly say the first name and the initial.

Anybodys (*West Side Story*, 1957). What's her real name? That's anybody's guess.

Joe Wellington (*Golden Boy*, 1964). When Clifford Odets wrote his 1937 play *Golden Boy*, he named his leading character Joe Bonaparte. For the musical version, the character would not be Italian, but African American, so he changed the name to Wellington.

Considering that the Duke of Wellington bested Napoleon Bonaparte in the Battle of Waterloo in 1815, was this Odets' way of saying the musical would be better than the play?

Christmas Eve (*Avenue Q*, 2003). No explanation was given how this day of the year became a young woman's name. Was she born then? If so, she shares the honor with Harry Warren, composer of "Lullaby of Broadway."

Ann Harada, as Christmas Eve, did introduce a Broadway lullaby: "The More You Ruv (*sic*) Someone (the more you want to kill them)."

She started in perfunctory fashion before suddenly moving into a rendition that would have made Judy Garland smile in admiration.

Author's Choice: Usnavi (*In the Heights*, 2008). A great percentage of Broadway theatergoers may well have assumed that Usnavi was a genuine Latinx name; for all they knew, there could be a Usnavi on every block of Washington Heights.

The joke was on them when they learned how the young man got his name. When his parents sailed to New York from the Dominican Republic, they saw a ship that had "US Navy" emblazoned on it. In an effort to assimilate, they chose this name for their son.

It was another subtle but significant way of showing the attendees that they had much to learn about their fellow Manhattanites.

What Musical Made the Most Memorable Commercial?

Pippin (1973). Stuart Ostrow, the musical's producer, had tried the television commercial route once before for his *1776* but saw no perceptible results.

Broadway wasn't surprised. The time-honored way to go was by buying space in major newspapers.

Ostrow wondered if the *1776* spot had failed because it was animated. What about live action? He certainly had the right director-choreographer for it: Bob Fosse, who was then riding high with the film version of *Cabaret*.

Fosse actually handed the job to an associate who had Candy Brown and Pam Sousa buttress castmate Ben Vereen. On a New Jersey sound stage, they rehearsed a minute's worth of soft-shoe enhanced by those shoulder and hip thrusts for which Fosse had become famous.

They'd do even better when Fosse dropped by and made some improvements.

And so, in September 1973, eleven months after the opening, viewers saw "a free minute from *Pippin*," as the voiceover proclaimed. "You can see the other 119 minutes of *Pippin*, live at the Imperial Theatre, without commercial interruption."

People did, to the tune of 1,944 performances. That figure was more than three times the run of that season's commercial-free Tony winner *A Little Night Music* that finished at 601. Indeed, *Pippin* closed as the tenth longest-running book musical in Broadway history.

Ever since, a television commercial for a musical has been *de rigueur*; one that doesn't have one suggests it's an also-ran.

And also-rans don't run.

42nd Street **(1980).** Lead from your strength, it's said, and this hit did just that.

Julian Marsh (a pre–*Law & Order* Jerry Orbach) must entice young newcomer Peggy Sawyer (Wanda Richert) to take over for his ailing star. Peggy waffles until Julian gives his most potent argument: "Think of musical comedy—the most glorious words in the English language!"

New Yorkers who were fans of Broadway musicals loved hearing this sentiment night after night on television. Aside from attending the show once again, there was no other place for them to hear it; in one of the great mysteries in the history of original cast albums, those immortal words weren't included on the recording.

Singin' in the Rain **(1985).** "The big musical Broadway has been waiting for," said the announcer, as the show's three leads were seen singing and dancing to the classic 1952 film's "Good Mornin'."

Then came man-in-the-street interviews. One said "I thought it was fantastic and *that*," he added, "is coming from a person who's seen *quite* a few Broadway performances."

That grizzled and wise veteran was a redheaded lad whose bar mitzvah or confirmation was still some months ahead of him. Yet in this boy-on-the-street interview, the kid spoke with such imperiousness and assurance.

As Stephen Sondheim wrote, "Everybody has to go through stages like that."

Teddy & Alice (1987). Theodore Roosevelt, via Len Cariou, roared out with his famous "Charge!"—just before viewers were told how to do just that by telephone.

(Not that many did . . .)

Author's Choice: *Grand Hotel* (1992). An effective commercial didn't necessarily need a celebrity. Paula Glogau proved that through her enthusiasm for this long-running hit two years after it had opened.

After the sixty-one-year-old Kew Gardens cafeteria worker was approached for her woman-in-the-street opinion, she gave it in no uncertain terms.

"Cyd Charisse is fabulous, wonderful!" she said in complete and unshakable earnestness. "I'd like to see the show two more times!"

The interviewer was amused by her passion. He pseudo-innocently goaded her by asking "Why? What could possibly be that good?"

Glogau didn't catch the irony. "I loved it! *So much*! She is fantastic! Her movements! Her dancing! Her voice! Everything about her is terrific!"

The interviewer continued to provoke: "So you didn't like her very much."

Glogau was still too enamored to notice the put-on. "I loved her!" she reiterated with the force of a drill sergeant. As the interviewer laughed in delight, she added, "I'm going to see it twice more!"

"When?" he challenged.

"As soon as I can get tickets!" she immediately responded. Lest anyone worry how that would happen, Glogau said, "My husband works in this area."

She and he could have seen it many times more than twice with the $935 she was paid for her twenty-eight seconds of fame.

WHAT'S THE BIGGEST MISTAKE THAT THE CREATORS OF A MUSICAL MADE?

My Favorite Year (1992). A musical set in 1954 was made in the style and tradition of the Golden Age. Thus it belonged in a traditional theater.

The thrust stage at the Vivian Beaumont serves many maverick shows well, but not one that needed a genuine frame in which musicals of yore comfortably sat.

The Secret Garden (1993). The first act ended with Mary using a key to unlock the door to the eponymous garden. No, the curtain should not have come down there and then. Mary should have opened that door and found not the beautiful collection of plants and flowers she'd expected, but a devastated and dead garden.

Now *that's* a first-act curtain.

13 (2008). Evan Goodman, recently transplanted from Manhattan to Indiana, makes a friend named Archie, who is disabled and must walk with crutches. But Aaron Simon Gross, the appealing actor who played him, trotted out at the curtain call and showed that he was able-bodied.

What a shame that a genuinely disabled lad wasn't cast, given that there aren't many opportunities for such young actors.

Head over Heels (2018). Here comes what might well be a generalization with no inherent merit: The Go-Go's fans, who helped the group to selling over seven million records, probably don't know or care much about Sir Philip Sidney's 1593 pastoral romance *The Countess of Pembroke's Arcadia.*

The idea of putting new songs to a tale of Ancient Greece may not in itself have been a bad one; after all, *Arcadia* deals with issues still very much with us today: sex, politics, and cross-dressing.

Original bookwriter Jeff Whitty and his successor James Magruder kept the show in those long-ago times. What they shouldn't have done is retain such cumbersome names as Basilius, Dametas, Gynecia, Musidorus, Philoclea, and Pythio. Such unfamiliar sounds tend to confuse and ultimately alienate audiences.

Ancient Greece had many names that we still hear today, ones that would have given theatergoers a much easier time in keeping track of everyone: Hector, Jason, Penelope, Alexandra, Nestor, and Chloe.

Needless to say, if Whitty or Magruder had made the changes, Sir Philip Sidney would not have filed a lawsuit.

Author's Choice: *The Fig Leaves are Falling* **(1969).** In 1962, the unknown Allan Sherman issued an album that parodied well-known songs. "Frere Jacques" became "Sarah Jackman," in which she was asked such questions as "How's your Uncle Sidney?" to which she answered "They took out a kidney."

My Son, the Folk Singer was the fastest-ever album to sell a million copies. The following year, Sherman's single of "Hello, Muddah, Hello, Fadduh," in which a homesick lad writes a letter from summer camp, couldn't quite hit number one, but its reaching number two for three weeks straight was accomplishment enough.

With Sherman's superb sense of humor, could a musical comedy be far behind? He also dared to do what comparatively few Broadway rookie lyricists have done: write an original libretto.

Some have alleged that his character Harry Stone was a stand-in for Sherman himself and that the plot came from his own life. Whatever the case, it was the story of middle-aged executive, Harry, who was pursued by Pookie, an attractive *young* office worker.

Many men would have immediately succumbed; Harry, however, was loyal to his wife Lillian. He decided that a second honeymoon was in order.

When Harry made the suggestion, all Lillian could do was give reasons why the plan was impossible. Who'd watch the kids, the dog, and what about their other commitments, too?

Harry had tried; Lillian's pouring arctic-cold water on the idea was enough to push Harry into Pookie's arms and beyond. And wouldn't you know that after their first tryst, Lillian apologized at being so unfeeling at her husband's wanting to do this nice romantic gesture. She'd go on that second honeymoon.

Too late; now that Harry had tasted the delicious forbidden fruit, he couldn't go back—well, not until he saw that sex was all that he and Pookie had in common. The wife you know is better than the devil you've come to know.

That may not be such a surprising plot, but it is one that would have resonated with audiences. The problem was composer Albert Hague. He'd had modest hits with *Plain and Fancy* (1955) and *Redhead* (1959), which were steeped in the Broadway musical tradition. Thus his songs for Harry and Lillian had the right classic sound.

The ones for Pookie, however, were much too old-fashioned for a just-out-of-her-teens lass who's come of age in the rock era. A completely different musical sensibility was needed to contrast the two women in Harry's life.

In the first third of the twentieth century, many hit shows had two different composers: *Poppy* and *Rain or Shine* mean nothing today, but each ran over three hundred performances, which, in the 1920s, was enough to make money for everyone. *Wildflower* and *Rose-Marie*, with two different composers and two different lyricists, in the same decade stayed on Broadway even longer.

Felix Caviliere ("How Can I Be Sure?"), Bob Crewe ("Let's Hang On"), or Neil Diamond ("I'm a Believer") would have served Pookie well. If one of them or their contemporaries had signed on, *The Fig Leaves are Falling* might not have fallen after four performances.

WHAT'S THE MOST CLEVER DECISION MADE BY THE WRITERS OF A MUSICAL?

"Home Sweet Heaven" (*High Spirits*, 1964). In Noel Coward's 1941 comedy *Blithe Spirit*, Elvira is a ghost who returns to greet her now-remarried husband. She mentions that only a few moments earlier she'd been "playing backgammon with a very sweet old Oriental gentleman; I think his name was Genghis Khan."

How wise of Hugh Martin and Timothy Gray to make more of this one joke and have Elvira elaborate on her neighbors in this dynamic eleven o'clock number: "We all sit 'round King Arthur's table, Freud and Cain and Abel, Barnum and Bailey, Oscar Wilde and me!"

Considering how charming Tammy Grimes was, we can see why those luminaries would want to rub elbows with her.

The Wiz (1978). When you're working on a new version of *The Wizard of Oz*, what do you do when you get to the spot where Dorothy has been famously singing "Over the Rainbow" for thirty-five years?

How can you top or even match the Oscar winner that the American Film Institute named Best Movie Song on its "100 Years/100 Songs" list? The Recording Industry Association of America and the National Endowment for the Arts were even more effusive, choosing it as number one on their lists of the best songs of the entire twentieth century.

Charlie Smalls, composer-lyricist for *The Wiz*, solved the problem by not writing *anything* for the analogous moment in the musical. Call him as cowardly as a certain lion, but Small could have pointed out that MGM Chief Executive Officer Louis B. Mayer didn't want the song in the 1939 film because it "slowed down" the story—and what was good enough for L. B. was good enough for Smalls.

La Cage aux Folles (1983). Even in 1983, many in the Broadway audience wouldn't want to see two grown men kiss, despite their being a couple for decades.

You might expect at show's end, after everything has worked out splendidly for the couple, that the two would kiss then and there. Instead, George and Albin regarded each other with affection, put their arms around each other's shoulders, and exited chuckling.

However, in the ensuing decades since the Tony winner's premiere, many productions now do have them kiss.

The best of times is now.

Author's Choice: "Il Mondo Era Vuoto" (*The Light in the Piazza*, 2005). As soon as Fabrizio sees Clara, it's love at first sight—exactly what so many musical theater heroes have experienced long before him.

So what can he say that we haven't heard before? Composer-lyricist Adam Guettel knew that any observation that Fabrizio would make would only be a variation on "Your lips, your eyes, your cheeks, your hair are in a class beyond compare."

As a result, he wisely decided to let Fabrizio sing in Italian, knowing that anyone in the audience who didn't even know a *parola* of the language would pretty much know what he was saying, anyway.

What Musical Was Most Impacted by History?

Star Dust (1932). In 1931, Cole Porter's "I Get a Kick out of You" contained the lyric "I get no kick in a plane; I shouldn't care for those nights in the air that the fair Mrs. Lindbergh goes through."

However, on March 1, 1932, twenty-month-old Charles Lindbergh, Jr. was kidnapped and later found dead. So when *Star Dust* wasn't getting anywhere while *Anything Goes* was in 1934, Porter wanted to place the song in there.

Mentioning anything to do with Lindbergh, however, would be in questionable taste. So, in the category of "It's an ill wind that blows no one any good," the tragedy allowed Porter to come up with an even better line: "Flying too high with some guy in the sky is my idea of nothing to do." Now he had five "I" sounds that rhymed and a new show in which to put them.

The Girl Who Came to Supper (1963). The opening number of Noel Coward's new musical was "Long Live the King If He Can" when the show had its world premiere in Boston on September 30.

Grand Duke Charles started the song in typically droll Noel Coward fashion: "As Regent of a Balkan state, I have to be realistic. My loving people cultivate an impulse to assassinate that is positively sadistic."

Very funny in Philadelphia, where the show opened on November 5. On November 22, it ceased to amuse when President John F. Kennedy was assassinated in Dallas.

Coward had to work in a hurry to rewrite an old song of his so that when performances resumed on November 23, Grand Duke Charles was singing about "My Family Tree" which had no such misfortune.

Six (2021). Catherine Parr, the sixth of Henry VIII's half-dozen spouses, asks some good questions to her five predecessors.

"Why does anyone know who we are? Who was Henry VII's wife? Henry VI's? Henry V's?"

Parr answers the question for them: "We don't know. The only reason people know who we are is because there's six of us."

(You know, she's right?)

Author's Choice: "November 22, 1963" (*Assassins*, 1990). In this surreal scene, John Wilkes Booth is encouraging Lee Harvey Oswald to assassinate President Kennedy. "Fifty years from now," he says, "they'll still be arguing about the grassy knoll, the Mafia, some Cuban crouched behind a stockade fence."

John Weidman wrote those words more than thirty years ago, approximately twenty-seven years after the assassination. He wasn't overstating the case. As of this writing, we're closer to sixty years later and they're still arguing, especially authors who have collectively written more than forty thousand—yes, forty thousand—books on the subject.

What Question Would You Like to Ask Those Who Worked on a Musical?

John Raitt told this author that the rumor is true.

Richard Adler told this author that the rumor was false.

The question involves *The Pajama Game*, which had Raitt as the leading man who sang the score that Adler had co-written with Jerry Ross.

The question: Did they write the *entire* score? Some have alleged that Loesser, who did mentor the two young songwriters, wrote "A New Town Is a Blue Town" and "There Once Was a Man."

Raitt sang the former as a solo and duetted in the latter, so he might be more reliable than Adler, who undoubtedly would have wanted to save face.

"A New Town Is a Blue Town" *does* sound somewhat like Loesser's "My Time of Day" from *Guys and Dolls*. "Big D," for *The Most Happy Fella* that Loesser would write after *The Pajama Game* opened, does seem as if it was cut from the same bolt of cloth as "There Once Was a Man."

Betty Comden and Adolph Green. In *Bells Are Ringing* (1956), they wrote about dramatist Jeffrey Moss who, with his writing partner, has been very successful. Now, however, the two have ended their collaboration, and he can't write a thing.

The question: Were Comden and Green referring to themselves? Did each of them fear working without the other, and that either one wouldn't be able to come up with something if they went at it alone?

Ruth Kobart. From the World War II era until late 1963 (when the *New York Daily Mirror* folded), critics from New York's seven newspapers gave only seven musicals unanimous raves.

In October 1961, *How to Succeed in Business without Really Trying* was the last of them.

One of its highlights was the exuberant eleven o'clock number "Brotherhood of Man." Halfway through it, Ruth Kobart, as executive secretary Miss Jones, stood on a desk and did a good deal of brio and belting.

The show was primed for a long run, which it eventually had: 176 weeks.

Kobart stayed for only fifteen of them. She left to play Domina, the harpy wife, in *A Funny Thing Happened on the Way to the Forum*.

The question: Why leave a smash hit that guaranteed lengthy employment? A hit in the hand is worth two just starting out. Granted, *How to Succeed* didn't offer Kobart much stage time. But neither did *Funny Thing*. A look at the published text shows that Domina exits on page twenty-five and doesn't return until page eighty-two.

What did Kobart feel at that now infamous tryout performance in Washington where many have alleged that a mere fifty attendees were in the house? Regrets, she had a few, to be sure.

Of course, the show did work out its problems and ran for 120 weeks. And—funny thing—Ruth Kobart was there for all of them. Apparently she now knew the value of holding onto a job.

Author's Choice: Harold Prince. In 1968, fewer than three years after Lila Kedrova won an Oscar for portraying Madame Hortense in *Zorba the Greek*, Prince cast her as Fraulein Schneider in his London production of *Cabaret*.

The question: Given that his next project would be a musical version of *Zorba the Greek*, why didn't he have her repeat her role? By then, Prince knew she could sing well enough, for she sold her four songs in *Cabaret*. When *Zorba* was revived on Broadway in 1983, Broadway learned that Kedrova could do a musical. She even won a Tony to boot.

WHAT'S THE GREATEST INSULT A BROADWAY MUSICAL HAS EVER ENDURED?

Nowhere to Go but Up **(1962).** Tom Bosley and Martin Balsam starred as Izzy and Moe, federal agents who during the Prohibition took on many disguises to fool bootleggers and bring them to justice.

Recalled Bosley, "We were in Philadelphia when Mel Brooks came to see the show. After the performance, Mel rushed into our dressing room and pulled our suitcases off the shelves and threw our clothes in them. 'With a show like this,' he said, 'you guys gotta get out of town right away. It's hopeless.'"

The next morning, producer Kermit Bloomgarden introduced Brooks as the show's new director. Bosley said to him, "But you told us it was hopeless." Brooks responded, "I need the money."

Fade Out–Fade In **(1964).** Steven Suskin, in *Opening Nights on Broadway*, said that this show received positive notices from five out of the six critics on May 27. It immediately began outgrossing *Funny Girl* and *Hello, Dolly!*

With a hit of that magnitude, people tend to stay a while. One featured player, however, left less than a month later: Tina Louise, to play Ginger on *Gilligan's Island*.

As Vittorio Vidal says when (Sweet) Charity quotes a line from one of his films, "The things I do for money."

The Wizard of Oz **(2012, London).** At a January performance eleven months into the run, few are seated in the London Palladium. Often when attendance is low, performers are inclined to walk through the performance.

No: Michael Crawford, playing the title character, gives 100 percent. So does every other performer with one exception: the white-haired dog that was non-traditionally cast as Toto.

When time came for him to walk the Yellow Brick Road (an oval treadmill), he hung his head low and perfunctorily put one foot ahead of the other. The expression on his face said, "I hate this part of the show."

Compare that to Terry the Terrier, who originated the role in the 1939 film. Watch her as the others cavort on their way to Oz. She's looking up at them, keeping pace and in the moment.

For the rest of that London performance, Dorothy didn't depend on him to walk the walk, but literally and figuratively carried him. On the occasions when this Toto barked, he actually relied on the sound system to do his work for him. At the end of the show when he did deign to give a couple of yelps, the difference in sound left no doubt.

We hear a lot about the atrocious and unethical practice of lip-synching in today's theater, but who'd ever expect it from Toto?

Author's Choice: *Dangerously Funny: The Uncensored Story of The Smothers Brothers Comedy Hour* **(1967).** David Bianculli's excellent book *Dangerously Funny: The Uncensored Story of The Smothers Brothers Comedy Hour* stated that when the Smothers Brothers debuted on CBS on Sunday, February 5, 1967, at nine p.m., they were pitted against NBC's then-wildly popular *Bonanza*. The brothers were given no chance to ever win their time slot.

Ah, but they eventually did—on Sunday, March 19, 1967. However, that was a night on which *Bonanza* was pre-empted. The show that the brothers bested? Sad to say, the televised Ethel Merman revival of *Annie Get Your Gun*.

WHAT WAS THE MOST UNEXPECTED GENESIS OF ANY MUSICAL?

The Boys from Syracuse **(1938).** In the early 1930s, Teddy Hart, Lorenz Hart's younger brother, couldn't expect to be recognized when he walked down the street. Each of his first four Broadway outings couldn't even run two months.

Starting in January 1935, however, Hart was in *Three Men on a Horse*, which ran nearly two solid years, and *Room Service*, which stayed put for fourteen months.

Now Hart was being recognized, but only in a manner of speaking. People would stop and ask him "Aren't you Jimmy Savo?" There was a resemblance between him and the then-famous comic. When Teddy told big brother Lorenz of the problem, a musical version of *The Comedy of Errors*, about two sets of identical twins, began to take shape.

So did a song that had to be at least somewhat biographical: "Big Brother."

***They're Playing Our Song* (1979).** This was not the project that Marvin Hamlisch expected to write with Neil Simon. They had meeting after meeting about musicalizing Simon's 1970 comedy-drama *The Gingerbread Lady*.

Hamlisch was often late for meetings. When he arrived, he blew off a great deal of steam in talking about his current and volatile relationship with lyricist Carole Bayer Sager. This went on for a few weeks.

One day Hamlisch showed up for a work session and Simon handed him a sheaf of papers. They dealt with a composer named Vernon Gersh and a lyricist named Sonia Walsk who were having the toughest time professionally and personally.

Those characters worked it out. Hamlisch and Bayer Sager did not. If they'd only severed their relationship before the show was produced, *They're Playing Our Song* would have undoubtedly had a better lyricist who would create rhymes that truly rhymed.

Well, as a song in *Barnum* wisely states, "Love Makes Such Fools of Us All."

Author's Choice: *Show Boat* (1927). Producer Winthrop Ames' name was attached to thirty-five Broadway productions in the first thirty years of the twentieth century. Yet his most significant contribution to musicals was one he didn't produce.

The first tryout performance of his production of *Old Man Minick* did not go well. Ames joked at the opening night party that next time he'd open a production on a show boat.

Edna Ferber, who had written *Old Man Minick* with George S. Kaufman, had no idea that such a thing as a show boat existed. She was interested . . . then intrigued . . . then possessed. Her 1926 bestseller *Show Boat* spurred the first truly significant musical of the twentieth century. *Old Man Minick* led to "Ol' Man River."

WHAT MUSICAL HAS THE BEST INSIDE JOKE?

New Faces of '52 (1952). In "Boston Beguine," a woman tells of her unsuccessful liaison in "Boston: land of the free, home of the brave, home of the Red Sox."

Non-sports fans may see this as a non sequitur. But in 1952, Boston still had two baseball teams: the American League's Red Sox, and the National League's Braves.

Ten months after the show opened (and only fifteen days before it closed), the Boston Braves moved to Milwaukee (and later to Atlanta, where they remain today). So much time has passed that many don't get Sheldon Harnick's excellent play on words.

"But yes," Harnick has said, "that's what I meant!"

Wish You Were Here (1952). The musical was set in upstate New York, where, from the early 1900s to the late 1960s, Jews from Manhattan and other boroughs would avoid the heat by traveling 130 miles upstate to such hotels as the Concord or Grossinger's.

Always on hand was a tummler, who was, as the dictionary informs, "a professional entertainer or comedian whose function is to encourage an audience and guests at a resort to participate in the entertainments or activities."

Harold Rome's "Ballad of a Social Director" had a tummler state that his occupation demanded him to be a combination of twenty-five people, starting with "Emily Post, Sigmund Freud, Superman, William Boyd, Moss Hart, Danny Kaye, Sir Laurence Olivier . . ."

Kaye and Olivier were often said to be lovers. Did Rome want to show that he was in on the joke by listing them next to each other?

Drat! The Cat! (1965). Ira Levin, in his 1967 landmark novel *Rosemary's Baby*, characterized Guy Woodhouse as a jealous actor who was "touchy reading the theatrical page. Everyone else is out of town with *Skyscraper* or *Drat! The Cat!*"

For the latter musical, Levin wrote the book and lyrics.

In 1997, Levin wrote *Son of Rosemary* as a sequel to his bestseller. One line stated "Joe had managed to get house seats for the first solid hit of the Broadway season, a revival of a failed 1965 musical. . . . The show was a charmer."

In case there's any doubt that Levin meant *Drat! The Cat!*, he mentioned it by name only a few pages later.

Up in One (1979). Peter Allen's one-man show did need a voiceover, and according to the program, it was provided by Vernon Gersch.

Although somewhere in the land there may well be one, two, or more individuals named Vernon Gersch, musical theater enthusiasts associate it with the character that Robert Klein originated in *They're Playing Our Song*.

Klein took time off during the run to record, but to mask his identity (and have some fun in the bargain), Klein chose to use his character's name instead of his own.

The Boy from Oz (2003). In a domestic scene in Peter Allen's house, a bulletin board sported a card that had the logo of *Soon*, the 1971 musical that lasted all of three performances.

The cast may not have been to blame; it featured Barry Bostwick, Nell Carter, Richard Gere—and Peter Allen.

Author's Choice: *Bye Bye Birdie.* Rose Alvarez, taunted by her would-be mother-in-law because she's Latina, declared a Spanish American war on the woman. In her eleven o'clock number, Rose vowed "I'll be more Espanol than Abbe Lane!"

Lane was a sultry movie star from the late 1940s until the early 1960s, gracing such films as *The Americano, Susana y yo,* and *Maricaibo.* For eleven years, she was married to Francisco de Asís Javier Cugat Mingall de Brue y Deulofeo, better known as bandleader Xavier Cugat, with whom she recorded some of her many albums. One, *The Best of Abbe Lane*, included "Babalu," "Malaguena Salerosa," and "Pan-Amor E Cha Cha Cha."

Abbe Lane was born in Brooklyn as Abigail Francine Lassman. As a result, Rose Alvarez wouldn't have much trouble being "more Espanol than Abbe Lane."

WHAT TITLE OF A BROADWAY MUSICAL WAS CHANGED FOR THE BETTER?

My Fair Lady. That *My Lady Liza* was a working title is well known, and would have been a perfectly decent alternative.

For a while there, though, Lerner and Loewe were considering *Fanfaroon*.

What?!?!

It's a British term for a person who brags; to be sure, Henry Higgins does just that after he transforms his student into his fair lady.

But *Fanfaroon*? Does this sound like a hit to you? Can you hear someone saying "You won't believe it, but I got two for Saturday night for *Fanfaroon*! Sure, I had to go to a scalper and pay a fortune, but come on: this is *Fanfaroon*!"

The Sound of Music (1959). For a while there, Rodgers and Hammerstein were calling it *The Singing Heart*.

Can you imagine what those who have endlessly branded this musical as much too sticky sweet would say if the show had retained its original name?

Applause (1969). Three-sheets in the lobby of the Mechanic Theatre in Baltimore during the last week of 1969 were advertising the upcoming Lauren Bacall vehicle as *Applause, Applause*.

The show's wonderful title song does use the word "applause" twice in a row. The problem is that "Applause, applause" has become a droning expression that people use when someone says something that doesn't impress them: "Applause, applause," they sardonically respond.

One *Applause* was quite enough. Always leave 'em wanting more.

Author's Choice: *Musical Husbands.* No, it never was an actual musical; it's the mythical one that marked the Broadway debut of composer Franklin Shepard and bookwriter-lyricist Charley Kringas in *Merrily We Roll Along.*

Actually, *Merrily*'s bookwriter George Furth originally called his show-within-a-show *Musical Husbands: The Barbara Hutton Story.*

Barbara Woolworth Hutton, actually. She was heir to the chain of stores casually known as "The Five and Dime." But she was more famous for having no fewer than seven husbands, and was marrying the last one in 1964—the same year that *Musical Husbands* supposedly opened.

As the show got closer to production, someone let better taste prevail; the second half of the title was dropped. Would Hutton have minded if they hadn't? No—she'd died two years before *Merrily* died, before she could even consider marrying Number Eight.

Now you know.

WHAT WAS THE MOST MISLEADING MOVE THAT A MUSICAL MADE?

Allegro **(1947).** The second performance of the New Haven tryout. Lisa Kirk, when singing the dynamic "The Gentleman Is a Dope," falls into the orchestra pit. She climbs back on stage so deftly that she receives what we call admiration applause.

Kirk had done it the night before, too—but accidentally. This time, it was accidentally-on-purpose. She wanted that appreciative applause that first-nighters had given her twenty-four hours earlier.

This time, bookwriter-lyricist Oscar Hammerstein was waiting backstage to tell her that if she ever tried it again, she'd be fired.

(*Allegro* was having enough problems as it was.)

No Strings **(1962).** Richard Rodgers' musical claimed to have just that: no strings in its orchestra. And while there were no violins in the on-stage band, orchestrator Ralph Burns did write parts for a harp, guitar, and bass. (The bass is most noticeable at the end of "You Don't Tell Me.")

Ironically, when Burns decided to record his own album of the score, he included strings in his orchestra.

Half a Sixpence (1965). Opening night, when there's so much on the line, during the charming dance section of "If the Rain's Got to Fall," a chorus boy spins a little too fast which makes his boater hat fly off his head and onto the stage. The number still has some minutes to go; he can't hold up the dancers behind him so he must leave it there.

But star Tommy Steele comes to the rescue. During one of his circular moves around the stage, he quickly bends over, retrieves the hat, and Frisbees it over to the hatless chorus boy.

The first-nighters go wild. Is there anything that Tommy Steele can't do?

Be honest, for one thing. This routine was perfected during the Boston tryout and continued through each of the Broadway's 511 performances.

At least Lisa Kirk did her trick only once.

Tommy Tune: White Tie and Tails (2002). Tune takes questions from the audience and is surprised when a woman says she was his student in the days when he taught dance. He invites her to join him on stage to enact some choreography of yore and the audience applauds enthusiastically when she turns out to be terrific.

She should be; she's a plant. As Inspector Clouseau once said, "Every move I make is carefully planned."

The Cher Show (2018). Given the title of the musical, fans of the former Cherilyn Sarkisian must have been furious after they'd paid top dollar for their tickets, settled in their seats, and only then discovered that, despite that title, Cher herself wasn't in it.

Author's Choice: *Band in Berlin* (1999). The sad story of The Comedian Harmonists, a German sextet that began entertaining in 1927 and would have continued beyond 1934 had the Nazis not condemned them for having three Jewish members.

Making matters more heartbreaking was seeing the last surviving Harmonist telling the tale on a black and white film. The picture and soundtrack are marred by nips and crackles. But the audience is so moved to see that Hitler hadn't totally succeeded.

At the curtain call, the six performers who'd played The Harmonists took their bows. They were followed by the real-life actor who had played the survivor on film.

What's the Funniest (if Cruelest) Line that a Daily Newspaper Critic Wrote When Reviewing a Musical?

Because we're talking about *daily* newspaper critics, John Simon, the meanest of them all, is not eligible; most of his career was spent at *New York*—a weekly magazine.

Besides, much of what John Simon wrote should never be repeated.

We're not just looking for cleverness, such as what Clive Barnes delivered in the *New York Times* in his review of *How Now, Dow Jones* (1967). He termed this Wall Street–centric musical "How to Try in Business without Really Succeeding."

No, we're talking *mean*.

Walter Terry for the *New York Herald Tribune* on *Oh Captain!* (1958). Well, a devoted and dedicated dance critic only goes to a musical for one thing. So while he didn't elaborate on the star's acting or singing, he did decree that "When Tony Randall dances, he tortures the air."

Stanley Kauffmann for the *New York Times* on *Pousse-Café* (1966). This musical version of *The Blue Angel* opened not long after Burt Bacharach and Hal David's title song for the film *What's New, Pussycat?* had climbed the charts.

So Kaufman began his review "What's new, *Pousse-Café?*"

His next words were "Answer: nothing good."

Kauffmann missed a good opportunity, though, to be even meaner. Considering that "What's New, Pussycat?" has its singer warble over the next seven notes "Woh, oh, woh, oh, woh, oh, woh"—which Kauffman could have turned into "Woe, woe, woe, oh, woe."

Clive Barnes for the *New York Times* on *Via Galactica* (1972). The musical set in 2972—a thousand years in the future—had performers jumping on trampolines to give the illusion that they were weightless in space.

What they really resembled were people jumping on trampolines. *Via Galactica* was nevertheless a major event, not because the music was written by Galt MacDermot of *Hair* fame; he'd already been tainted a few weeks earlier with the wretchedly received *Dude*.

What set the musical show apart was its opening the first new Broadway theater since 1928.

One expects a review to begin with a comment about the show in question. Barnes' began "Well, there is always the theater."

Not that people could visit it after the week was out. *Via Galactica* never had to update its time frame to 2973 or 2974.

Frank Rich for the *New York Times* on *Legs Diamond* (1988). After Peter Allen's musical had slogged through nine weeks of staff-firing previews, Rich called it "a sobering interlude of minimum-security imprisonment that may inspire you to pull out a pen and attend to long-neglected tasks, like finishing last Sunday's crossword puzzle or balancing a checkbook."

Despite the mention of a checkbook, this was not a money review.

Author's Choice: Walter Kerr for the *New York Herald Tribune* on *My Fair Lady* (1956). The Lerner-Loewe masterpiece opened on March 15, 1956, proving that one didn't always need to beware the Ides of March.

Kerr, like so many of his brother wizards, raved, using such words as *electrifying, glorious, magnificently, exuberant, delight, jubilantly,* and *joy.*

So why is Kerr's review included here? He reported that after "The Rain in Spain," "you couldn't have stopped *My Fair Lady* if you'd invited the authors of *Buttrio Square, Hit the Trail,* and *Carnival in Flanders* to work over the second act."

Buttrio ran seven performances in 1952, *Hit the Trail* amassed four in 1953, and *Flanders* made it to seven in 1954. In the following two to four years, perhaps the authors were j-u-s-t healing from the critical and financial wounds. Then Kerr had to go and rip off the Band-Aids.

Shouldn't there be a statute of limitations on being criticized for your flop?

HOWEVER, WHICH MUSICAL THEATER PROFESSIONAL DELIVERED CRITICISM HARSHER THAN ANY CRITIC?

Me and Juliet (1953). Oscar Hammerstein didn't like what Richard Rodgers was proposing for their next show: an original musical *about* a musical that's been running on Broadway for a while. Rodgers wanted to give audiences a look backstage.

Despite his objections, Hammerstein began work on the book and lyrics; after all, a few years earlier Rodgers had reluctantly agreed to write a show based on Hammerstein's idea. *Allegro* became their only flop in six tries.

The reviews for what became *Me and Juliet* included "It needs work" (Atkinson, *New York Times*) and "a big disappointment" (Coleman, *New York Daily Mirror*). Walter Kerr in the *New York Herald Tribune* used the words *limp, restless, failing,* and *loss* before he concluded with "Rodgers and Hammerstein have come perilously close to writing a show-without-a-show."

Nevertheless, Hammerstein was a pro who made a habit of dutifully attending a performance of his currently running musicals each week to ensure that the cast was continuing to do its utmost. After one matinee, he returned home where his sister-in-law matter-of-factly asked how *Me and Juliet* had played that afternoon.

Hammerstein was uncharacteristically silent for a long moment before snarling "I hate that show!"

Here's Love (1963). After Meredith Willson had adapted *Miracle on 34th Street* into this musical, he stated in the show's souvenir program that his goal was to change the recent tendency for writers who "create plays that do not entertain audiences." That's why, he said, "audiences stay home."

After this essay was reprinted in the *New York Herald Tribune*, Stephen Sondheim took time out from penning the score to his maverick *Anyone Can Whistle* to write a letter to the editor.

Among his observations were "Look at statistics, Mr. Willson: freshness is even commercial. *Who's Afraid of Virginia Woolf?* is bringing back the audiences that *The Unsinkable Molly Brown* drove out."

This is even more biting when one considers that the score to *The Unsinkable Molly Brown* was written by Meredith Willson.

Do I Hear a Waltz? **(1965).** What goes around sometimes comes around. It did for Stephen Sondheim when this new musical was in New Haven, Connecticut, the norm for a Richard Rodgers show. For the first time in twenty-two years, Rodgers was working with a new lyricist. Sondheim came to rehearsal with a lyric to a recently minted Rodgers melody.

According to Arthur Laurents, the show's bookwriter, Rodgers looked at the lyric and, in front of the entire company, said "Do you think I can give this piece of shit to my actors?"

Sondheim couldn't go complaining to the producer. He was Richard Rodgers.

Gone with the Wind **(1972).** Bonnie Langford played Bonnie Blue Butler, the young daughter of Rhett and Scarlett in this musical version of the famous novel and film.

On opening night at the Drury Lane Theatre in London, Noel Coward wasn't impressed with the seven year old. Some claim that he said of the overlong show "Two things should be cut—the second act and the child's throat."

Others report that during the burning of Atlanta when a horse defecated on stage, Coward said "They could solve two problems at once if they shoved the child up the horse's ass."

Of course, that he made both observations—or neither—is entirely possible.

Despite them, Langford went on to a lifelong career, ranging from Baby June in the 1974 Angela Lansbury revival of *Gypsy* to Roz in the 2019 London edition of *9 to 5*. As a result, in the category of "Living well is the best revenge," she today finds Coward's remarks quite amusing.

Oh, Brother! **(1981).** Donald Driver's adaptation of Shakespeare's *The Comedy of Errors* was set in the volatile Middle East.

Lew's wife gave birth to identical twins, which means more than twice as much work as having one baby. So what do the new parents do? They go out and adopt another set of twins.

There wouldn't be a show if they hadn't, which would have been fine with Frank Rich of the *New York Times*.

"What's funny about the Middle East today?" he wrote. "Why bother to set a show in a region where there's no room, right now, for humor?" Judy Kaye felt there *was* humor, although she put it differently at the memorial for deceased castmate David Carroll: "We called it the *stupidest* show on Broadway."

Author's Choice: *Molly* (1973). Much was revealed in *How I Lost 10 Pounds in 53 Years* by Kaye Ballard—or Kay Ballard, as she was known "for the first, last and only time in my career."

The reason? Said Ballard in her audiobook, "Well, let's just say I will never go to a numerologist for advice again!"

Molly was the musical version of the radio and television hit *The Goldbergs.* Ballard played Gertrude Berg's famous character Molly Goldberg—"a Yiddish answer to *I Remember Mama*," she said.

But Ballard, born Catherine Ballotta, found that "many prominent Jews objected to that"—she wasn't Jewish.

Ballard insisted that *Molly* had "a very good score" but conceded that it had "a so-so-book" and "an inept director." Paul Aaron, she said, "wanted the cast to play patty-cake games before every rehearsal to relax us." What's more, she said, "We would spend weeks rehearsing only one number and ignoring the rest."

It apparently showed. After the Boston opening (and pans), Ballard said Aaron left and didn't return. Noted character actor Billy De Wolfe urged her to have Aaron fired. Ballard didn't explain why she didn't, considering that she had already lost confidence in him.

Aaron did return. "Two days before we were to preview on Broadway!" Ballard exclaimed, to "throw an entire new first act at us right before our first New York performance. I became a screaming Shelley Winters," she said before demanding, "Where were you the last three weeks?"

(If Aaron had a new first act, he was apparently rewriting.)

Aaron rebutted that they had three more weeks; Ballard saw matters differently: "The first preview tells people exactly what is going on and the word 'bomb' spreads like wildfire."

True enough for shows that *don't* go out of town. For those who followed Broadway, *Molly*'s Boston run had already let the bomb out of the bag.

"Somehow we actually managed to learn the new first act," Ballard said without revealing if she thought it better or worse. What she did say was that "I also called in another writer named Norman Martin to do some songs." (Why, if it was a "very good" score?)

At the first preview, producer Alexander H. Cohen and Ethel Merman were both in the first row until intermission. Ballard was livid, and later confronted Merman, who didn't apologize but urged "Ballard! Get out of this thing!" which was much the same sentiment that Maureen Stapleton told her.

Ballard was buoyed when Michael Bennett agreed to attend, giving her "hope that he would take over." She then confessed that "he heard the Overture and walked out."

Alan Arkin was recruited and stayed. He'd only directed one show, but it was a hit: *The Sunshine Boys* by Neil Simon. However, it was neither a musical nor did it have a script by *Molly*'s Louis Garfinkle and Leonard Adelson.

Ballard praised Arkin's efforts before admitting "we had run out of time and out of money. They didn't even have enough money for orange juice on the set," she groused before also criticizing the scenery as "very dark and gloomy" because the show was set during the Great Depression.

(But the Goldberg's could have painted their flat with bright colors before then, couldn't they?)

Also blamed for poor business was "a gas crisis." Indeed, one did start in October 1973, only weeks before *Molly*'s November 1 Broadway opening: the Organization of Arab Petroleum Exporting Countries had levied an oil embargo against countries that had supported Israel during the Yom Kippur War.

"So," said Ballard, "the bus (*sic*) and tunnel people couldn't get there." (They apparently could get to *Grease* and *Pippin*.)

There was one brief shining moment: "Gertrude Berg's son Cherney," Ballard related, "told me I had really captured the essence of his mother."

(Coincidentally, Cherney Berg would die on April 23, 2003: Paul Aaron's sixtieth birthday.)

Ballard mentioned "standing-room-only during matinees. It was really a woman's show; it appealed to the average person rather than"— and here her audiobook reveals a most pretentious voice—"the socially elite'—just as the Goldbergs had."

Does "the socially elite" mean the critics, whose reactions she doesn't mention? "The unfortunate look of a warmed-over corpse" (Watt, *New York Daily News*); "A mess—unamusing, untouching, uninteresting and unnecessary" (Gottfried, *Women's Wear Daily*). As for the two appraisers from the *New York Times*, they ranged from "mediocre" (Clive Barnes) and "a muddle" (Walter Kerr).

Sixty-seven performances later, it came to an end. "On closing night," Ballard said, "I believe I suffered a slight nervous breakdown when singing 'Go in the Best of Health.'"

She undoubtedly didn't dedicate the song to Paul Aaron.

WHAT BROADWAY MUSICAL CHANGED ITS TITLE EN ROUTE TO BROADWAY BUT SHOULDN'T HAVE?

Rainbow. Today, this musical version of N. Richard Nash's 1954 play *The Rainmaker* would be called *The Rainmaker: The Musical.*

Actually, *Lizzie and Starbuck*, referring to the main characters, may sound trite, but it would have been better than *110 in the Shade* (1963). More awkward still was the way the *New York Times* A-B-C ads put it: *One Hundred and Ten in the Shade.*

The cumbersome title didn't even center on the main event. The musical takes place during a blisteringly hot summer, but it's not the heat, it's the humanity that's important.

A father and his two sons know that Lizzie, deemed "plain" by them and many in this Texas town, wants to be a wife and mother and not, to use the term of the day, "an old maid." Their hopes that Sheriff File will be the man to change that status-to-be, but he doesn't seem to care.

Enter Starbuck, a con man who claims he can make rain to soothe the town's parched ills. His apparent romantic interest in Lizzie spurs the previously reluctant Sheriff File to action. Eventually each man is on one knee proposing.

"Pop, what am I going to do?" Lizzie pleads.

"Well, whatever you do," her father says, "remember, you've been asked. You don't never have to go through life a woman who ain't been asked."

Tom Jones and Harvey Schmidt did an estimable job in transforming Nash's play. Of course, it wouldn't have been called *The Rainmaker: The Musical* back then, for creators usually retitled a musical adaptation to inform audiences that they were offering something new and exciting.

Rainbow, an optimistic and audience-friendly word, got as far as the first ads in the Boston newspapers. As for *110 in the Shade*, it did squeak by with a tiny profit. Would *Rainbow* have resulted in a pot of gold?

Cat and Mouse. Alice Van Guilder is a late nineteenth-century debutante who's thoroughly bored with high society. So she becomes a jewel thief.

On the case is Bob Purefoy, a woefully insecure and incompetent policeman. He's smitten with Alice and unaware of her extracurricular activities.

She's the cat; he's the mouse. Perfect title!

Soon, however, it became *Drat! the Cat!* (1965).

This original musical with book and lyrics (by Ira Levin) and equally terrific music (by Milton Schaefer) closed after a week mostly because the producers just didn't have the money.

It received more good reviews than bad, but it might have garnered even better ones if the title hadn't been changed—because the *Drat* in the title suggested a Keystone Kops–like take. That's what director-choreographer Joe Layton delivered, making matters arch and spoofy.

Had it remained *Cat and Mouse*, it most likely would have had a straightforward style that could have pleased the critics even more; after better reviews, some money may have been raised to keep it alive.

The star was Elliot Gould, Barbra Streisand's then-husband. She invested fifty thousand dollars, which may have come up in arguments when they were discussing their divorce a few years later. Gould may have resented that he got nothing out of it while his wife turned "She Touched Me"—*his* song in the show—into *her* hit song "He Touched Me."

At least that recording must have returned to Streisand some of the fifty thousand dollars.

Come Back! Go Away! I Love You! This was an evening of three one-act musicals, so that title at least obliquely suggested three separate stories.

Then this Bock and Harnick musical became *The Apple Tree* (1966).

Strange, for the first story was the only one centered on such a sapling: Mark Twain's *The Diary of Adam and Eve*. In it, Adam tried to get Eve to go away before coming to the conclusion that he loved her.

The Lady or the Tiger offered a medieval princess who had the choice to see her beau either married to someone else (a sacrifice that would show "I love you!") or put to death (the ultimate "Go away!")

No apple tree was in sight.

Passionella was a variation on the Cinderella story where Ella, a chimneysweep, yearned to be a movie star. Once her fairy godmother made it magically happen, Passionella was ready to say "I love you!" to the Bob Dylanish star she met, but he turned out to have been a meek and mild man who'd been magically transformed by *his* Fairy Godmother. When both were unmasked, not much time would pass before they said "I love you."

Without an apple tree *anywhere* in sight.

Century of Progress (1985). In the first twenty years of the Tonys, a mere four Best Musical winners had one-word titles.

But five did in merely the next ten years.

Short, punchy, direct titles were in, which may be one reason why *Century of Progress* was dropped in favor of *Grind*.

The word did give the musical a pungent double meaning. It referred to the daily and seemingly incessant grind of hard work endured by the entertainers at Harry Earle's Burlesque in Chicago. It was, to use the term for a theater that offered neither an elegant setting nor top-notch entertainment, a "grind house."

The musical's real issue, however, was segregation. This was 1933, when Blacks couldn't even perform on the same stage with whites, let alone share dressing rooms. All this was happening when only a few streets away, the forward-thinking "Century of Progress" Exposition—Chicago's World's Fair—was on display.

That the century hadn't progressed very much with racial relations was a more important message than entertainers had to work hard in a less-than-lofty venue.

Author's Choice: *Home, Sweet Homer.* After spending every week of 1975 on the road, *Odyssey*, the musical version of Homer's epic poem, came to Broadway in 1976 with this title.

It suggested a spoof, which the show wasn't; it was a sincere attempt to bring music to the epic story. (*Les Miserables* and *Ragtime* later proved that such a lofty goal could be accomplished.)

With such a silly title, no wonder that Erich Segal, who'd been a professor of Greek and Latin literature at Harvard, Yale, *and* Princeton, removed his name as bookwriter. This title was catnip to those who insist that Broadway musicals are ridiculously silly trifles.

Shows now routinely close after the Sunday matinee—but not on the same Sunday afternoon that they open. This simplistic, off-putting, and banal title may be the main reason why audiences, despite the star power of Yul Brynner, gave it the shortest possible Broadway run. Let the punishment fit the crime.

WHAT MUSICAL HAS THE MOST UNBELIEVABLE SITUATION?

On the Town **(1944).** Gabey, a sailor on the subway, is so smitten with a poster of the alluring Miss Turnstiles that he tears it down. This infuriates a Little Old Lady straphanger who lectures Gabey about vandalism and then calls a policeman to arrest him.

Gabey bolts at the next station, and for the rest of the musical, the two pursuers unflaggingly try to catch him and see that justice is done.

Although the 1940s may have been a time when there was more respect for law and order, would these two actually take all that time and energy to chase someone all over town for this petty crime? Wouldn't the cop have bigger criminals to catch?

There could have been a better motivation for Little Old Lady. As Gabey removed the poster, she could have said "Hey! That's my *grand-daughter*!" Then we'd better understand the motivation for a show-long chase.

***Guys and Dolls* (1950).** Miss Adelaide has been telling her mother, a Rhode Island resident, that she's been married to Nathan for years and that they have five children.

Now the most distant point in Little Rhody is at the most 186 miles away from New York and a four-hour ride by car or train. A five-time grandmother would certainly have enough curiosity and affection to make at least *one* trip to see a grandchild, let alone five, in these many years.

***Mamma Mia!* (2001).** Sophie wants to learn which of the three foreigners with whom her mother consorted some twenty-one years ago is her father. She invites them to attend her wedding in faraway Greece.

Would these strangers spend so much time and money to get there? Plenty of people won't go to weddings that are even a state away. Yet Sophie gets perfect attendance from her request.

Once they're there, why doesn't anyone at least mention DNA testing? That started in earnest in 1986, more than a dozen years before *Mamma Mia!* saw the light of production.

Oh, well; people attended just to hear those ABBA songs, didn't they?

***13* (2008).** Evan Goodman, a West 92nd Street resident, is looking forward to all his friends attending his bar mitzvah. His world caves in when his parents divorce and his mother whisks him away to Appleton, Indiana. Now Evan is hoping to make some nice new friends to populate his Midwestern bar mitzvah.

Hadn't the family made plans for the bar mitzvah in New York? Certainly by now, they'd at least have booked the hall.

Evan's mother could have eased the pain of taking him away from his friends by giving him this one, big farewell party. Even if the bar mitzvah had been scheduled for after the moving date, a smart mother would have undoubtedly arranged for both of them to return to New York. There Evan would have been greeted warmly by his friends who'd missed him.

No wonder during the show's entire ninety-five minutes, we never saw Mrs. Goodman. She was probably too ashamed to show her face.

Author's Choice: *The Producers* (2001). The musical dropped the character of Lorenzo St. DuBois, who in the original film won the title role in *Springtime for Hitler*. But in the stage musical, Franz Liebkind, the Nazi sympathizer who authored the work, interrupted an auditioner to show how the song should be done. Franz does such a good job (read: a bad one) that conniving Max Bialystock decides, "That's our Hitler!"

Franz doesn't open the show because he breaks his leg shortly before the curtain, thus forcing director Roger DeBris to take over. But if Franz has been cast as Hitler, he's obviously been to rehearsals and has seen Roger changing his play into a travesty with such lyrics as "I'm the German Ethel Merman, doncha know?" So why does he show up the next morning, furiously toting a gun, shooting at those who ruined his precious and sincere script when he'd been there all along?

Needless to say, this lapse of logic didn't keep *The Producers* from becoming a smash hit. Still, the show would have been better if bookwriters Mel Brooks, Thomas Meehan, or anyone else had thought to add two mere lines:

Bialystock: "Franz, you were there every day. Why didn't you say anything?"

Franz (meekly): "Vell, y'know, somehow things look different when you see the show from out front."

What Musical Has the Most Historically Inaccurate Character?

As Kurt Vonnegut wrote in his 1963 novel *Cat's Cradle*, "God never wrote a good play in His life."

Peter Stone was even more critical of the Deity in his afterword for the published edition of *1776*: "God writes lousy theater."

Stone improved what the Deity wrought by having John Adams send for Martha Jefferson to come to Virginia so Thomas could, to use Richard Henry Lee's expression, "refresh the missus." Then he'd be clear-headed enough to write the Declaration of Independence.

Martha never came to Philadelphia.

Historical musicals can't be relied on to tell the truth, let alone the whole truth and nothing but the truth. For the sake of dramatic interest and conflict, writers must take liberties and license with the facts.

And they have.

Author's Choice: A tie between *The King and I* and *Gypsy*.
Leslie Smith Dow's biography, *Anna Leonowens: A Life Beyond "The King and I,"* admits that Ann Harriet Emma Edwards (1831–1915) was "creative with the truth" and that "her finished portrait may still prove to be painted more in the style of the Impressionists than the realists."

Anna did have a husband named Tom, but his middle one was Leon and his surname Owens. Smith Dow suggests that Anna merged those two names and made them her last one "perhaps as a way of making herself seem more exotic and less easily traceable."

They were married seven years before Tom died. Anna did have some offers of marriage, but turned them all down—including one from Captain Orton, who commanded the boat that had taken her and Louis to Siam.

Louis wasn't an only child. Anna had two daughters who had perished in infancy before Avis was born. A big surprise is that Anna relegated Avis to boarding school before heading to Siam.

As for that house that Anna fights for, the King's initial offer said that she could "live in this palace or nearest place thereof" if she would "desire to live with her husband or mail (*sic*) servant." In actuality, the King gave her a house a mere week after she'd arrived, albeit a dilapidated one.

The musical never pinpoints why a house is so important to Anna, but Smith Dow does: Anna was afraid that living in the palace would lead to her becoming part of the harem. She didn't wish to become one of the King's more than six hundred wives, many of whom gave birth to his eighty-two children.

Although "to be part of King Monghut's harem was the greatest honor a Thai woman could hope for," Anna disagreed: "I have pitied these ill-fated sisters of mine," she wrote in a letter. How ahead of her time she was in putting racial differences aside and referring to these women as "sisters."

The King had his own fears about Anna's living off premises. He felt that she'd be in the company of missionaries who'd pressure her to convert him to Christianity. If His Majesty sounds paranoid, Smith Dow admits that the missionaries precisely did ask that of Anna who "hated their attempts." As time went on, Anna in fact came to prefer some tenets of Buddhism.

The King also gave Anna slaves. She either freed them or retained them as paid employees, *but* she did this more slowly than we might have expected.

Many have assumed that Oscar Hammerstein was making a joke when he had the King offer to send Abraham Lincoln male elephants to help win the Civil War. No, the King did just that, right down to limiting his gift to bull pachyderms.

Lady Thiang was not Prince Chulalonghorn's mother; she never met Anna, for she'd died years earlier. There was a Tuptim, but her Lun Tha was actually named P'hra Balat. For his part in their illicit romance, he was burned at the stake. Smith Dow adds that the King later regretted ordering the execution and that she could find no record of Tuptim's being whipped for her part in the forbidden romance.

Anna's complaint that the King treated her as a servant was one she indeed made. After he had bestowed a post to a diplomat and then changed his mind, he demanded that Anna write the man and say that *she* had mistakenly made the offer. Anna refused, not once, but twice; when she arrived at the palace the following day, soldiers greeted her with rocks in hand. Anna retreated. Only after an advisor urged the King to reconsider was she out of danger.

However, the Kralahome's brother and others "were bitterly resentful of what they perceived as her growing power" over the King.

Chulalonghorn was not first in line for the throne; Prince Nooyai was, but he died young. Although the musical shows Chulalonghorn and Louis as bosom buddies, at first they didn't get along. They even had a vicious no-holes-barred fight, and Louis, although two years younger, emerged victorious.

After five years, Anna left Siam, stating that she would only return if given more money and less work. Besides, Louis was now eleven and Chulalonghorn was getting him interested in the harem.

After nearly a year of negotiations through slow-traveling letters, the King died (not in her presence). Fifteen-year-old Chulalonghorn assumed the crown as King Rama V. He did abolish bowing and scraping to royalty but, more significantly, he outlawed slavery as well. After his ol' pal Louis got in trouble in Australia (where some say he'd been jailed), he offered him a job, which Louis returned to Siam to take.

Anna moved to America where she wrote *The Romance of the Harem*. Imagine her excitement when, in 1872, she met Harriet Beecher Stowe, whose *Uncle Tom's Cabin* was indeed the book that Anna had introduced to her students. Stowe thrilled Anna by saying she'd read and had enjoyed her book, too.

The *Atlantic Monthly* also published four of Anna's stories, but money from writing wasn't enough to support her and Louis. Anna was forced to take a job teaching on Staten Island, but also "spearheaded prison reform and founded schools for the blind."

Ms. Leonowens didn't bear any resemblance to Gertrude Lawrence or the other actresses who've played her on Broadway or film. Anna had "hair parted in the middle, braided upward and coiled like a pretzel on the top of her head."

Let's be grateful that all the hair designers of every production of *The King and I* veered from reality, too.

As for *Gypsy*, thanks to Carolyn Quinn's *Mama Rose's Turn*, we find where the life of Rose Hovick and Arthur Laurents' libretto differ.

"Dainty June and Her Pals," as the act was actually called, was once quite successful, raking in $1,250 a week at a time when a Coke cost a nickel.

Herbie's real name was Gordon, and he was married when he first hooked up with Rose.

Rose actually made her kids older, not younger, on their birth certificates; that way, they could circumvent child labor laws.

Mr. T. T. Grantziger, who offered to take June under his wing, was actually mogul Roxy Rothafel, celebrated in Rodgers and Hart's marvelous (if irrelevant to the plot) "At the Roxy Music Hall" in *I Married an Angel.*

When June didn't arrive at the train station, Rose immediately inferred that the kid had eloped.

Most intriguing of all: Louise was recruited to do burlesque by the theater's staff and that it wasn't Rose's idea at all.

Incidentally, Quinn knows that Rose is never called Mama Rose in *Gypsy.* Madame Rose, yes. Momma, yes. Mama Rose, no. But when your editor and your publisher insist on a title . . .

WHAT'S THE BEST DOCUMENTARY ABOUT A MUSICAL?

Original Cast Album: Company **(1970).** When musical theater enthusiasts remember this film, they usually center on Elaine Stritch and her difficulties in doing a definitive rendition of "The Ladies Who Lunch."

Also worth watching is leading man Dean Jones.

Jones would later admit that he had lost faith and interest in *Company* after the first performance in Boston. The audience had reacted coldly to "Happily Ever After," his original eleven o'clock number, in which his character Bobby equated marriage with "hell."

Sondheim's "Being Alive" ameliorated the situation, but Jones still wanted out. So notice his expression after he lays down the last note of "Being Alive." You can see that he's thinking "That's it. I'm done. I'll never have to do this again."

Actually, he did, in 1993, when *Company* had a reunion both in Long Beach, California, and Lincoln Center, New York. Jones participated, and he looked mighty happy and proud to be there.

Life after Tomorrow (2006). Prepubescent girls who played Annie and the other orphans recall that fateful day when they were told "You're too old and tall."

The film's most intriguing part occurs at the end. A group of those fortysomething stage orphans have a reunion and do "You're Never Fully Dressed without a Smile."

In other words, they've become the aging Weismann Girls from *Follies* who try to recapture the past in "Who's That Woman?"

Every Little Step (2008). Directors Adam Del Deo and James D. Stern take us through most every little step that performers take while auditioning for a 2006 revival of *A Chorus Line*.

Three thousand audition for the twenty-four spots. Seven of the roles aren't much, for these characters are eliminated before the show's first scene has ended.

The revival's semi-bored assistant tells everyone how the auditions will proceed: "We can just sorta bang it out so then you can move on with your lives."

Translation: "You don't have much of a chance."

Inside, sitting at the long table, are the much nicer director Bob Avian, choreographer Baayork Lee, and a few other staff members. One could argue that they're nicer because they know the cameras are rolling, but the all-too-frank assistant knew that too.

Besides, Avian, who'd worked with *Chorus Line* conceiver Michael Bennett on eight musicals and two plays, was always considered the good cop to Bennett's bad one.

Avian is intent on not replicating the performances delivered by the original cast but admits that he must find the same types. Lee is sympathetic when she admits "Those auditioning for Connie really have it rough"—because *she* was the original Connie.

Video clips from the original production are interspersed among poignant interviews with the hopefuls. ("Every person thinks of that song 'I Hope I Get It' every time he goes in to audition.")

Reactions at the table are carefully measured. ("It was very interesting, your choices.")

Avian and Lee became the keepers of the flame after Bennett died in 1987. And yet, neither he nor she was at the famous first taping session when Bennett brought a number of dancers together to talk about their lives. One bonus of this documentary is hearing Bennett on tape from that night; these revelations hadn't before been made public.

There's also a clip of Bennett when he made his one appearance in 1966 on the short-lived variety show *Hullabaloo*. We know from his musicals that he was an unparalleled director-choreographer; *Every Little Step* reveals that he was also a dazzling dancer. If those auditioning for the 2006 revival saw what he could do so amazingly and seemingly effortlessly, they might very well have gone home and got on with their lives.

***Ghost Light: The Year Broadway Went Dark* (2021).** On March 12, 2020, composer Tom Kitt, Tony and Pulitzer Prize winner for *Next to Normal*, was only hours away from seeing the first preview of his new Broadway musical *Flying over Sunset*. That would be followed a few weeks later with his new off-Broadway musical *The Visitor*.

Both shows were indefinitely suspended on that day that will forever live in theatrical infamy. The COVID-19 pandemic prevented Broadway from building on the previous 2018–2019 season, which had accommodated 14.8 million theatergoers who spent $1.8 billion in tickets.

Most shows had planned to resume. Eventually the producers of *Mean Girls* decided that theirs wouldn't. In the documentary, cast member Maria Briggs told of learning of the permanent shuttering ten months after the previous performance. Getting her belongings from the theater was "the first time I was going back to midtown," she said. "We had 20 minutes to clear out our station. There was no closing night party."

Don Darryl Rivera has been Iago in *Aladdin* from day one (meaning February 26, 2014). With his wife, Kate, a stage manager at *Beetlejuice*, they were able to buy a house in New Jersey.

Now they had to pay for it. So Rivera went into real estate "and joined the group that sold us our house."

Shereen Pimentel was playing Maria in *West Side Story* and knew that an incontrovertible COVID-19 barrier was her having to kiss the actor portraying Tony. She'd never do it again, for the revival that had only officially opened twenty days before the shutdown eventually announced that it was permanently closed.

Dan Micciche, the musical director and conductor of *Wicked*, mused that when performances resumed, G(a)linda's opening line "It's good to see me, isn't it?" would get a sensational response from the crowd. His prediction was accurate, for footage of that September 14, 2021, first performance showed Ginna Claire Mason saying those seven words and receiving cheers and a standing ovation.

What was most remarkable about the documentary was the courage that everyone showed in the face of dire adversity. Although Rivera admitted that he spent "a third of my time in tears," he showed none of them here but offered as brave a smile as he could muster.

So did all the other performers as they told their sad stories. Yes—they are actors. How well they proved Irving Berlin's other famous point—that show people "smile when they are low."

Author's Choice: *Best Worst Thing That Ever Could Have Happened* **(2016).** Lonny Price's film examines the making—and breaking—of *Merrily We Roll Along* (1981), the Stephen Sondheim-George Furth-Harold Prince musical that ran sixteen performances.

Price was with the musical from the first experimental reading, playing Charley Kringas, composer Franklin Shepard's bookwriter-lyricist and a good friend to budding writer Mary Flynn. More than thirty years later, Price reconnected with many of his twenty-five castmates and interviewed them for this extraordinary film.

It started out like a song. Sondheim says after the first reading that "By the fourth scene, you forget they're kids." That was important, for *Merrily* introduced its characters as high school graduates and followed them through adulthood.

Could they find teenagers who could convincingly age?

Certainly there were hundreds of young adults who believed they could. Some who waited for long hours in a longer line to audition got the perfunctory "Thank you!" that so many get after warbling just a few bars of music. Here's where these youths learned that Irving Berlin lied when he wrote "There's No Business Like Show Business," for not everything about it is appealing.

Others kids were asked to stay around. When casting director Joanna Merlin told Maryrose Wood that she was on the short list, the lass naïvely assumed that the remark referred to her height. Terry Finn makes clear she wanted in so she could meet and sleep with Kevin Kline.

All auditioners feared associate producer Ruth Mitchell. "The Angel of Death," as they called her, had the task of breaking the bad news to those hundreds who weren't cast. Then the day arrived when Hal Prince had the much nicer job of telling the golden twenty-six that "You're all in the show."

They all whooped with joy. Cast member David Cady stated, "I expected that the next Stephen Sondheim show would be the best-ever." Prince too admitted that he believed that he'd had a hit throughout rehearsals and up to *Merrily*'s first preview.

After that October 8, 1981, night, he wasn't so sure.

Changes and chaos continued through forty-four more previews. Ann Morrison, playing Mary, couldn't believe that Prince, already the possessor of eighteen Tonys, was asking little ol' her for advice about the costumes.

The show greatly improved after Jim Walton replaced James Weissenbach as Franklin. So after the opening night final curtain fell, the cast members celebrated in a circle; to their surprise, Sondheim jumped in and joined them in joy.

The happiness lasted only a few hours. The film shows negative television reviews and a snippet from Frank Rich's *New York Times* pan. Even Clive Barnes' *New York Post* rave was headed by a pull-quote that acknowledged *Merrily*'s already bleak reputation: "Forget what you've heard and go see for yourself."

Not enough people did. Only twelve days after the official November 16 opening came the November 28 closing. Yet castmate Abby Pogrebin defiantly knew that someday the world would catch up to *Merrily*'s wonders. She was right, as end credits reveal: thousands of productions have since been mounted.

Most astonishing is that Weissenbach participated in the film. Apparently time healed this wound. Even all these years later, tears emerged from Morrison's eyes as she recalled losing her self-esteem. She got it back, though, and has made a fine career in helping the disabled.

The film caught up with some others, now squarely in middle age, and discovered, to paraphrase another Sondheim song, the roads they did take.

One did go on to household name fame: Jason Alexander, thanks to a show about nothing in which he played a nothing. That's ironic, for *Merrily* saw him as a wildly successful and powerful Broadway producer.

Footage from 1981 shows Alexander making a prediction that certainly came true: "If this doesn't go," he says of *Merrily*, "there'll be a better one."

The most potent moment may well be Sondheim's frankly stating that his previous success with Prince—especially after they'd tackled seemingly impossible ideas for musicals and had made them fly—caused many to hope they'd fail with *Merrily*. Yes, everything about show business is *not* appealing—but *Best Worst Thing That Could Have Happened* is certainly arresting.

WHO'S THE MOST HEROIC LEADING CHARACTER IN A MUSICAL?

To many, the first person on this list was someone living in Jerusalem at the start of the millennium—no less than the central figure of *Godspell* as well as the title character of *Jesus Christ Superstar*.

A great many theatergoers would have a different take on Mr. Christ, so we'll make Him ineligible.

But still in the game are the following.

Meyer Rothschild (*The Rothschilds*, 1970). This musical has been accused of being about a family that just wants to make money. Sure, Meyer wants to give his wife and children the best that he can. But his goals are far, far more loftier and important than that.

Meyer wants the Jews to have freedom from the oppressive Austrian government, which keeps his people in the ghetto. They must be locked in each night at a certain time and worse, whenever a Jew approaches a Gentile—even if it's a child—he must tip his hat.

That's the reason why Meyer wants to build a fortune. He does, and by the end of the show, the Gentiles are taking their hats off to the Rothschilds.

Annie (*Annie*, 1977). To really appreciate how heroic Annie is, compare her to the orphan who was previously musical theater's most famous: Oliver Twist.

Annie is on a quest to find her parents, as impossible as that would seem. Her youth, however, keeps her from realizing how difficult this mission is. And yet, after she meets the cold streets of New York, she'll still continue, unleashing a courageous anthem in "Tomorrow."

Instead, Oliver's "Where Is Love?" is plaintive. He does mention a "she" in "Where Is Love?" but we can't be sure if he means his mother or some woman who'll provide tenderness.

Annie more specifically establishes that she wants both her parents in "Maybe." She's so resolute about this that she won't immediately accept Warbucks as her father when he offers to be just that.

Meanwhile in London, Oliver does show substantial backbone in asking for his orphanage oppressor for more food. Later at the undertaker's establishment, he wallops his tormentor. Subsequent scenes, however, show him pretty much allowing events to happen to him.

That wasn't initially composer-lyricist-bookwriter Lionel Bart's intention. "I'm Going to Seek My Fortune," Oliver originally sang after he'd escaped. Eventually Bart settled on having Oliver mostly listen to the Artful Dodger tell him to "Consider Yourself (part of the family)."

To be fair, beggars can't be choosy. Oliver's falling in with his fast friend puts him in a trajectory to become a victim. Yet Annie could be a victim, too, after a policeman captures her and returns her to the orphanage. However, Annie seizes her chance to re-escape when Grace Farrell, secretary to uber-wealthy Warbucks, comes there to find a boy who'll enjoy a Christmas vacation at the industrialist's mansion.

Annie's clever quips inspire Grace to change her mind and accept a girl, which leads her to—to reference a song from *Oliver!*—a fine life.

Oliver too winds up in a nice home surrounded by love, but it happens through a needle-in-a-haystack-like chance and an even more extraordinary coincidence. Annie instead earns what she gets.

As David Benkof, who teaches musical theater in Israel, says, "*Annie*, not *Oliver!*, should be the musical that has the exclamation point at the end of its title."

Bill Snibson (*Me and My Girl*, 1986). He and fiancée Sally Smith are very much in love. Both are members of the working class until Bill learns that the father he never knew was a lord. Bill is now heir to a fortune and the title of lord, too.

When Robert Lindsay's Bill entered the mansion and saw such high-ups as Duchess Maria and Sir John Tremayne, he wasn't the low-class blowhard that would cause the audience to dislike him and even want him taken down a peg. The shy and nervous way in which Lindsay came down the marble steps allowed audience members to relate to his plight. Every one of us has had the experience of walking into a room where we didn't know anyone and feared what these people would think of us.

Lindsay had us feel for him as he stood hat in hand, nodding "hello" almost imperceptibly to those whom he considered his betters. He made an ever-so-tiny social gaffe by occasionally lifting up a thumb, which in his world was a symbol for "Everything's all right," but one considered vulgar by these so-called high-borns.

To our surprise, Duchess Maria doesn't try to connive and get Bill out of the picture, will, and mansion. She educates him while fully expecting that he'll give up Sally.

No, no matter how much she tries. Lord knows millions of men who have suddenly come into wealth and power discard their girlfriends or boyfriends with a shrug and the claim that they've outgrown him or her. Not Bill Snibson. Sally will still be his girl when she's a nonagenarian.

Mother (*Ragtime*). A 1906 husband would leave his wife on her own for a year as he decides to explore the North Pole? That seems difficult to comprehend, but so be it.

Mother has the experience that many wives have had when their dominant husbands leave or are removed: they now have the chance to think for themselves, make decisions, and come into their own.

Few ever have as monumental a decision that's brought before Mother. She finds a Black newborn in her backyard; when the child's mother is found, the police are on the scene. Mother could have the baby and his mother carted away and never given them another thought as many in her position—and her husband—would do. Mother adopts them instead and puts herself on the road where she'll never go "Back to Before."

Bat Boy (*Bat Boy*, 2001). Who expected that we could come to care for that eerie creature so often pictured on the cover of *Weekly World News*?

In a small Appalachian town, Bat Boy is captured and brought to local veterinarian Thomas Parker, who wants to kill this newly arrived freak of nature. His wife Meredith is dead set against it and gets her way by promising to have sex with her husband (which hasn't happened in quite a while).

Meredith makes Bat Boy her pet project, slowly but surely teaching it—no, *him*—how to be a functioning and productive member of society. At first he's more bat than boy, emitting animal-like cries of pain and advancing to primitive "oooh-ooohs" that back up Meredith's lullaby. What a wonder to watch him become so easily assimilated as an elegant gentleman who knows how to drink his tea while smiling and engaging in polite conversation.

What theatergoers would have never expected before the houselights dimmed comes to pass: Bat Boy becomes someone they come to care about and love.

(If only the plot didn't turn against him.)

Author's Choice: John Adams (*1776*). Thanks to William Daniels on stage and screen, have we ever seen anyone who's so determined to refuse to take no for an answer? (All right, Robert De Niro in *New York, New York*, yes. But the stakes are so much higher and the goal seemingly impossible. And Adams won't give up or give in.)

What does he get for it? "You're obnoxious and disliked," Franklin tells him.

Does Adams become furious at being so harshly insulted? A lesser man would, but he's very much beyond that: "I am not promoting John Adams; I am promoting American independence."

And he got it, through the greatest stick-to-it-iveness of any character in a musical.

Who's the Most Impressive Featured Character in a Musical?

Steve Barker (*Show Boat*, 1927). He discovers that his wife, Julie LeVerne, is not white as she's been pretending. Laws against miscegenation would separate them, so Steve purposely cuts Julie's finger to suck out a bit of her blood. He knows that anyone with even a drop of black blood is considered Black. How heroic he is in giving up so much of his life and career to be with her.

Dolores Dante (*Working*, 1978). The musical version reinforces what Studs Terkel's oral histories revealed: many people complain about their jobs, be they an office worker, mill worker, teacher, prostitute, supermarket box boy, or housewife (which is quite a job, too).

In contrast, waitress Dante loves her work. She sings that "It's an Art" to serve people: "You carry your tray like it's almost ballet-like." Dante even provides "a twist to my wrist if I let a fork drop or cut up a porkchop or serve a New York chop. It all needs be stylish and smart. That's what makes it an art." Stephen Schwartz wisely set his lyrics to a waltz, still the most romantic of tempi.

One passage may seem forced: Dolores sings "Tips? Ha! Tips are important for people like captains and barmen. For them, it's a tip; see, for me, I'm a gypsy. Just toss me a coin and I suddenly feel like I'm Carmen."

Before you assume Schwartz chose "Carmen" simply as a rhyme for "barmen," take a look at Terkel's actual interview with Dante: "Tips? I feel like Carmen. It's like a gypsy holding out a tambourine and they throw the coin."

A personal note: I was so taken with Dante's healthy point of view that on my next trip to Chicago, I grabbed a phone book, found her name and number, and dialed it. I wanted to tell her how much I admired her attitude.

This was before every home had an answering machine, so the phone just range and rang.

Of course Dolores wasn't home. She was *working*.

Almost Everyone Else (*Me and My Girl*, 1986). With the slight exception of benign gold diggers Lady Jacqueline and the so-called Honorable Gerald Bolingbroke, the other characters always try to do the right thing.

One might expect that the royals will try anything and everything to cheat Bill out of his money and position (only to have the Country Rube outsmart them).

But as we've seen, Duchess Maria states that Bill's entitled to everything and she will now educate him so he'll be worthy of his new station. When she wants him to break with Sally, Bill won't.

Sally decides that she won't stand in his way: that's love and true nobility. To have Bill turn against him, she gets Bill's working-class friends to join her in crashing the posh party that the Duchess and Sir John have planned in Bill's honor. This, she feels, will drive Bill to say "You've embarrassed me! You and I are through!"

Hardly. Bill instead leads her and everyone else in "The Lambeth Walk," a glorious number that celebrates their modest neighborhood.

There's only one solution, as Sir John sees it. He'll see that Sally is educated to come up to Bill's new level. What a novelty: nobles who really are noble.

The residents of Gander, Newfoundland (*Come from Away*, 2017). The moment that these people hear that seven thousand people are stranded as a result of the 9/11 terrorists attacks, all they can do is think about how they can help them. Nothing else matters.

Has any musical ever shown such self-sacrificing people?

Author's Choice: The members of the Continental Congress (*1776*). How smart of bookwriter Peter Stone to see to it that after they dared sign their names to the Declaration of Independence, a dispatch immediately arrives from General George Washington saying how hopeless the cause seems to be.

And yet no one relents, to our eternal gratitude.

WHAT'S THE BEST LINE IN A MUSICAL?

Annie. Don't our hearts go out to Annie when she's taken to the Daddy Warbucks' mansion and secretary Grace Farrell asks her "What do you want to do first?"

The poor kid, who can't conceive of being a guest, says, "The floors."

Kiss Me, Kate **(1948).** Soon after Fred Graham spanks Lilli Vanessi on stage, she phones her new lover and urges him to "Send an ambulance!" What a drama queen!

Mame **(1966).** After Beauregard Jackson Pickett Burnside makes such an effort to find Mame (who so injured his fingers during a manicure that she was fired), he offers to take everyone to dinner. Mame, of course, says yes, and Beauregard exits to deal with the taxi. Agnes Gooch immediately advises Mame, "Marry him the minute he asks you!"

(By the way, there was a rock group called Agnes Gooch. Its foursome made one album in 1997 and then called it quits.)

Blood Brothers **(1993).** The abandoned Mrs. Johnstone, now expecting twins, agrees to give one away to the upscale but barren Mrs. Lyons. Eddie enjoys a life of privilege while Mickey sweats and strains.

When Mickey discovers the truth, he looks at his mother, and in a voice half-pleading and half-castigating, says the heartbreaking, "Why didn't you give me away, mum? I could have been him."

The Prom **(2018).** Trent, a New York actor, finds that the Indiana teens he wants to inspire have no native interest in theater.

"We don't have a drama program at our high school," one student tells him.

Trent's response: "That explains your lack of empathy."

Christopher Sieber said it as if his high school had spent money on new decals for the football team's helmets instead of funding a theater program.

Author's Choice: *Hamilton.* "Immigrants. We get the job done." Performances of the already legendary musical often have attendees applaud this line.

It's their tribute to those who came to this country from another, endured hard work, and sacrificed themselves so that their successors could have better lives and enough money to afford tickets to *Hamilton.*

WHAT MUSICAL SPURRED THE MOST CLEVER PRINT AD?

Subways Are for Sleeping (1961). When there were seven daily newspapers in New York, getting seven critics to rave about a show wasn't easy. But the ad after the Styne, Comden, and Green musical opened proudly proclaimed that "7 out of 7 are ecstatically unanimous about *Subways Are For Sleeping.*"

Indeed Taubman, Kerr, Chapman, and the rest were. However, they weren't the actual drama critics for their papers; these namesakes were recruited by press agent Harvey Sabinson for producer David Merrick. After he gave each of these ringers a free sumptuous dinner and comps to the show, seven out of seven agreed to lend their names to whatever quotations Sabinson cared to use, including "One of the best of our time" and "The best musical of the century."

Betty Comden—co-librettist and co-lyricist—wasn't amused. "It wasn't a nice thing to do," she said, standing by her work. "It wasn't a nice thing to do at all."

Man in the Moon (1963). The new Bock and Harnick musical proclaimed in its *New York Times* A-B-C ad that it had "a cast of 200."

Broadway had to be impressed by that. And who were among those two hundred?

The ad didn't provide names of stars, but instead cited the "gangsters, ghosts and gollywhoppers."

As Jennifer sang in *Paint Your Wagon*, "What's going on here?"

Man in the Moon starred the then-famous Bil and Cora Baird Marionettes. None of the two hundred puppets demanded a payday or a raise.

State Fair (1996). "When the big victor is announced, it won't be fair."

This was the season when the much-lauded *Rent* and *Bring in 'Da Noise, Bring in 'Da Funk* were considered locks as nominees for Best Musical. That left *Big*, *Victor/Victoria*, and *State Fair* jockeying for the other two slots.

Instead they went to *Swinging on a Star*, which was indeed an excellently put-together revue of Johnny Burke songs as well as a musical version of Gabriel Garcia Marquez's *Chronicle of a Death Foretold*.

What a shock. *Swinging* had managed only ninety-six performances and had been closed for three months; *Chronicle* tallied fewer than even half that many showings and had been closed for three-quarters of a year.

In contrast, *Big*, *Victor/Victoria*, and *State Fair* were still running and could have used the boost in business that Tony nominations tend to give. They didn't get it, causing David Merrick, in his last-ever producing effort, to take the ad that reiterated the slight.

Curtains (2007). In addition to the usual A-B-C ads for which the *New York Times* is famous, this musical created a large mock-up of an A-B-C ad that actually shows musicals that were running in 1959—the year in which *Curtains* was set.

The ad played fast and loose with billing. Dolores Gray's (notoriously difficult) mother would have been pleased to see her daughter's name placed above Andy Griffith's, who in 1959 had actually held first place in *Destry Rides Again*.

Several performers who were actually billed under the title were promoted, such as *West Side Story*'s leads (including Chita Rivera) and *Take Me Along*'s Robert Morse, right next to Jackie Gleason. And if Morse hadn't parted company with *Wicked* as its Wizard prior to Broadway, this ad may have bestowed him top-billing.

In reality, Robert Preston, Gwen Verdon, Mary Martin, and Ethel Merman were respectively all alone over the titles of *The Music Man*, *Redhead*, *The Sound of Music*, and *Gypsy*, but this ad had Barbara Cook, Richard Kiley, Theodore Bikel, and Jack Klugman joining them, respectively. Their post-1959 success was obviously responsible.

The Most Happy Fella was included, not because of its original run, but due to its 1959 revival at City Center. What's underneath the title would cause a smile: "with Bernadette Peters." Granted, she *was* in that production, but in the small role of Tessie.

Each ad stated "Tonight at 8" but in those days, shows began at 8:30 p.m. No ad boasted a critic's quotation—not even *Gypsy*, which in those days often trumpeted "Best damn musical I've seen in years" by Kerr of the *Herald Tribune*.

What's conspicuously missing were ticket prices that had been routinely listed in these ads. *Curtains* didn't want to remind anyone that a theatergoer wouldn't even have to spend ten dollars to see all the aforementioned stars and shows in front-row orchestra seats. On matinee days, fewer than five dollars would swing it.

Believe it or not, the ad neglected a musical that ran from early 1956 to late 1962. One can only imagine the hell someone caught next day: "How could you forget *My Fair Lady*!?!?"

Author's Choice: *Livin' the Life* (1957). The musical version of Mark Twain's *The Adventures of Tom Sawyer* published quotations from the critics:

"Conventional . . . Mock battle is not only arch and irrelevant but fuzzily executed . . . The rumor that Mark Twain's Mississippi stories had been turned into a musical comedy was exaggerated" (*New York Herald Tribune*).

"Most of the dancing lacks the earthiness of Mark Twain" (*New York Times*).

"The authors have been looking at their source material through a pair of stove-lids . . . Casting Timmy Everett in the part of Tom doesn't strike me as being a happy notion . . . Comes to a dead stop with monotonous regularity" (*New York Daily News*).

"A macabre minstrel interlude" (*New York Mirror*). "I certainly wish that Alice Ghostley never tackled the role of Aunt Polly" (*New York World Telegram and Sun*).

T. Edward Hambelton and Norris Houghton, co-founders of The Phoenix Theatre that had produced the musical, bought a quarter-page ad in the *New York Times* that included all these quotations.

Were they masochists? No; at the top of their ad they offered a Twain quotation: "It were not best we should all think alike. It is difference of opinion that makes horse races."

So Hambleton and Houghton went to the races with this ad, which then offered nine enthusiastic rebuttals to the nine knocks cited previously.

"Extraordinary choreography and musical numbers" (*Associated Press*).

"Excellent casting, principally in the selection of Timmy Everett as Tom Sawyer . . . Adaptation is spirited and colorful . . . the production ranks as one of the best original productions presented at the Phoenix thus far" (*Variety*).

"When the spry and agile youngsters are staging mock battles, they become infectiously joyous" (*Women's Wear Daily*).

"A minstrel show number that is gay and invigorating" (*New York Post*).

Two were from the same papers that had been responsible for the earlier negative quotations: "The authors have made a clever musical romp out of folklore" (*New York Times*), "All action-packed and amusing . . . off-beat . . . Alice Ghostley, who can sing and act, is well-cast as the spinster Polly" (*New York Mirror*).

Next came a quotation from Hambleton and Houghton: "We were amused—and thought you might be, too—by the startling contradiction among New York critics on aspects of *Livin' the Life*. We think the show is a lot of fun, a treat for the eye and ear. We know that those younger in spirit than some of its detractors will enjoy it. Audiences who have seen the show before and after its opening have proved this to us."

Although none of the positive quotations would ever be confused with "Best damn musical I've seen in years!" the experiment was the best damn publicity stunt Broadway had seen in decades.

Or was it? *Livin' the Life* stopped livin' and called it a life after twenty-five performances.

By the way, the musical's book and lyrics were written by Bruce Geller. Would you expect that from the creator of *Mission: Impossible*, a franchise still very much with us? He also wrote the book and lyrics for an off-Broadway musical version of *The Rivals: All in Love* (1961). His first musical wasn't recorded, but the second was, and deserves to be re-released in some format; its music by Jacques Urbont is as marvelously tuneful as Geller's lyrics are deft.

But let's give an honorable mention to an advertising campaign that would have made the list if all had gone as planned for *Two Gentlemen of Verona* (1971).

The New York Shakespeare Festival's musical opened to plenty of good reviews that could have been quoted in ads. But every hit does that, doesn't it?

Associate producer Bernard Gersten, bookwriter-lyricist John Guare, and press agent Merle Debuskey decided to try something new. They'd challenge musical theater fans to pen limericks about the show, submit them, and vie for a nice grand prize: a free trip to New York, dinners, the musical's original cast album, as well as a pair of tickets not only to *Two Gentleman* but also to the festival's much-lauded production of David Rabe's *Sticks and Bones*.

The plan was that each day in the *New York Times*, the alphabetical ads would sport a new *Two Gents*–centric limerick.

Then a funny, fortunate, and frankly unexpected thing happened on the way to the final decision: *Two Gentlemen* managed to win the Tony for Best Musical. As a result, management decided to trumpet that achievement in the A-B-Cs rather than a fanciful limerick each day.

Nevertheless, festival producer Joe Papp did make good on the prizes, which was fine publicity in itself.

What Flaw in a Musical Did You Not Notice Until You Thought More About It?

The Music Man. When Winthrop gets his cornet from the Wells Fargo Wagon, he emerges from his years-long funk and comes alive. Marian is so grateful to see the boy's excitement that she on the spot falls in love with Harold Hill, who made this happen.

Ah, but Marian has always had her feet on the River City ground. Why doesn't she think that, yes, Winthrop's happy right now, but how will he feel when he discovers that Harold is a con man who can't teach him how to play?

Meredith Willson wrote in *But He Doesn't Know the Territory*, his book about the making of the show, that after it was a smash hit, Ernest Martin, who once had an option on producing it, wrote him to say "You still haven't licked the book." This situation might have been what he meant.

Peter Pan (1954). Why does Peter give Wendy, Michael, and John the fairy dust to fly when he's not given it to any of his gang of Lost Boys?

West Side Story. Wouldn't someone tell the Jets and the Sharks not to pick up and remove Tony's body and that they had to wait for the authorities to perform that task?

School of Rock (2015). Considering that substitute teacher Mr. Finn has his students playing ear-shatteringly loud music, why isn't the teacher in the next room barging in to complain and put a stop to all that noise?

A solution: Finn arrives for his first day and is apologetically told that a water main has broken in the classroom he was to occupy. Now the only room available is in the windowless, cinder-blocked basement. Out of earshot, out of mind.

Author's Choice: *Annie.* How does Daddy Warbucks manage to find Sandy as a Christmas present for Annie? After all, she's never mentioned to him that she'd ever bonded with a pooch from whom she was separated. Locating him would be harder than finding Annie's parents, and yet there he is, jumping out of the box at Christmas to be reunited with his mistress.

James Lapine's direction for the 2012 revival was highly criticized, but at least he addressed this issue. Early in the musical, Lapine had Grace Farrell, Daddy Warbucks' secretary, see Sandy and instructed a police officer to catch him. He apparently did.

WHAT CHANGE MIGHT HAVE MADE A MUSICAL'S PLOT EVEN BETTER?

The Apple Tree. Bock and Harnick's adaptation of Frank R. Stockton's 1882 short story *The Lady or the Tiger* told of a barbaric and simplistic king.

When any of the king's male subjects was accused of a crime, he'd be put into an arena where he'd face two doors. Behind one was a beautiful woman; behind the other was a most hungry tiger. The monarch believed that if a man were innocent, he'd be divinely inspired to choose the door with the woman, whom he'd immediately marry. If he chose the door with the tiger, well, then he was obviously guilty.

Complications ensue when the king's daughter comes to love a man daddy deems far below her station. He'll put the would-be lover into the arena, which horrifies the princess. She makes certain to discover which door is which.

Then what? The lady whom he'd marry was her rival for her beau's affections. Certainly she doesn't want to see him wind up with her. But "Better dead than wed?" she asks in one of Harnick's lyrics.

Princess discovers which door houses the lady and which the tiger. When the dreaded day comes, she gestures to her lover the door to select.

Stockton ended his tale with "Which came out of the opened door—the lady, or the tiger?"

That's how the musical ended, too, which offered no surprise to 1960s audiences who were most familiar with the story from their youth when it seemed to be in every anthology of short stories. What a nice shock they would have had if Princess had gestured to the door that then revealed a snarling, raging, panting jungle beast.

Then she could have looked fourth wall to us and said, *"Are you kidding?"*

Cabaret. Because director Hal Prince and choreographer Ron Field delivered a brilliant opening number in "Willkommen," the audience was well within its rights to assume that the Kit Kat Club was a top-notch venue.

Usually in a musical when an emcee introduces a singer who then enters to perform, audiences assume that he or she is at least very good or even a star. So when the Emcee in *Cabaret* told us that we were about to see "Sally Bowles, the toast of Mayfair," we took him at his word and expected that she'd be wonderful.

Cabaret's creators have since revealed that they saw Sally as a mediocre talent. So Jill Haworth, the original Sally who was called the show's "wild wrong note" by Walter Kerr in the *New York Times*, was doing her job when not doing well by "Don't Tell Mama" and her subsequent songs.

Audiences, however, came to the conclusion that Haworth, not Sally, was the deficient one.

So during "Don't Tell Mama," perhaps Prince should have shown the nightclub's customers who were seated ringside to look at each other, exchange glances, and even pinch their noses—the universal symbol for "It stinks!" That would have immediately told us what we needed to know about Sally Bowles and the Kit Kat Club.

West Side Story **(1980, 2009, 2020).** When Sondheim originally had "Gee, Officer Krupke" end with the famous F-word, composer Leonard Bernstein hastily suggested "Krup you!"

In it went, which had to be the case in the Eisenhower era. Audiences wouldn't endure genuine profanities even from the Jets, who would have spoken far more harshly to express their anger and frustration with the hands they'd been dealt.

They wouldn't say "lousy" to describe "a Puerto-Rican chicken." The object they imagined hitting the fan wouldn't be "spit" any more than "bugging" would be their go-to adjective.

However, the show was pushing enough boundaries so even a little vulgar language in "The Jet Song" could have sent audiences speeding out of their seats.

After films became more frank in the late 1960s, audiences became accustomed to obscenities. So when the 1980 revival rolled around, Sondheim could then have appropriately altered his lyrics. After cable television brought more strong language into homes, the 2009 and 2020 revivals certainly wouldn't have offended many with realistic language. All three Broadway revivals seemed toothless for not having the Jets and Sharks say what we all knew was really on their minds.

The Who's Tommy (1993). Certainly we feel bad for four-year-old Tommy who's so traumatized by seeing his father kill his wife's lover that the lad becomes deaf, mute, and blind.

However, before this tragedy happened, if happy-go-lucky Tommy had sung a cute, life-affirming song, we'd feel even more for the lad. Years later, when he miraculously recovered, seeing the adult version and return of the charming kid we once knew would be so moving.

Author's Choice: *Gypsy.* After Rose, Rose Louise, and Her Toreadorables land at Wichita's one and only burlesque theater, let's see a despondent Rose go into the street. There emerging from the theater is Mr. Goldstone, the booking agent whom she tried so hard to impress years earlier.

Having Rose try to explain what she's doing there—and have Mr. Goldstone seriously doubt her—would make for a devastating scene. The situation could be humbling for Mr. Goldstone, too, who wouldn't want to be caught attending burlesque. He'd claim that he was "scouting talent," but he'd fear Rose wouldn't believe him.

Finally, we'd also get a payoff on why we were introduced to Mr. Goldstone in the first place, whom we never see again after the song in his honor concludes.

WHAT MUSICAL BEST PROVED OSCAR WILDE'S BELIEF THAT "IMITATION IS THE SINCEREST FORM OF FLATTERY"?

The dream ballet in *Oklahoma!* (1943). After this Agnes de Mille piece, "Laurey Makes up Her Mind," became the talk of the town (and reached towns as far away in Oklahoma and beyond), many, many musicals suddenly sported a dream ballet. A scant six months later, de Mille herself created another for *One Touch of Venus*.

Other musicals followed suit: *On the Town, Brigadoon, A Tree Grows in Brooklyn, The Pajama Game, West Side Story, Goldilocks, Flower Drum Song,* and *Bye Bye Birdie* (although Rose's "How to Kill a Man" in that last-named musical is usually omitted these days). Even in 2021, *Mrs. Doubtfire* had one.

There were plenty of others in between and after. Also embracing them were film musicals, be they as lofty as *Singin' in the Rain* or as inconsequential as *Snow White and the Three Stooges*.

The tornado sequence in both *The Wiz* and *The Wizard of Oz* can also be said to count, for (here comes a most unnecessary spoiler alert) Dorothy Gale is dreaming, isn't she?

***Platinum* (1978).** It made good on its name during the finale in which a chorus line featuring every cast member had each bedecked in a platinum-colored costume.

How impressive that would have been if *A Chorus Line* had not cast its cast in gold-colored costumes for its finale.

This was one case in which platinum was far less valuable than gold—or, to paraphrase Senator Lloyd Bensten's famous remark to Dan Quayle in a 1988 vice presidential debate, "*Platinum*, you're no *Chorus Line*."

***Is There Life after High School?* (1982).** Whether there is or isn't, there was plenty of life, worth, and introspection in Craig Carnelia's pungent score.

Perhaps critics and longtime theatergoers resented that Act Two showed a high school reunion. A dozen years earlier, they'd had the ultimate reunion musical—*Follies*—and this low-budget enterprise paled in comparison.

Too bad, for the reunion allowed "Fran and Janie" to reunite. They were best friends in their youth and then (as we've all experienced with certain friends) they grew apart. Now, though, they'll share a lovely nostalgic night and—let's face it—go their separate ways once again.

Victor/Victoria (1995). Henry Mancini was another Hollywood superstar composer who became a Broadway neophyte. His melody for his title song suggested that he said to himself, "Oh, I guess every Broadway show has a big number for its star in the manner of 'Mame' and 'Hello, Dolly!'"

That's probably why Mancini aped it, and why it was more of a bore than a knock-off.

Author's Choice: *Shrek* **(2008).** No book musical that wasn't an out-and-out parody borrowed more from other musicals than this millions-of-dollars money-loser.

At the end of "Forever," the Dragon's final line was a reference to the *Dreamgirls* song "And I Am Telling You I'm Not Going."

During "Story of My Life," Mama Bear sang "Mama's in the mud, Mama's in distress," in a nod to "Rose's Turn."

In "Freak Flag," the banner that was waved showed a face that greatly resembled the Cosette logo of *Les Misérables.*

At the end of "What's up, Duloc?"—an expression lifted from both an animated rabbit and a film—the resolute Lord Farquaad suddenly decided "And no one's going to bring me down"—which brought us two blocks down to a far more successful musical.

By the time *Shrek* began its tour, its creators had thought of more: Donkey, in "Don't Let Me Go," interpolated some of *Rent*'s "Take Me or Leave Me" and "I'll Cover You"—presumably without paying any rent to the Jonathan Larson estate.

As Madame Armfeldt observed, "Where is skill? Where is forethought?"

Virtually Every Musical Involves Some Controversy. At Which One Would You Most Like to Have Been a Fly on the Wall to Witness?

The answer shouldn't be as mundane as "I'd love to have attended the opening night of *West Side Story*." The more specific implication of "Oh, to be a fly on the wall!" means that (1) you'd be in surreptitious position where you wouldn't be noticed; (2) you had no business being there; and (3) you'd observe a situation as sticky as flypaper.

So . . .

***Porgy and Bess* (1935).** In Boston, after the first performance of the ambitious new musical, it's around one a.m. The late hour doesn't stop composer George Gershwin, director Rouben Mamoulian, and musical director Alexander Smallens from walking in the Boston Common for many hours more. All were arguing heatedly over what should be cut. Gershwin was adamant that none of it should, while the others felt differently.

And yes, the Boston Common has many a retaining wall on which a fly could eavesdrop.

***By George!* (1945).** Fifteen-year-old Stevie Sondheim arrives at Oscar Hammerstein's summer house. He's anxious to hear what his mentor will think of his new musical.

Sondheim has often said that after Hammerstein judged his pupil's first-ever attempt as utterly terrible: "I really learned more about musical theater in one afternoon than most people learn in a lifetime."

Wouldn't you have liked to have been a fly so you too could have learned a thing or two hundred about musicals, too?

***Carnival in Flanders* (1953).** Backstage before the first (and only) Wednesday matinee. The morning reviews called the musical "stupid," "draining," and "a loss."

Although star Dolores Gray very much likes her song "Here's That Rainy Day" (which will, despite the show, become a standard), it has a l-o-n-g introduction called "It's a Fine Old Institution," which she doesn't like. As a result, Gray refuses to perform today. Understudy Susan Johnson is alerted that she'll have to go on.

In an interview with your author, Johnson said that she was raring to go until Gray saw her in costume, which made her relent. And yet in another interview with your author, co-star John Raitt remembered that Johnson said she didn't know the role and couldn't possibly go on.

Only a fly on the wall would know for sure.

Sunset Boulevard (1994). Patti LuPone, while reading a London newspaper, notices an article about this musical in which she's been playing Norma Desmond. The columnist says that Andrew Lloyd Webber has decided that another actress will do the part when the show opens on Broadway.

Actually, being in the place where LuPone eventually confronts Lloyd Webber would be worth braving the widest and longest fly-swatter.

Rent (1996). The show is in rehearsals, and, to Jonathan Larson's thinking, it's not going well. So he calls his mentor Stephen Sondheim and says he wants to have director Michael Greif fired.

Now—which wall would you rather be on: Larson's or Sondheim's?

Author's Choice: *West Side Story*. During an on-stage note session after a difficult rehearsal, director-choreographer Jerome Robbins is on stage with his back to the house. He starts aimlessly walking backwards, getting closer and closer to the orchestra pit. He doesn't realize that he's soon to fall in and do himself some serious harm.

During the torturous weeks of rehearsal, Robbins has so angered and humiliated so many Jets, Sharks, and Anybodys that no one on stage decides to warn him.

And down he goes.

However, Grover Dale, the original Jet known as Snowboy, claims that the cast was so mesmerized by what Robbins was saying that they didn't notice that he was walking toward the pit.

Could a fly corroborate?

Which Broadway Musical Was the Most Unexpected Flop?

Breakfast at Tiffany's (1966). Once the musical received terrible reviews in both Philadelphia and Boston, perhaps producer David Merrick felt that simply putting the heralded 1961 film on stage was all-too-expected.

So he asked Edward Albee to come in and rewrite Abe Burrows' libretto. It became a story about a writer who once knew a woman as wild and crazy as Holly Golightly, tried writing about her, but could never quite capture her essence. Albee probably didn't know that a recent musical had used a similar device. At the end of *Cabaret*, we saw Cliff writing his book recapping what he and we had just experienced.

A more compelling musical might have filled in the blanks we never knew about Holly. Both Truman Capote's 1958 novella and George Alexrod's 1961 screenplay show the surprising scene where Southern veterinarian Doc Golightly comes to Manhattan to reclaim Holly as his wife. They had married when she was fourteen, and Holly became an instant stepmother of four.

How did you get here from there, Ms. Golightly? The woman, who clearly admitted that she'd been "stealing turkey eggs and running through briar patches," would seem to have no idea of what New York was or entails. Even getting to the next town would seem to have been impossible. So how did Holly reach New York? Once she arrived, how did she even begin to conquer the city? Where did the initial money come from? Did she sleep her way from south to north? If so, what adventures or misadventures did she have along the way? Granted, this musical may not have been what 1966 audiences would have wanted to see. But both out-of-town engagements showed that this business-as-usual treatment of *Breakfast at Tiffany's* wasn't what they fancied, either.

Mr. President (1962). Here's Irving Berlin's first musical since *Call Me Madam* (1950), for which he won the Tony for Best Score. The book will be by Howard Lindsay and Russel Crouse, whose previous musical was *The Sound of Music*, and who then (and now) hold the record for Broadway's longest-running play: *Life with Father*.

Joshua Logan, who steered two of Broadway's most famous musicals—*Annie Get Your Gun* and *South Pacific*—will direct this one, too.

How can it miss?

For one thing, the nation then had its youngest elected president, John F. Kennedy, but *Mr. President* chose as president, Stephen Decatur Henderson (Robert Ryan), who more resembled aged presidents of yore. All the potential drama of difficult White House decisions and compromises were lost when Henderson lost the race near the end of Act One. After that, it was *Mr. Ex-President*, which makes for a far less compelling character.

Someday, Aaron Sorkin's excellent screenplay for *An American President* will morph into a musical. The story of a widower president who falls in love with a journalist who can't approve his every move—and his opponent who'll take advantage of it—is a natural.

(Budding bookwriters, composers, and lyricists, stop reading and start getting the rights right now.)

***The New Mel Brooks Musical Young Frankenstein* (2007),** to use its official title.

To be fair, following a smash hit isn't easy. Irving Berlin's *Miss Liberty* (1949) ran 308 performances to his *Annie Get Your Gun*'s 1,147. Michael Bennett's *Ballroom* ran 109 performances to *A Chorus Line*'s 6,137.

So we shouldn't be so surprised that *The New Mel Brooks Musical Young Frankenstein* at 485 performances ran little more than 19 percent of *The Producers: The New Mel Brooks Musical*'s 2,502 showings.

Notice the change in the billing. Now Brooks was above the title.

The concept of premium seats began with *The Producers* (beg your pardon, Mr. Brooks, for shortening the name). The cost: one hundred dollars.

For *Young Frankenstein*, the price was suddenly $450. Granted, six years had passed, but inflation calculators reveal that one hundred dollars in 2001 was equivalent to $117 in 2007.

Charity organizations and theater parties traditionally need upwards of two hundred seats to happily accommodate their patrons. *Young Frankenstein* limited group sales to fifty seats at most weekend performances—prime time for when these theater parties like to attend.

That policy would change five months into the run, after lukewarm reviews and fewer theatergoers charged the box office or charged their tickets. Premium seats were dropped, making Brooks' current musical the only show on Broadway not to offer what Brooks' previous musical had originated.

Neither the cast album nor the published script offered the ditty that the cast sang after the curtain call. It informed the audience that Brooks would musicalize *Blazing Saddles*, his 1974 film hit. It didn't specify whether it would be called *The New Mel Brooks Musical Blazing Saddles* or more modestly *Blazing Saddles: The New Mel Brooks Musical*.

That issue turned out to be moot; the musical never happened, which may have been all for the best, even if it didn't turn out to be, to quote a previous Brooks song, "the worst show in town."

Prettybelle (1971). Composer Jule Styne and lyricist Bob Merrill's previous score was *Funny Girl*. Director-choreographer Gower Champion's *Hello, Dolly!* had recently become Broadway's longest-running musical. The star: Angela Lansbury, who'd won Tonys for two Jerry Herman musicals: *Mame* and *Dear World*.

The latter was produced by Alexander H. Cohen, who would do this one, too. Because he's never had a musical hit, he's the only Achilles heel.

That is, until proper Bostonians heard Lansbury's Prettybelle tell them she was sleeping with Blacks and Mexicans because her late husband, a bigoted sheriff, had oppressed them. Despite a stunning score, stony silence greeted the book scenes from the crowd that wishes that the city's "Banned in Boston" policy were still in place. *Prettybelle* never gets the chance to be banned in New York.

War Paint (2017). Patti LuPone, always on the very short list of nominees for First Lady of the American Musical Theater, would play cosmetics magnate Helen Rubinstein.

Portraying her arch-enemy Elizabeth Arden would be Christine Ebersole, who'd matched LuPone's two Best Actress in a Musical Tonys.

Ebersole would reunite with the team that wrote *Grey Gardens*: composer Scott Frankel, lyricist Michael Korie, and bookwriter Doug Wright (who, for *I Am My Own Wife*, not only won a Best Play Tony but also a Pulitzer Prize). The director would once again be Michael Greif, the only man to stage two musicals that had won Pulitzers: *Rent* and *Next to Normal* (2009).

Rubinstein and Arden each believed she was the greater giant and hated whenever the other had a success. Given that a substantial part of the Broadway audience included women over forty for whom cosmetics were of interest, this had to be a smash.

The official reason for closing after a mere 236 performances was that LuPone needed the aforementioned hip surgery. However, there were plenty of musical theater actresses who could have replaced her and sold tickets (Bernadette Peters, Betty Buckley, Bebe Neuwirth).

The real reason *War Paint* closed was because in its final thirteen weeks on Broadway, it never sold better than 49 percent of its gross potential.

WHAT BROADWAY MUSICAL HAD THE BEST SPECIAL EFFECT THAT DIDN'T INVOLVE TECHNOLOGY?

42nd Street **(1980).** During the fetching song "Dames," one showgirl after another came through the opening in the back wall.

Dance assistant Kari Baker recalled that the first dresses were yellow, followed by a series of orange, red, pink, lavender, violet, purple, blues, and greens. They eventually lined up and only then did audiences realize that each color was not quite the same. The colors became progressively darker and then lighter, making for a spectacular rainbow spectrum.

Dreamgirls **(1981).** The Dreams finished an engagement in one city, disappeared behind a tinseled curtain, and reappeared as the announcer told us they were now in a different city.

After they emerged, those in the audience could feel something had changed, but they couldn't quite put their finger on it—for a long second, that is. Then they figured out what had happened and broke into applause.

Although The Dreams had only been behind that tinseled curtain for a very few seconds, they'd emerged wearing totally new costumes. If there were a Tony category for dressers, *Dreamgirls* would have won seven awards instead of six.

The Tap Dance Kid (1983). William Sheridan is one of those boys who wants to be a dancer. His father is one of those who forbids it. What exacerbates matters for Dad is that his brother-in-law Dipsey is a successful dancer, who's now rehearsing a show in Manhattan.

Father would prefer that Willie stay put on Roosevelt Island. Fat chance. Willie decides to visit Dipsey, which means a tram ride from the island.

The stage was filled with large squares that sported pictures of various Roosevelt Island locations. Then, as the tram slowly took Willie to his promised land, the pictures changed one by one to Manhattan landmarks. Many in the audience were reminded of that heavenly first time they saw the city's skyline.

Cyrano—The Musical (1993). Rostand's 1897 play (and the many musical versions that followed) usually opened with a little stage positioned against the back wall. There actor Montfleury would perform to an audience whose backs were to us.

Scenic designer Paul Gallis had a better idea. He had Montfleury at the edge of the stage with *his* back to us. His audience was in front facing the actor, so we saw *their* faces—and not much more of them, for they were standing in a recessed area five or so feet below.

If only the musical itself had had such imagination . . .

Author's Choice: *Sunday in the Park with George.* Georges Seurat has been feverishly working for all of Act One on *Un dimanche près-midi à l'Île de la Grande Jatte.* Just before intermission, Georges puts the finishing touches on the painting, moving one of his subjects here, another one there, and even deciding to remove another's eyeglasses at the last moment. We then have a three-dimensional representation of the painting we all go to see at the Art Institute of Chicago.

(By the way, if you go to the institute to see the painting, you needn't ask "Where's *Un dimanche près-midi à l'Île de la Grande Jatte?*" Just say "Where's 'Sunday in the Park with George'?" and they'll know what you mean and quickly say "Gallery 240.")

WHAT MUSICAL MOST JUMPED THE SHARK?

Here's expression that's been handed down to us from *Happy Days* (the 1970s sitcom, not the Samuel Beckett play).

According to Webster, it means "a point at which far-fetched events are included merely for the sake of novelty, indicative of a decline in quality."

Some musicals did it long before Mr. Fonzarelli catapulted over a *carcharodon carcharias* in 1977.

Mr. President. "The Only Dance I Know" is Irving Berlin's poorest excuse for an eleven o'clock number. Out of nowhere, belly dancers from the Middle East show up at the White House to do their stuff.

"You don't need an Arthur Murray," one sings, citing the host of a then-popular television show that encouraged viewers to dance.

That rhymed with "just the fringe that's on a surrey."

Had Arthur Murray and *Oklahoma!* really made it to their part of the world?

Breakfast at Tiffany's (1966). David Merrick needs a new bookwriter for his breezy musical comedy.

So he asks Edward Albee, author of the ferocious *Who's Afraid of Virginia Woolf*, to do the fixing.

Once Albee agrees, it was, to cite the title of one of his own future plays, *All Over.*

Illya, Darling (1967). The score stinks, so let's insert "Never on Sunday," the Oscar-winning song from the movie of the same name.

Little did we know at the time that taking an established song from a famous film and adding it to a new score would eventually become standard procedure. "Never on Sunday" was Patient Zero.

I Remember Mama (1979). With Martin Charnin bowing out of the picture, Richard Rodgers needs a new lyricist.

Raymond Jessel gets the job.

If you were passing by the meeting room where this information was disclosed, you might have assumed a coven of owls had invaded the premises, what with all the "Whos!?" that were emitted from everyone present.

Jessel was a co-composer-lyricist of the 1965 musical *Baker Street*, which didn't win plaudits for its score. In fact, it had to be buttressed with songs by Bock and Harnick.

That Rodgers even took a meeting with Jessel would have seemed unlikely. But this was his last musical, produced only seven months before he died, so he may not have cared very much.

***Senator Joe* (1989).** A character named "Fatty Deposit" danced in Joseph McCarthy's stomach.

This was no dream ballet; it was a terpsichorean way of showing the distress that the troublemaker was enduring while hunting Communists.

(Not as much as the stress he had caused.)

***The Scarlet Pimpernel* (1997).** So many changes are made during the run that subsequent versions are dubbed *The Scarlet Pimpernel 2.0* and *The Scarlet Pimpernel 3.0*.

That brings to mind the joke about the American opera soprano who, after singing her opening aria at La Scala, heard the audience demand encore after encore. After doing a few, the soprano finally said, "Oh, please, thank you, but I just can't do even one more!"

An audience member then yelled, "You'll do it until you do it right!"

Author's Choice: A tie between two 2005 musicals.

First, ***Chitty Chitty Bang Bang*.** So who gets the final bow at the curtain call? One of the three performers who receive Tony nominations for the show: Erin Dilly, Jan Maxwell, or Marc Kudisch?

Previous Tony nominee Raul Esparza?

Previous Tony winner Philip Bosco?

No. The cast parts as the Red Sea did for Moses so that the show's title "character"—the car—can drive on and take the final bow.

In My Life. A musical that's so frank about mental disorders, death, Tourette's, and unfortunate growths ("There's a little rumor someone's got a tumor") wouldn't seem to have any skeletons in its closets.

However, when our hero opens a closet, out comes a skeleton, and the choreography begins for "The Skeleton Ballet." Perhaps it was book-writer-composer-lyricist-director and co-producer Joe Brooks' way of saying that his character was being liberated.

Instead, *In My Life* was liberated from The Music Box after sixty-one poorly attended performances.

IF YOU WERE RECRUITED TO REWORK ANY MUSICAL, WHICH SHOW WOULD YOU CHOOSE AND WHAT WOULD YOU DO?

Sweet Charity (1966). This musical has had more endings than the number of Broadway performances of *Kelly*, *Gantry*, and *Dance a Little Closer* combined.

The first one: Oscar learns that the woman he thought was "sweet" has had many, many lovers over the years and thus ends their engagement. Charity was then visited by her Fairy Godmother—or so it seemed; the ethereal spirit turned around and wore a sign on her back that advertised "Watch *The Good Fairy* tonight at 8 p.m. on CBS."

No. We cared too much about Charity by this point to have her be the victim of a punch line.

The second one. In the 1969 film, Charity was mollified by flower children, much as Cabiria, her counterpart in the Fellini film, was cheered by a troupe of strolling players.

The third one: an alternate ending was filmed in which Oscar returned, but it was discarded.

The fourth one: Broadway's 2005 revival again had Oscar dump Charity, but had her castigate him, making us admire the backbone she'd never shown.

If in 1966 bookwriter Neil Simon had been married to Marsha Mason, *Sweet Charity* might have that reconciliation that was almost used in the film. Remember, Mason called *A Chorus Line* auteur Michael Bennett during the show's early previews to strongly advise him not to deny veteran Cassie the job because she was overqualified. Mason believed that everyone should have the right to start again.

Bennett never agreed that Cassie would get the job, but understood that the ray of hope was necessary for audiences.

Too bad that Mason's marriage to Simon was still seven years away when he was writing *Sweet Charity*. If she'd been there, she might have given him similar advice: everyone should have the right to start again in love, too; love can return to anyone's life at any time.

Simon could have had Oscar break up with Charity, but a day or so later return and admit that he was naïve to assume that at her age (Gwen Verdon was forty-one) that she didn't have a past and that his life would be all the poorer without her. We'd then admire Oscar for giving both of them a fresh start, and "I Love to Cry at Weddings" would have been a joyous, no-strings attached eleven o'clock showstopper that would send a message as positive as Cassie's getting the job.

You're a Good Man, Charlie Brown **(1967).** Lucy along with the other Peanuts sing the title song as an opening number. But during the nearly fifty years of the comic strip's existence, had she or any of the kids in the neighborhood ever thought of Charlie as "a good man"?

Not that the show has suffered for it; for many moons, it was the most produced musical in schools and community theaters.

Still, the song should have been placed at the end of the show—ideally after Charlie came through with a game-winning home run or touchdown. Why must we always see him fail?

Wicked. At one point, the Wizard deftly mentions "philanthropists." However, in the 1939 film that inspired the musical, the Wizard famously says, "There are men who do nothing all day but good deeds. They are called phil . . . er . . . phil . . . er . . . er . . . good-deed-doers!"

Had *Wicked*'s Wizard endured the same trouble—or had over-carefully articulated the word—the audience would have cackled in delight.

What Was the Worst Idea for a Musical?

Chee Chee **(1928).** Rodgers and Hart didn't always pick the right property, as is proved by their musicalizing a novel called *The Son of the Grand Eunuch*.

(And no, this is *not* the musical that has a song that begins "What did I have that I don't have . . .")

Because of the position that Li-Pi Tchou's father held until his death, the son is now entitled to inherit dad's job and live an easy life as an esteemed member of the Chinese court. But Li-Pi does love Chee Chee. Should he sever relations with the aristocracy or get severed himself?

Only thirty-one audiences could ever say for sure.

Casablanca. David Merrick's biography on the back cover of the original Broadway cast album of *Oliver!* stated that he'd produce a musical version of the classic film.

According to Ken Bloom's *American Song*, Arthur Schwartz (composer of *A Tree Grows in Brooklyn*) and Leo Robin (lyricist of *Gentlemen Prefer Blondes*) at least wrote three songs: "Lucky to Be Alive," "To Love and to Lose," and "Why Should I Care?" Perhaps the first was for Ilsa or Victor; the latter two were probably for Rick.

Merrick eventually scheduled a September 26, 1967, opening at the Mechanic Theatre in Baltimore. George Segal was mentioned as Rick, but nothing came of it.

Perhaps *Casablanca* could never be a musical success, and not solely because audiences would have trouble imagining anyone but Humphrey Bogart, Ingrid Bergman, Paul Henreid, and Claude Rains in the leads. Two failed television series suggest as much; one in 1955 lasted ten episodes; another in 1983 amassed only half as many.

In the 1990s, fledgling songwriters brought a few songs from their *Casablanca* to the ASCAP Musical Theatre Workshop. Said Marvin Hamlisch, "And what happens when you get 'As Time Goes By'? When Rick says 'Play it!' do you instead have your own new song? If Sam plays that, I can just hear Rick saying, 'No, no, no—not that song! Play "As Time Goes By"!'"

Actually, since that time, films made into musicals think nothing of interpolating a hit song from a film; a musical *Casablanca* today would do the same.

Incidentally, *Casablanca* was based on an unproduced play called *Everybody Comes to Rick's*. In it, Rick doesn't say the much-misquoted "Play it again, Sam," or "Play it, Sam," or even "Play it."

What playwrights Murray Burnett and Joan Alison had Rick say was "Play it, you dumb bastard."

Kentucky Lucky. The life of Colonel Sanders. Sounds crazy, no? But here was a man who dropped out of school in seventh grade and left home at thirteen because he hated his stepfather. Thanks to an uncle, he landed a job as a streetcar conductor but soon lost interest. He then lied about his age to enlist in the army and married at eighteen.

So maybe a story about a man seemingly doomed to a dull life who became a household name (especially in kitchens) isn't such a bad idea.

What doesn't instill confidence is that Jay Livingston and Ray Evans were writing the score. Although they'd won three Oscars (for "Buttons and Bows," "Mona Lisa," and "Que Sera, Sera"), their Broadway track record includes the uneven *Oh Captain!* and the woebegone *Let It Ride!* Considering the lack of worth of these two, how did they dare add an exclamation point after each title?

Welcome to the Club **(1989).** In *Merrily We Roll Along,* when Franklin Shepard is in the process of splitting from his wife, he exclaims "Divorce court! What a fascinating setting for a musical!"

Is it? Cy Coleman and A. E. Hotchner's musical started there and then moved to the jail where wives had their husbands incarcerated for nonpayment of alimony.

And we were expected to believe that once they paid up, most of them would reconcile with their exes?

No, there's no love lost—nay, no love at all—for any wife who had a husband jailed (even when they have Coleman's jaunty melodies to sing).

The show was called *Let 'Em Rot* before making it to Broadway as *Welcome to the Club.* Later it was retitled *Exactly Like You* and later still *Lawyers, Lovers, and Lunatics.* The lunacy was the creators continuing to rework the show.

Author's Choice: ***Yours, Anne*** **(1985).** A musical based on *The Diary of Anne Frank?*

The real problem arose when Anne and her family were shown sitting and crooning. Singing implied that they were content. Of course they weren't. Their need to be deathly quiet most of the time left little opportunity for dance, too.

Not everything needs to be musicalized.

WHAT'S BEEN THE CLEVEREST DEROGATORY NAME FOR A MUSICAL?

Admit it: You've mocked the names of musicals you haven't liked.

Some corruptions have been better than others. *Screamgirls* for *Dreamgirls* isn't apt, considering that only one "girl" screams much of the time.

***The Red Shoes* (1993),** the great Jule Styne's last musical, was dubbed *Jule's Last Jam*, cruelly referencing the recent musical *Jelly's Last Jam*.

(Much kinder would have been *The Shoes as Red as Blood*.)

But then there have been the following.

***Into the Light* (1986).** This six-performance disaster concerned the Shroud of Turin, the cloth in which Jesus Christ was wrapped prior to burial. Some have claimed that it still shows the imprint of His face.

Broadway wags mocked it by calling the show *Jesus Christ Tablecloth*. But Peter Stone of *1776* fame preferred to dub it *A Face in the Shroud*.

***Mack & Mabel* (1974).** Robert Preston would play Mack Sennett and Marcia Rodd would portray Mabel Normand—that is, until director-choreographer Gower Champion saw Kelly Garrett in *Mother Earth* (1973).

"That's our Mabel!" he thought, so he put Rodd through a couple of perfunctory rehearsals to pretend he was giving her a chance—then he could tell her that she just wasn't working out. Perhaps she wasn't, but as it turned out, Champion eventually found Garrett genuinely incapable.

By the time Bernadette Peters was found and hired, many longtime Broadway observers were dubbing the show *Mack & Maybe*.

***Prince of Central Park* (1989).** Gloria DeHaven, not seen on Broadway for thirty-four years, will make her return in this musical of Evan Rhodes' novel.

Alas, she's found wanting, so Joanne Worley replaces her—causing the future four-performance flop to become known as *Ain't Miss De Haven.*

***James Clavell's Shogun* (1990).** Unlike so many others that receive mocking names while they were experiencing birthing pains, this one didn't receive its moniker—and couldn't have—until its seventy-second and final performance came and went: *James Clavell's Show Gone.*

Author's Choice: *The Yearling* (1965). You may have read Marjorie Kinnan Rawling's 1938 novel *The Yearling* (about a boy's beloved deer) or seen the 1946 Oscar-nominated Best Picture.

However, you probably didn't see the musical version, for it lasted only three performances. Under those circumstances, writer-director Barry Kleinbort says that the logical name for the show would have been *Oh, Deer.*

WHAT'S THE BEST FUN FACT ABOUT A MUSICAL?
Annie. It won the Tony, Drama Desk, and New York Drama Critics Circle Award for Best Musical, but it was denied that prize by the Outer Critics Circle (the appraisers who write in New Jersey, Connecticut, and points beyond).

Many nominators must have resisted giving it that prize, for the ultimate designation was "Most Refreshing Musical."

Theatergoers, who have tired of *Annie's* ubiquitous household name success, may now feel that that honor was an even worse one than Best Musical.

Not Thomas Meehan, Charles Strouse, and Martin Charnin. "We hope," wrote Meehan, "that Annie would do for us what daughters are supposed to do for their fathers—support us in our old age."

Needless to say, none of the three collaborators' children ever had to put out a dime for their daddies' care.

The Music Man. And what is situated directly across the street from Meredith Willson's boyhood home in Mason City, Iowa?

The town's library.

Was seeing this book repository day after day the inspiration for his making Marian a librarian?

Follies opened on April 4, 1971, which was also the thirtieth birthday of David Edward Byrd, who designed its great logo. Although many of his generation were then warning people "Don't trust anyone over 30," the producers of *Godspell*, *Jesus Christ Superstar*, *The Robber Bridegroom*, *The Grand Tour*, and *Little Shop of Horrors* entrusted him to do their art-work—and weren't sorry that they did.

Terry Beaver, *Nice Work if You Can Get It* (2012). The actor was born on June 2, 1948, in West Palm Beach, Florida. On that very same day 1,676 miles away in Sioux City, Iowa, Jerry Mathers was born.

What a coincidence that Mr. Beaver shares a birthday with an actor who'll always be known as Beaver. And yes, that's Terry's real surname.

Author's Choice: *The 1959–1960 Tonys*. So what song opened the show? Did Ethel Merman belt *Gypsy*'s "Everything's Coming up Roses"? Was Mary Martin there singing the title song from *The Sound of Music*? You may even guess "The Name's LaGuardia" from *Fiorello!* in honor of New York City where the man was mayor and the ceremony took place.

Because *Take Me Along* had the double star power of Jackie Gleason and Walter Pidgeon, could their singing the title song have been the choice? Or was that too modest? A big production number, such as Joe Layton's witty choreography for "The Spanish Panic" in *Once upon a Mattress*, would get things off to a spirited start.

Neither any of these nor any other song from these musicals was chosen. The ceremony began with a song whose melody was then already 180 years old, albeit with a lyric written "only" 146 years earlier: "The Star-Spangled Banner."

WHAT MUSICAL SPORTED THE MOST INGENIOUS COSTUME?

The King and I **(1951).** If Mrs. Anna hadn't worn a hoop skirt, we wouldn't have had that marvelous moment during "Getting to Know You" when the children encircle her and emulate the dress.

The Wiz (1975). Perhaps the Tin Man should have been called the Aluminum Man in this version. Instead of sterile sheets of metal, his "tin" came from an upturned trash barrel and a variety of beer cans.

Howard Crabtree's Whoop-De-Doo! (1993). In this off-Broadway revue, Crabtree designed and wore a costume for a Native American (whom he played) who had a baby strapped to his back.

The father's face, however, was a plaster mask; when Crabtree turned around, we saw that the face of the "baby" was actually his, filling the oval above the plaster body of the child.

Crabtree's 1996 death at only forty-one makes many wonder what innovative costumes he might have designed but have been forever lost to us.

The Lion King (1997). To paraphrase the title of a Leslie Bricusse song from *Doctor Dolittle*, you've never seen anything like it in your life, thanks to Julie Taymor.

Which one in particular do we mean? All of them, friends, all of them.

Author's Choice: The Bright Red Dress. It's worn by Anastasia, Annie, Desiree Armfeldt, Dolly Levi, Ella Peterson, Phyllis Rogers Stone, and the unsinkable Molly Brown. Mother (Edna) and daughter (Tracy) each wear one at the end of *Hairspray*.

In fact, all those characters named don a red dress rather late in their musicals. Costume designers know enough to save the best for last.

WHAT'S THE BEST MUSICAL ABOUT TEENAGERS?
This has become a genre in itself, so it deserves its own category.

Smile (1986). With a little brains and a little talent, a high school senior girl could win the Young American Miss Pageant.

Doria's the seen-it-all contestant and veteran of many such competitions; Robin's the rookie. And yet, Doria's dream (beyond winning, of course) is to get to Disneyland.

Now Robin's the smart one. She's been to Anaheim and back and knows the place is mostly "gift shops and people wearing very big heads."

They and all the girls from Antelope Valley to Yuba City work so hard at being sophisticated. Then Marvin Hamlisch's music and Howard Ashman's lyrics convey the intense nervousness they feel in "Until Tomorrow Night." This first act-closer, written during the Baltimore tryout, show that their mounting frustrations lead to a good ol' fashioned pillow fight.

At heart, these Young American Misses are just little girls.

Bring It On (2012). *All about Eve* goes to high school. The nearly identically named Eva is just as Machiavellian. And yet, bookwriter Jeff Whitty did a marvelous job in not letting us suspect what's she's been planning until the very end of the musical.

That's when she crows about her sabotage. Whether it was Amanda Green or Lin-Manuel Miranda who thought of having Eva sing "I'll have the trophy in my hands and all you'll have is friends," the lyric was worthy of its own trophy.

The Prom (2018). *Eleanor*, a musical about Mrs. Roosevelt, closed on opening night. The critics had also taken aim at stars Dee Dee Allen and Barry Glickman, calling them narcissists. So they, along with fellow thespians Trent and Angie, go to an Indiana town that had recently made the news.

Emma, a senior at Edgewater High, wanted to bring her girlfriend to the prom. She was told that even if she were to try, the event would be canceled. The New Yorkers would help, solely so they could get publicity that would make them "appear to be nice people."

To their surprise, they all became emotionally involved with the young lovers. Once Barry heard that Emma's parents cut her out of their lives, he felt her pain, for his family did the same when he came out. Barry now needed to care for his new surrogate daughter.

Dee Dee, who seemed shallower than the water in a drained swimming pool, was ready to drop the crusade when matters involved money. Trouble is, she and everyone else were needed to combat Mrs. Greene, who ensured that Emma would not attend the prom and told the press what so many like-minded people have said in such situations: that she was really "worried about the child's safety."

Mr. Hawkins, Edgewater High's principal, supported Emma's rights, even as he endured intense pressure from Greene and townies who literally cringed in fear when gays and their supporters walked near them.

"It wouldn't be high school without a test," Emma sang bravely. Far less brave was Alyssa, Emma's girlfriend—and Mrs. Greene's daughter.

Bookwriters Bob Martin and Chad Beguelin played fair with Mrs. Greene, who established at the end that she tried to protect her daughter from having a harder life. In the end, *The Prom* wasn't only about LGBTQ_rights but also celebrated how much can be accomplished when adults and teens work together.

Author's Choice: *The Scottsboro Boys* **(2010).** You don't think of this as a teen musical, but history shows us that eight of the nine lads falsely accused of rape were teenagers.

The other one was twelve. The poor soul was so naïve that when an officer mentioned that a Black man looked a white woman in the eye, the child innocently asked, "Is that what rape is?"

Here was Kander and Ebb's intelligent musical about racism in America and politicians who failed to do the right thing. It showed the famous 1931 case and its multiple trials for those nine young men who hopped a train and were accused of raping two white women. Victoria Price and Ruby Bates accused the lads just to deflect suspicion that they'd been engaging in prostitution.

The young men cooperated with the authorities. One deferentially said, "Anything we can do for you, sergeant?" in a most polite voice only to be castigated by his friend: "Take off your hat!" Librettist David Thompson made clear that in those days, a Black man always had to intently watch his step with whites; forgetting to include even one respectful gesture could lead to trouble.

"When I want your opinion," the sergeant snarled, "I'll give it to you." The audience laughed because it was a funny line, but the sound of the laughter was hollow and joyless. Any humor was eclipsed by the realization that this was indeed the way things once routinely were—and that isn't funny.

Ruby Bates eventually recanted, but the Southern bureaucracy wouldn't accept her revised testimony. What sadness there was in her line "Why did everyone believe me when I was telling a lie, but nobody believes me when I'm telling the truth?"

Now the bigoted Southern attorney general had to attack the defense attorney for being Jewish. The song the attorney general sang was euphemistically called "Financial Advice," but a more apt title would have been "Jew Money." So we not only saw bigotry against Blacks but against Jews, too.

(If that sounds hyperbolic, the actual court records of April 13, 1933, show that Wade Wright, a county solicitor who was assisting the attorney general on the Scottsboro case, asked jurors "whether justice in this case is going to be bought and sold with Jew money from New York.")

Most of the story centered on Haywood Patterson, whom the irascible judge wanted to admit guilt; if he did, the judge would be lenient on him.

The judge and prosecutors knew a mistake had been made and wanted to save face by having Haywood say he was guilty. Then they could have been considered merciful good guys who grandly let him go.

Haywood wouldn't. This was a story that was a bottleful of bitter pills to swallow. Perhaps that's why the collaborators settled on framing it with a corny-joke-filled minstrel show. They always began with the line, "Gentlemen, be seated!" so Thompson had the judge say the same words to those in his courtroom.

If only someone had stood up instead.

WHAT'S THE BEST MERCHANDISE THAT A MUSICAL HAS EVER OFFERED ITS PATRONS?

Oliver! (1984 revival). Many musicals offer mugs with various lines of dialogue or lyrics. The ones for this production sold mugs that quoted Oliver's famous request: "Please, sir, I want some more!"

Beauty and the Beast **(1994).** Sure, every show hawks very expensive T-shirts, but one in a very small size was very much worth the price.

It said "My First Broadway Show."

Company **(1993 reunion concert).** Merch wasn't much offered in the days of the Golden Age, so the original production of the Sondheim-Furth masterpiece didn't take advantage of one of the show's most famous lines.

This two-performance event did. It sold magenta baseball caps that said in that stylized fuchsia-colored lettering of the original logo: "Does anyone still wear a hat?"

Hamilton. Keychains have become popular, even those heavy, extra-large ones that replicate theater tickets of yore.

Far more modest in size—if not in egocentricity—are the ones that sport a quotation from Lin-Manuel Miranda's mega-hit: "I am the one thing in life I can control. I am inimitable. I am an original."

So many musicals are described as "feel-good." So why not a keychain that makes its owners feel good about themselves?

Author's Choice: The Declaration of Independence (*1776*). After each performance, all a theatergoer had to do was go to theater's stage door and ask for the faux-parchment paper on which the cast had affixed its fourteen signatures at that performance.

(And yes, the actor playing John Hancock did always sign with the biggest signature, as his counterpart had in real life.)

The best part of all is that it was given gratis, absolutely free. Who'd think that any Broadway show would give away any souvenir, especially one as distinctive?

WHAT WAS BROADWAY'S GREATEST SPECIAL PERFORMANCE?
The 1970–1971 Tony Awards. Not because *Company* won Best Musical or that Sondheim won one for Best Music and one for Best Lyrics. (It's the only time, incidentally, that two separate awards were bestowed for Best Score. How fitting that they should be given to Sondheim.)

What was special about the twenty-fifth anniversary of the awards that took place on March 28, 1971, was its musical retrospective of the awards' first quarter-century.

It started with David Wayne replicating his "When I'm Not Near the Girl I Love" (*Finian's Rainbow*), followed by Nanette Fabray doing "Papa, Won't you Dance with Me (*High Button Shoes*). He'd won; she hadn't, but she did what we inferred was Jerome Robbins' Tony-winning choreography.

Neither show had won Best Musical, because, bizarrely, the category didn't exist until the next awards in 1949, when *Kiss Me, Kate* emerged victorious. Alfred Drake represented it with "Where Is the Life That Late I Led?"

From then on, with only two exceptions, every performer did a song from a Tony-winning musical. Some had won Tonys themselves: Ray Walston (*South Pacific*), Alfred Drake (*Kismet*), Gwen Verdon (*Damn Yankees*), Robert Preston (*The Music Man*), Verdon and Richard Kiley (*Redhead*), Tom Bosley (*Fiorello!*), Robert Morse (*How to Succeed . . .*), Zero Mostel (both in *A Funny Thing Happened* and *Fiddler on the Roof*), Carol Channing (*Hello, Dolly!*), Kiley (*Man of La Mancha*), Leslie Uggams (*Hallelujah, Baby!*), and Lauren Bacall (*Applause*).

Even those who didn't win Tonys for themselves represented their musicals: Vivian Blaine (*Guys and Dolls*), Edie Adams (*Wonderful Town*), John Raitt (*The Pajama Game*), Stanley Holloway (*My Fair Lady*), Paul Lynde (*Bye Bye Birdie*), Jill Haworth (*Cabaret*), and William Daniels and Virginia Vestoff, "Yours, Yours, Yours" (*1776*)—although the former would have won had he not taken himself out of contention because his billing placed him in the Best Featured Actor in a Musical category.

Two Best Musical losers were represented. Verdon danced to the title song of *Can-Can* (splendidly, to no one's surprise). Angela Lansbury did "Open a New Window" (*Mame*). This wasn't only because she'd won a Tony in the musical's losing cause; she was one of the evening's hosts.

And although Florence Henderson had never done *The Sound of Music* on Broadway, she'd performed it in enough places that she was welcomed to sing the title song.

Or was it because the television audience would find her the biggest name there, thanks to her then-current but forever immortal stint as Mrs. Carol Martin Brady.

Ichabod (1977). It was a Sunday afternoon in May at the Boston Repertory Theatre. For the lanky Ichabod Crane, Washington Irving's hapless victim in *The Legend of Sleepy Hollow*, Tommy Tune and his six-foot-six-inch frame makes him ideal casting for this one-man musical.

On this day, it really would be a one-man show. Fifteen minutes after the scheduled showtime, Tune entered with a worrisome look on his face. He told the audience that the pianist simply hadn't arrived. "I'll do it *a capella*," he said.

Indeed he did, but only a few seconds later, wished that he hadn't. A capella would work decently enough in coming decades with off-Broadway's *Avenue X* (1994) and Broadway's *In Transit* (2016). Those musicals, however, respectively had a company of eight and eleven, so beautiful harmony filled out the sound.

Tune had no such luxury. His eyes soon widened as he realized how unentertaining a capella can be and how unresponsive the audience already was.

About three minutes later, a frantic young man ran onto the stage holding a batch of sheet music. He apologized while still on foot and hurriedly sat at the piano.

We'd later learn that he'd been resting under a tree in Boston Common and had fallen asleep. No cell phones in those days, remember.

Tune just gave him a no-hard-feelings smile and said "Let's start again!" They did—and both they and the audience enjoyed the show.

The 1996 Easter Bonnet Competition. This annual fashion fest offers millinery of which Irene Molloy could only dream.

The event began in 1987 when *La Cage Aux Folles'* cast members asked performers in currently running Broadway shows to write a sketch or parody a song, perform it, *and* design and make a hat that both represented their shows and what the bonnets parodied.

Case in point: In 2016, *Hamilton* set the melody of its opening number to rap lyrics about *Sweeney Todd*, played by Lin-Manuel Miranda himself. The show's bonnet was a Revolutionary War tricolor bisected by a generous triangular slice of brown pie (which presumably did *not* come from a little priest).

For more than three decades, delightfully outrageous headwear and self-deprecating humor have yielded dozens upon dozens of laughs from such comedians extraordinaire as Nathan Lane, Andrea Martin, and Tracey Ullman.

Never, however, did a laugh come so quickly or loudly as it did at the tenth edition at the Palace Theatre. Only two words needed to be spoken by the first emcee of the afternoon: Elaine Stritch, who droned "Does anyone ..."

***Sondheim: A Musical Tribute* (1973).** This star-studded event actually came halfway through Sondheim's career; he'd had his name on eight Broadway musicals to that point; in the next twenty-one years, he'd write nine more that would play New York.

Appearing on that March 11 night were thirty-four performers who'd appeared in Sondheim shows—two of whom had won Tonys in them (Larry Blyden, *A Funny Thing* ... ; Alexis Smith, *Follies*) and three who would (Glynis Johns, *A Little Night Music*; Len Cariou and Angela Lansbury, *Sweeney Todd*; add in *Gypsy* for her).

The highlight came deep in the show after Ron Holgate sang *Follies'* "Beautiful Girls" and then introduced Smith, Lansbury, Johns Hermione Gingold, Dorothy Collins, and Nancy Walker. The last-named made the biggest impression with "I'm Still Here." It would result in the first-ever recording to feature the lyrics that had been inexplicably dropped from the truncated original cast album.

Author's Choice: *A Chorus Line* **#3,389.** On September 29, 1983, 332 performers who'd appeared in various productions of the musical came back to break the record that *Grease* had been holding for the previous three years.

Those who attended the afternoon dress rehearsal actually got the better deal, after the show was officially over, NBC would reassemble everyone and tape the finale for a broadcast later that night.

So "One"—performed by everyone, be they on stage or in the aisles—was done twice.

WHAT MUSICAL WAS NEVER PRODUCED THAT YOU WOULD HAVE MOST LIKED TO HAVE SEEN?

Arsenic and Old Lace. "Oh, everybody wanted me and Merman to do it as a musical," Mary Martin told *The Washington Post* in 1977. Richard Rodgers was interested in composing, too, but instead opted for *I Remember Mama* (to his chagrin).

Having those two blockbuster names above the title might have been enough to raise tickets from the twenty-five dollar high that had just been set by Liza Minnelli in *The Act.* However, although Martin would seem right for a sweet and demure Brewster Sister, such a character wouldn't seem to be in Merman's wheelhouse.

A better match for these two would have been a musical version not of *No, No, Nanette*—no, no—but of Don Dunn's aforementioned tell-all *The Making of "No, No, Nanette"* with Merman as avaricious producer Cyma Rubin and Martin as demure Ruby Keeler.

Bullets over Broadway. Wait, you're saying, this was on Broadway in 2014. Yes, but with a jukebox score filled with song hits (and misses) from the 1920s and 1930s.

Despite a production helmed by the much-heralded Susan Stroman, the musical lost in all six categories in which it was Tony nominated; it shuttered after a mere 156 performances.

Ah, but if Marvin Hamlisch had written the music as was originally planned, and if auteur Woody Allen not settled for a secondhand score, matters might have turned out very differently.

I Picked a Daisy. "Daisy" refers to Daisy Gamble, a cigarette-addicted heroine with ESP—yes, the same character that Alan Jay Lerner wrote with Burton Lane for *On a Clear Day You Can See Forever.*

That score is marvelous, yet we can't help wonder how Lerner's lyrics would have sounded with the music of the first composer with whom he worked on this musical: Richard Rodgers.

Rodgers eventually complained that Lerner was working too slowly and severed the collaboration. No question that Lerner wasn't speedy, but his taking speed—meaning methamphetamine—was a greater problem for Rodgers; after all, Lorenz Hart, his first partner, had had an addiction (albeit to alcohol) that had caused the composer many, many problems.

The official "works too slowly" excuse doesn't ring true when one considers that *On a Clear Day* opened only seven months after the musical Rodgers had chosen in its stead: *Do I Hear a Waltz?*

Considering that sturm and drang we hear about *Waltz*, were there times when Rodgers wished that he and Lerner had continued, even if they had to duel to the meth?

Star Wars. For a musicalization of George Lucas' brainchild, Charles Strouse and Lee Adams wrote at least two songs: "Han's Your Man" and "My Star."

Nothing much happened after that.

If it had come to fruition, however, would the premium seats have been R2 and D2?

Vicki for President. Jerry Herman would provide the score and Carol Channing would star. It would be the biomusical of Victoria Woodhull (1838–1927), an early feminist.

Woodhull was also a staunch advocate of free love. Considering what Channing told us about her forty-three-year marriage to Charles Lowe, she would have been miscast.

Author's Choice: *Scandal.* Michael Bennett's workshop had a book by Treva Silverman, a 1973 "Writer of the Year" Emmy for a *Mary Tyler Moore Show* episode (in which Lou Grant and his wife were having problems). Jimmy Webb, who'd written "Up, Up, and Away" and *seven* other platinum hits, provided the score.

Many of us could relate to the story. When a person's on vacation, especially in a foreign country, he or she becomes a different person—and often a far more sexual one. Swoozie Kurtz would play a woman who rebels against her unhappy marriage and takes her pleasures wherever she could find them overseas.

Such a scenario was in the promiscuous Bennett's wheelhouse; the choreography he devised for the 1984 workshop was said to be especially erotic. Bennett was telling friends that this musical—not *A Chorus Line*—would be the one for which he'd most be remembered.

In January 1985, Bennett canceled *Scandal*. AIDS had put a stop to much promiscuity, so audiences would be worrying about their heroine rather than enjoying her. But the real reason, of course, is that Bennett himself was enduring AIDS, which would kill him in 1987.

WHAT IS THE SADDEST LOSS THAT MUSICALS (AND WE) HAVE ENDURED?

Follies. With a score of this scope, the many missing or abridged songs shouldn't be called cuts but amputations. The saddest aspect of all this is that Stephen Schwartz, a year before he wrote *Godspell*, was scouting projects for RCA Victor, and urged the company to do the cast album— and as a two-record set that we all would have loved.

Musicals have shrunk. There are fewer in a musical's cast, fewer in the orchestra, and fewer square feet on the sign over the Winter Garden so those who are experiencing fine dining at Applebee's can have a view.

The Nederlanders Sell the Mark Hellinger Theatre (1989). The original agreement that Jimmy and his brood had with the Times Square Church was bad enough: a five-year lease. But at least by 1994 we would have had it returned to us. By now, a quarter-century's worth of musicals could have played there.

Somewhere along the way, however, the lease became an outright sale. To quote Sondheim, "Gods of the theater, smile on us"—and see that the Hellinger is returned to musicals.

The Palace Theatre. Did the powers-that-be who controlled the legendary showplace make a mistake in raising the theater to allow retail stores to nestle underneath? Time will tell.

Author's Choice: Leonard Bernstein's musical theater output. Serge Koussevitzky, music director of the Boston Symphony Orchestra from 1924 to 1949, mentored Bernstein and told him not to waste his time and talent on déclassé Broadway musicals.

Although Koussevitzky died in 1951, he continued to cast a long shadow over his pupil's career.

So what works did Bernstein compose outside of Broadway that the general public knows as well as *West Side Story*? Here's betting that a man or woman on the street has heard of *On the Town*, *Wonderful Town*, and *Candide* much more than *Jeremiah*, *The Age of Anxiety*, and *Halil*.

We'll draw the line at the average person knowing the five-performance *1600 Pennsylvania Avenue*. But they might have if Bernstein had allowed an original cast album to be made. Perhaps Koussevitzky's ghost was somewhat responsible for Bernstein's refusal.

And while we're on the subject of people . . .

CHAPTER TWO

Debating the Personalities

WHAT PERFORMER HAD THE GREATEST ENTRANCE?
Ethel Merman, *Annie Get Your Gun.* We're startled by the sound of a gunshot, but not as unnerved as Dolly Tate, whose hat *had* been decorated with a bird atop it.

We soon saw the perpetrator. In the spirit of less is more, Merman walked on v-e-r-y slowly, all so the audience could reward her for all those jobs well done in her previous nine Broadway appearances—that is, if we're talking about the original 1946 production. By the time she did the 1966 revival, the number had increased to twelve; the applause probably increased, too.

Ethel Merman, *Gypsy.* Entering from the back of the house and down the aisle past theatergoers is a cliché now. It was, however, brand new, startling, and unforgettable when Merman stormed in.

John Cullum, *On the Twentieth Century* **(1978).** Oscar Jaffee has missed the train—or has he? While his two henchmen are in their compartment wondering how to maneuver without their boss, they don't notice what we do through the windows: someone's outside the train, pulling himself to their compartment, hand over hand. Eventually he reaches where they are, and after a few knocks, they see him and pull him in—but not before his hat blows off in the wind (and we applaud).

Donna Murphy, *Passion* (1994). We hear three anguished and horrifying screams. A long staircase behind a scrim lets us know they've come from an unseen upstairs bedroom. Who could be in such pain, and what could she be like?

Many minutes pass before we see a shadowy figure behind that scrim descending slowly. What are we in for?

(A brilliant performance, that's what.)

Author's Choice: What can compare to those large windows opening wide to allow Peter Pan to fly into the Darlings' bedroom? Whether Mary Martin, Sandy Duncan, or Cathy Rigby entered, *that* was an entrance.

What Broadway Performer Had the Oddest Name?

Temple Texas (*Pipe Dream*, 1955). Her name is the same as a town that genuinely exists sixty-five miles north of Austin. Its population is 78,439 (which, coincidentally, was the approximate number of curtain calls that Glenn Close took each night during her last stint in *Sunset Boulevard*).

And where was Ms. Texas born? Arkansas.

Lucky Kargo (*Li'l Abner*, 1956). Before playing an ensemble member in this hit, Mr. Kargo was a replacement pirate in *Peter Pan*. After that, Lucky tried his luck in Hollywood, where he appeared in *The Love Cult*, *The Hookers*, *Girl Smugglers*, and *Cauliflower Cupids* before turning to stunt work.

If all that doesn't sound impressive, remember we're talking about him and he's not talking about us.

Fluffer Hirsch (*Inner City*, 1971). 'Nuff said.

Dale Muchmore (*Sugar*, 1972). We'll be the judge of that. But we can understand someone who'd want much more than keeping house.

Author's Choice: Jill Streisant (*Gantry*, 1970). Perhaps this was her real surname; still, she should have changed it, for it does suggest someone more famous.

Streisant appeared as "Child" in this one-performance musical and never returned to Broadway (although she did do two productions of *Joseph* at the Brooklyn Academy of Music in the late 1970s).

She eventually married a man surnamed Younis. But wouldn't it have been something if she'd instead wed a man named Goult or Brolit?

If Performers Elected to the Theater Hall of Fame Were Pictured in a Costume, Which Would It Be?

In this era, when baseball players move from one team to another with the speed of summer lightning, a question arises to those elected to the Hall of Fame.

Which team's cap will the anointed player "wear" on the plaque on which he's memorialized?

Reggie Jackson: Yankees or A's? Greg Maddux: Braves or Cubs? Nolan Ryan: Angels, Astros, Mets, or Rangers?

The Theater Hall of Fame, which consists of a modest array of names emblazoned on the side lobbies of the Gershwin Theatre, offers no pictures, portraits, or sculptures of its inductees. But if it did, what costume would be chosen for those who'd be captured in bronze?

Angela Lansbury: Mame, Aurelia, Rose, or Mrs. Lovett?

Mary Martin: Peter Pan, Nellie Forbush, or Maria von Trapp?

Audra McDonald: Carrie Pipperidge, Sarah Brown-Eyes, Billie Holiday, or *Porgy*'s Bess?

Ethel Merman: Rose, Annie Oakley, or Dolly Levi?

Gwen Verdon: Lola, Anna Christie, Sweet Charity, or Roxie Hart?

Author's Choices: Lansbury won Tonys for all of the above, but because she didn't originate Rose, we'll eliminate that. As arresting as Lansbury looked as Aurelia "The Madwoman of Chaillot" in *Dear World*, its short run would have Hall of Fame visitors saying "Who's she supposed to be?"

That leaves Mame and Mrs. Lovett. Although the former role raised Lansbury to Broadway prominence, the latter has a more distinctive look, especially in the first act with those knobs of hair situated atop her head. Mrs. Lovett it is.

Martin must be clad in her forest-green Peter Pan outfit. Despite the fact that the musical's Broadway run was only a tiny fraction of her two other major hits, three much-publicized and highly rated television airings in five years, as well as subsequent appearances on VHS tapes and DVDs, make this the logical choice.

Billie Holiday for **McDonald**. Before she performed the role, many Broadway fans doubted that she could effectively imitate the legend's unique sound. The cast album, the HBO special, and the Tony proved naysayers *quite* wrong. Put a gardenia on her hair and on the plaque.

Merman should don the plaid coat that she wore in *Gypsy*. She said time and time again that Rose was her favorite role, so, as a lyric goes in another Jule Styne musical, "And who am I not to agree?"

Verdon would be seen in her bustier as Lola. You'll see it on the second pressing of the *Damn Yankees* cast album, which replaced the first one that had her wearing a baseball uniform. Sales for both the recording and tickets improved noticeably when Verdon was more seductively costumed.

WHO'S THE MOST DESERVING BROADWAY LEGEND WHOSE NAME SHOULD BE ON A BROADWAY THEATER?

Oscar Hammerstein. If we can have a Richard Rodgers Theatre, we should have one named for his most famous collaborator, who was also responsible for their greatest successes.

Note, too, that while Rodgers had one job—composing—aside from *The Sound of Music*, for which Hammerstein "only" wrote lyrics, he had two jobs (book and lyrics) on six musicals and was co-writer and lyricist of two other successes (*South Pacific* and *Flower Drum Song*).

One could effectively argue that Hammerstein was the *more* responsible for Rodgers and Hammerstein's greatest successes.

Ethel Merman. That we have one theater named for an Ethel (Barrymore, that is) should not preclude our having another.

Admittedly, Ms. Barrymore's theater career lasted fifty years to Merman's forty, but both were true theater artists.

The theater on West 47th Street that opened in 1928 was named Ethel Barrymore when the actress opened it with *The Kingdom of God*. Too bad that the St. James Theatre wasn't renamed for Merman on March 28, 1970, when she assumed the title role there in *Hello, Dolly!*

Chances are that we'll never see a Merman Theatre, for each day fewer who were dazzled by her are still alive to remember her. Although Merman did make fifteen films, she's really only remembered for *It's a Mad, Mad, Mad, Mad World* (in which, by the way, she's terrific).

Paul Robeson. By the time this book reaches print, there's an excellent chance that there will be a Paul Robeson Theatre; each of the three major theater chains have promised that they'd rename one of their houses for a Black theater artist.

Granted, he didn't originate the role of Joe in *Show Boat*, as many have assumed, but he was there singing "Ol' Man River" in the first revival; because of his galvanizing performance in the 1936 film, he's most associated with it.

In addition, Robeson did two important plays by Eugene O'Neill: *All God's Chillun Got Wings* and *The Emperor Jones*, which represented the first time an African American had a starring role in a play.

His most memorable success was as Othello, which, over two productions, he played for 320 performances, an astonishing run for a Shakespeare play. Here too he was an African American in a starring role that had been played (and, alas, for some time would continue to be played) by a white actor in blackface.

Robeson's politics and so-called Communist leanings did cause many to turn against him. As time went on, people understood that his intention was a noble one: to secure civil rights for African Americans.

The right time has arrived—or already has, depending on when you're reading this—for a Paul Robeson Theatre.

Alan Jay Lerner. It's one of Broadway's favorite fantasies. The theater where Lerner saw four of his musicals—*My Fair Lady, On a Clear Day*

You Can See Forever, Coco, and *1600 Pennsylvania Avenue*—is named for him.

It's not a fantasy because Lerner is unworthy; the theater in question was once the Mark Hellinger, which has been the Times Square Church for much too long.

Author's Choice: Harold Prince. The memorial held in his honor on December 16, 2019, was a marvelous tribute. More than a dozen Tony winners came to the Majestic Theatre, home to *The Phantom of the Opera,* Prince's longest-running hit (and Broadway's as well) to pay their respects.

And who deserved more respect than Broadway's greatest producer-director?

The event would have been so much better if it had concluded with a representative from The Shubert Organization sauntering on stage to tell us that from then on, the Majestic would be known as The Harold Prince Theatre.

(There's still time . . .)

OF THOSE WHO ALMOST APPEARED IN A CERTAIN MUSICAL, WHOM WOULD YOU HAVE MOST LIKED TO HAVE SEEN?

Judi Dench (*Cats*). She would have been the original Grizabella had she not torn her Achilles tendon during a rehearsal.

(Note: Achilles tendon, not Achilles heel. Where acting is concerned, Dench doesn't have an Achilles heel.)

Angela Lansbury (*The Visit*). Nothing against Chita Rivera, who did Claire Zachanassian proud in 2015. Lansbury, however, was the original first choice during the late 1990s when the McNally-Kander-Ebb musical expected to reach Broadway.

As a tune-up, Lansbury even recorded "Love and Love Alone" from the score. Her husband's illness became so severe, however, that she decided that she needed to be home and tend to him.

Had she been available, we'd have seen Lansbury return to the type of role for which she became famous in films: the insidious woman. (Exhibit A: *The Manchurian Candidate*.)

Roger Moore (*Aspects of Love*). Yes, the same Roger Moore who played James Bond in seven films in a twelve-year-span. In the original London production, he would have played "Dillingham … George Dillingham …" Then Andrew Lloyd Webber heard him sing at rehearsals.

Author's Choice: Judy Garland (*Mame*). She desperately wanted to do it because her finances were low and she needed a little Christmas then.

Jerry Herman lobbied for her, and later went on record saying that he regretted not persevering. But everyone from producers to stagehands worried that at many of the week's eight performances audiences would hear "At this performance, the role usually played by Judy Garland will be played by …"

Nevertheless, just imagine Garland singing "It's Today" and "If He Walked into My Life." That would have been more than a little Christmas for all of us.

WHAT MUSICAL BILLED ITS PERFORMERS IN A SURPRISING WAY?

Red, Hot and Blue! (1936). Here's the great-granddaddy of creative billing; Jimmy Durante and Ethel Merman were both big stars, so their names were criss-crossed into an "X" configuration to give both equal billing.

The irony is that the performer billed horizontally and matter-of-factly underneath them would be the one who'd become the most famous: Bob Hope.

The criss-cross hasn't been employed nearly as much the type of billing found on the original window card of *Wicked* where Kristin Chenoweth and Idina Menzel had their names carefully placed. The two had respectively scored in supporting roles in *You're a Good Man, Charlie Brown* and *Rent*, but Chenoweth won the Tony while Menzel had to settle for a nomination.

So for *Wicked*, Chenoweth was billed first on the left, while Menzel finished second on the right—but her name was positioned a bit higher than her co-star. It turned out to be a fine metaphor of her character Elphaba, who is, after all, an outsider and initially a higher-minded person—and flies, to boot.

Pal Joey (1957). The film version had Rita Hayworth listed before Frank Sinatra. Under such circumstances, those not familiar with the show might assume that Joey was a woman.

(Ever hear of Joey Heatherton?)

Pal Joey's billing was especially odd because Sinatra could make a boast that Hayworth couldn't. He'd won an Oscar (as Best Supporting Actor in *From Here to Eternity*). Although Christine Baranski's character in *Nick & Nora* insisted that "An Oscar for a supporting role is not a true Oscar," it was nevertheless enough of an achievement that should have catapulted Sinatra to top billing.

Hayworth did receive three awards that weren't as lustrous. For the film *My Gal Sal*, she won the 1942 Best Performance for the Month of July prize. She didn't even win it outright, but had to share the thirty-one-day honor with co-star Victor Mature.

Later Hayworth was the uncontested winner both in 1948 and 1952 for the Sour Apple Award, where she was crowned Least Cooperative Actress.

To be fair, Sinatra had won two Sour Apples, too, for Least Cooperative Actor in 1946 and 1951.

These "awards" suggest that these two may not have been pals on *Pal Joey*.

The Apple Tree. After dealing with agents who demanded certain billing for their clients, producer Stuart Ostrow agreed that Barbara Harris would be billed first, with Larry Blyden and then Alan Alda following—for the first month of the run.

From then on, Ostrow wouldn't play favorites; he'd rotate the three stars on a month-to-month basis. So for the show's second month, the marquee read Larry Blyden, Alan Alda, and Barbara Harris. In the third month, it read Alan Alda, Barbara Harris, and Larry Blyden before returning to the original lineup for the fourth month.

Buck White (1969). The biggest typeface on a window card of a new musical is usually the title.

Here, however, it went to its star: Cassius Clay, the 1964 heavyweight championship of the world who retained his crown through nine more bouts.

In late 1967, however, he was stripped of his title and had his boxing license revoked because the government didn't see him as the conscientious objector he claimed to be. In refusing to submit to the draft and the Vietnam War, he was convicted and sentenced to five years in prison.

Through appeals, he was able to stay free. With no immediate way of making a living, he turned to Broadway. This was surprising, but not nearly as surprising as his billing—not only because his name was bigger than the title, but also because of his choice of name.

In 1964, Cassius Clay became Muhammad Ali. And yet his original name was the one in boldface type on the window card, while a far more modest "a.k.a. Muhammad Ali" resting underneath.

Considering his devotion to the Muslim religion, it's a wonder that he agreed to this billing.

Destry Rides Again **(1982).** Jill Gascoine had recently played Dorothy Brock (to newcomer Catherine Zeta-Jones' Peggy Sawyer) in the London production of *42nd Street*. So when she agreed to star as Frenchy in the West End premiere of Harold Rome's 1959 musical, she was billed above the newcomer who'd portray Destry.

Alfred Molina.

At this point in his career, Molina's claim to fame was appearing as Harrison Ford's guide in the action-packed first scene of *Raiders of the Lost Ark* where he was killed.

"But when a later edition of the *Destry* album was released," said Gascoine in a 2004 interview, "Alfred in the interim had become a bigger star than I. Now he was billed first."

Gascoine said she didn't mind. Although Frenchy wasn't fated to be mated with Tom Destry, Gascoine, despite being sixteen years older than Molina, married him in 1986. They stayed husband and wife for thirty-four years. Only her death ended the union in 2020.

Who Delivered the Best Solo Tour de Force?

Two from *Lady in the Dark* (1941). It's opening night of the Boston try-out. Near the end of the show, legendary star Gertrude Lawrence is far upstage as the show's penultimate number begins. Once it's over, she'll step forward and do her big eleven o'clock finale.

Lawrence will wait longer than she'd expected, for after Danny Kaye rattles off in lickety-split fashion the names of more than four dozen Russian composers (including "Tchaikowsky"), the first-nighters go absolutely wild and ensure that a star is born.

Standing at the back of the Colonial Theatre is director-librettist Moss Hart. He doesn't join in with the titanic applause but says "Christ, we've lost our star." How could Lawrence ever top what Kaye has just accomplished?

Here's how: Lawrence comes forward, delivers "The Saga of Jenny" as she's never done it in rehearsal. She punctuates Ira Gershwin's lyrics with moves worthy of Gypsy Rose Lee at Minsky's Christmas show. The applause she receives K.O.'s Kaye's. A veteran star with plenty of stage dust on her feet can meet and conquer a challenge when faced with it. The "lost star" is reborn.

"The Coconut Girl" (*The Girl Who Came to Supper*, 1963). The European Regent to the Prince invites Mary, an American chorus girl, for a late-night meal—and perhaps more. She'd rather tell him about the musical in which she's performing. Without dozens of her co-performers to help, Mary must condense and do the entire show by herself.

Florence Henderson, long before she became the television mother of three daughters and stepmom to three sons, made the audience want to see *The Coconut Girl* in its entirety.

"I Can't Do It Alone" (*Chicago*). In fact, Velma must do the work of two in this very demanding number where she replicates the vaudeville act she did with her sister, playing both parts.

That so many, starting with Chita Rivera, have done it over ten thousand times is a testament to Broadway talent.

A fond memory: Ann Reinking was playing Roxie in the original production on August 27, 1977, which was Lenora Nemetz's last performance as Velma.

Nemetz finished this demanding number expecting to hear Roxie's line, "Boy, they got lousy floor shows in jails now-a-days." But at that performance, Reinking, considered to have been one of the nicest people in the business, said, "That was really good" as a lovely farewell present.

"Betrayed" (*The Producers,* **2001).** Max Bialystock (Nathan Lane) is in prison for his nefarious actions; Leo Bloom, his partner in crime, avoided jail. Hence, Max feels "Betrayed" and summarizes in a long solo harangue much of what we'd seen happen.

He does, however, call "Intermission" at the precise point where *The Producers* took its break.

The song—a musical scene in itself—takes nearly five minutes and would take everything out of a lesser performer. Nathan Lane had no trouble with it.

Actually, his achievement was even greater in the 2005 film. There he had to rip through the song without the few seconds respite of "Intermission!"

The film didn't have one.

"Model Behavior" (*Women on the Verge of a Nervous Breakdown,* **2010).** Candela calls Pepa and gets her machine. So she calls again. And again. And ten more times, too.

Laura Benanti's performance with this jawbreaker is just one of the reasons that producers and directors leave plenty of messages on her answering machine.

Author's Choice: "Duet for One" (*1600 Pennsylvania Avenue,* **1976).** Here's a Tale of Two First Ladies from lyricist Alan Jay Lerner and composer Leonard Bernstein.

They brought us to March 4, 1877, when Ulysses and Julia Grant were required to vacate the White House. Lucy Hayes, wife of Rutherford B., was only too happy to displace them—especially Julia.

For nearly nine minutes, both women criticize each other's looks (Julia: "Her fingers like ancient bamboo"; Hayes: "Her three little chins are out of style") and plenty more.

Bernstein's melody matches Lerner's achievement. What makes the number all the more astonishing is that Julia and Lucy are played by the same actress: Tony winner Patricia (*Darling of the Day*) Routledge. She wears a funky headpiece that's half hat and half hair, and moves it front-to-back, back-and-forth when she switches from one First Lady to the other.

On the closing Sunday matinee—fewer than three days after opening night—Routledge receives fifty-eight seconds of applause. That's six seconds longer than the entire length of "Rumson Creek" that Lerner had written for *Paint Your Wagon* a quarter-century earlier.

What Person Connected with Musicals Had the Best Luck?

Shirley MacLaine (*The Pajama Game*, 1954). Even many with no knowledge of Broadway know that Hollywood producer Hal B. Wallis specifically attended the Adler-Ross hit to see Carol Haney, but caught understudy MacLaine instead. He was so smitten that he rushed backstage after the show and offered her a five-year contract.

However, there's more to the familiar story. Earlier on that fateful June 29, 1954, night, MacLaine had accepted a job as Gwen Verdon's understudy in *Can-Can*. When she arrived at *The Pajama Game* to do her chorus stint, she planned to give notice.

MacLaine didn't have time. She had to get ready to play Haney's role.

A further irony is that MacLaine did wind up doing *Can-Can*—but in the 1960 film version. It was her tenth film in five years; she's since done almost four dozen others.

Haney appeared in all of two feature films, including reprising her role in *The Pajama Game*. She turned to choreography for the Broadway productions of *Flower Drum Song*, *She Loves Me*, and *Funny Girl*. The latter was her final job, for she endured a much-too-early death at thirty-nine, a mere seven weeks after the musical had opened.

This story is so emblematic of the successful understudy that Lee Adams, when writing the lyrics for a song in *Applause* (1970), referenced the situation after Eve Harrington went on for Margo Channing: "You got up early and pulled a Shirley MacLaine."

Betty Comden. One subplot in *Bells Are Ringing* (1956) involved a dentist who yearned to be a composer. Only a week after the show opened, *Happy Hunting* debuted with music composed by Harold Karr, DDS.

Many on Broadway wondered if Betty Comden and her writing partner Adolph Green had heard about Karr's day job and wrote such a dilettante into their show.

No. Comden stated that the idea originated from her own dentist. Whenever she arrived for an appointment, he'd take his air hose and maneuver it to play pop songs.

"That," she said to herself, "belongs in a musical."

Good thing that she didn't go to a different dentist.

James Kirkwood. One night he decided to see what Michael Bennett, who choreographed and codirected his *Follies*, had accomplished with Neil Simon's newest play *God's Favorite*.

At intermission, Kirkwood strolled into the lobby where Bennett saw and approached him. He needed an additional bookwriter for this musical he was creating: *A Chorus Line*.

Considering the results, Kirkwood might have felt that *he* was God's favorite.

Sutton Foster. Erin Dilly wasn't well on the day that she was to play the title character in *Thoroughly Modern Millie*'s first-ever full run-through at University of California, San Diego. Foster only knew the songs but hadn't memorized the dialogue, so she carried a script with her. Nevertheless, the show's team knew they'd found their ideal Millie.

Foster made such an impression that composer Jeanine Tesori and Dick Scanlan were motivated to write an eleven o'clock number, "Gimme Gimme," that became one of the show's highlights. It helped Foster to win her first Tony Award and a secure place on Broadway and in London.

Author's Choice: Matthew Sklar. In 1988, this fifteen-year-old was an usher at the Union County Performing Arts Center in Rahway, New Jersey. He wasn't scheduled to work on October 7—his birthday—but volunteered to help the ushers with the programs—"just on the off-chance that I might get an autograph from Marvin Hamlisch, who was doing a concert there," he says.

When Hamlisch arrived and overheard everyone saying "Happy birthday, Matt!" he joined in. Soon young Matthew was telling the Emmy, Grammy, Oscar, Tony, and Pulitzer Prize winner that he too wanted to be a composer. Hamlisch asked him to play a song he wrote, which he of course did.

Hamlisch was so impressed that during the concert, he called Sklar up to the stage.

"My parents had always planned to come to the concert that night," says the still-in-awe Sklar. "Weren't they surprised when I got on stage and played."

Sklar and Hamlisch kept in touch; the young man even asked him to write a college recommendation for him. Hamlisch did, and, needless to say, New York University accepted him.

So has Broadway—as the composer of *The Wedding Singer*, *Elf*, and *The Prom*.

Had Mrs. Sklar delivered her baby a day earlier—or if Hamlisch had appeared in Rahway any day later—Sklar's life may have turned out quite differently. As Stephen Schwartz wrote in *Pippin*, "It's smarter to be lucky than it's lucky to be smart."

WHAT PERSON CONNECTED WITH MUSICALS HAD THE WORST LUCK?

Patricia Routledge. At thirty-two performances, *Darling of the Day* ran more than four times longer than her other two musicals combined: *1600 Pennsylvania Avenue* (1976), seven performances; *Say Hello to Harvey* (1981), none, for it closed in Toronto.

For that matter, Routledge didn't have much luck when doing her one non-musical on Broadway. *How's the World Treating You?* (1966) closed after five and a half weeks.

(It involved a washing machine that had a piece fly off, penetrate its owner, and kill him as if it were a bullet. Does that sound like a hit to you?)

Karen Morrow. Those who post on musical theater–oriented sites on Facebook often give a YouTube link to the title song of *I Had a Ball* (1964).

Its centerpiece is Morrow, showing a brassy (and amazing) clarion voice.

How clarion? As Morrow recalled, "One time I entered a room, and Ethel Merman spotted me. She said 'Here comes Loudmouth!'"

(Look who's talking!)

In "I Had a Ball," Morrow sold a terrific melody and delivered lyrics that were almost dada-like; still, she made them sound sound.

Morrow didn't know then that *I Had a Ball*'s 199 performances would not only represent her longest-ever Broadway run, but that it would amass more performances than all her subsequent Broadway musicals combined. Even if she'd been cast as the female leads in *Little Me* and *110 in the Shade*—both of which she almost booked—she would have only done slightly better.

"I thought I'd have the same career as Mary Martin," she once said. "I envisioned composers coming to my villa in Brazil, auditioning their new shows for me, to which I'd say yes or no."

No. After *I Had a Ball* came *A Joyful Noise* (1966), which played its twelfth and final performance on Christmas Eve. ("We left the theatre and found there was a terrible blizzard. All we needed was a little girl selling matches in the snow.") *I'm Solomon* (1968) ran seven performances. ("On opening night, we each received a pendant that said, *I'm Soloman*—yes, *Solomon* misspelled!")

The Grass Harp (1971) matched those seven performances. ("Celeste Holm hated that she didn't come in until Act Two. She suggested five separate places where she could be accommodated in Act One. Instead, they went out and got me.")

The Selling of the President (1972) ran five. ("Jack O'Brien hired me after seeing me in *Grass Harp*. But the conceit was that none of the main characters would sing; all the singing would be done as the commercials for the candidate. Opening night, when I came out for a curtain call, a couple of guys in fifth row center yelled, 'You shoulda sung, honey!'")

Morrow was in one hit: *The Mystery of Edwin Drood*—but as a replacement. "I was the third Princess Puffer—and the last," she said. "Of course, after I went in, it soon closed."

Herbert Ross. In 1965, after choreographing nine musicals in thirteen years—all of which lost substantial money—Ross got his first chance to direct and choreograph.

The show was *Kelly*, which opened and closed on February 6, 1965. It turned out to be what was then the biggest Broadway flop of all time, losing $650,000.

And this wasn't even Ross' shortest-running show. Nine years earlier, his choreography for *The Amazing Adele* had closed in Boston.

Those two flops had scores by B-listers, so Ross must have been relieved when he signed to do subsequent shows with Rodgers, Sondheim, Lerner, Lane, Bock, and Harnick.

None of their shows were hits. No wonder that Ross went to Hollywood, where, after a shaky start with *Goodbye Mr. Chips*, he became a veritable hit machine with *The Owl and the Pussycat*, *The Sunshine Boys*, *The Goodbye Girl*, *The Turning Point*, and *Play It Again, Sam*, among many others.

Ross did return to Broadway to direct two Neil Simon comedies, but Broadway never again saw his choreography. Even contemporary cineastes with encyclopedic knowledge might well be astonished to hear that Herbert Ross could choreograph.

WHO IN A MUSICAL WAS THE MOST MISCAST?
Larry Blyden (*Flower Drum Song*, 1958). During the Boston tryout, when Caucasian Larry Storch was found wanting an Asian American Sammy Fong, Caucasian Blyden replaced him.

Why not Jack Soo (a future star, thanks to the television series *Barney Miller*)? He was already in the show, albeit in a minor role. For the record, Soo would later prove that he was worthy, for he played Sammy very effectively in the 1962 movie.

As for that film, the National Film Preservation Board has included it in its list. Its true significance was its casting all Asian Americans, in which Hollywood had been as lax as Broadway.

Time and awareness helped *Flower Drum Song*'s 2002 Broadway revisal see Asian Americans in all roles. The script was greatly rewritten and the revisal didn't do well, but at least the casting was correct.

Sammy Davis, Jr. (*Golden Boy*). Clifford Odets' play had an Italian American boxer in love with a WASP woman. In 1937, that was tantamount to a mixed marriage.

The stakes were considerably raised when producer Hillard Elkins asked African American superstar Davis to play the boxer. Composer Charles Strouse and lyricist Lee Adams gave him terrific songs to sing, including one that was dropped: "Yes, I Can," written to acknowledge the title of Davis' upcoming memoir.

In it, Davis sang that he was "133 pounds of confidence." That may be a great deal of confidence, but it doesn't amount to much in the fight game. Stories about boxers tend to be about heavyweight championships; a 133-pound boxer in the category literally called "lightweight." So the stakes somehow didn't seem as high when Davis' character took to the ring.

Credit where it's due, though; both Davis' performance and the Strouse-Adams score belong in the heavyweight championship division.

Irving Jacobson (*Man of La Mancha*, 1965). Why was a Yiddish theater favorite with a distinct Lower East Side accent cast as Spaniard Sancho Panza?

La Mancha was to be one of three shows playing in repertory at the Goodspeed Opera House during the summer of 1965. With a company of actors playing a part in each show, Jacobson was needed for the lead in the upcoming very Jewish *Chu Chem* (pronounced "Huck-um," which means "wise man").

Jacobson was cast as Sancho so he'd be available for *Chu Chem*. But that musical didn't get done at Goodspeed after all, and once *La Mancha* got rolling, no one had the heart (or the inclination) to fire the all-wrong Jacobson. When the Goodspeed engagement of *Chu Chem* was canceled, Jacobson had clear sailing to take his Sancho to Broadway.

Chu Chem did eventually make it to Broadway twenty-three years later in 1989. Jacobson still didn't get to do it, for he'd died eleven years earlier. The revival died in five weeks.

Raquel Welch as *Victor/Victoria*. Remember, Victoria must convincingly play a man whom she's named Victor. Welch's thirty-seven-inch bust got in the way.

No one said it better than Peter Marks in the *New York Times*. He started his review with "Oh, come on!"

Author's Choice: Imogene Coca (*New Faces of 1936*). Considering the revue's title, she had to be miscast; she'd already appeared in *New Faces of 1934*.

Apparently, being a New Facer wasn't like being a virgin; despite your past, you could return to your previous status.

WHAT'S THE BEST STORY ABOUT CASTING?
June Havoc (*Pal Joey*, 1940). Before she auditioned, she enticed Jerome Whyte, Richard Rodgers' assistant, to give her in advance the sheet music for "That Terrific Rainbow." Then she could learn it and make a better impression than those actresses who'd be seeing it for the first time.

Such a scenario has happened countless times. This story is more than of moderate interest when one considers who Havoc's mother was: Rose Hovick, immortalized in *Gypsy* as someone who didn't care about playing fair when she wanted something.

Guess Dainty June was more of a chip off the old block than we'd imagined.

(And she did get the part.)

Benay Venuta (*Hazel Flagg*, 1953). In the 1937 film *Nothing Sacred*, *Morning Star* reporter Wallace "Wally" Cook convinces his editor Oliver

Stone (!) that the paper should make a big story of Hazel Flagg, the Warsaw, Vermont, resident who's dying of radium poisoning. If the *Star* gives her a terrific send-off by bringing her to New York before she succumbs, circulation will skyrocket.

Bookwriter Ben Hecht, composer Jule Styne, and lyricist Bob Hilliard turned the editor into Laura Crewe.

But in 1954, when the musical was filmed and retitled *Living It Up*, the editor was once again Oliver Stone. Playing him was Fred Clark; his replacing Benay Venuta had an extra irony, for the two were husband and wife.

Did it affect their marriage? Not immediately, anyway. They didn't divorce until 1962.

Audra Ann McDonald (*Carousel*, 1994). After singing "Mr. Snow," all in hopes of landing the role of Carrie Pipperidge, she simply passed out. She awoke to the sound of Mary Rodgers saying, "Get her some orange juice!"

(And give her the part.)

Author's Choice: Estelle Parsons (*Happy Hunting*, 1956). In the 1950s, Parsons was a reporter on the *Today* show. She took a leave of absence to have twins. When she returned, she was told to fly to Monaco and cover Grace Kelly's wedding to Prince Rainier.

Parsons refused, because she needed to be with her newborns. She was fired. Could she find another job that would keep her close to her New York home?

Yes, on Broadway in this musical, where she played a reporter who goes to Monaco to cover Grace Kelly's wedding.

WHAT'S THE MOST SUCCESSFUL EXAMPLE OF STUNT CASTING?
Author's Choice: A tie between Anne Baxter (*Applause*) and Megan Hilty (*Gentlemen Prefer Blondes*, 2012).

Baxter, the original Eve Harrington in the Oscar-winning *All about Eve*, aged into the role of Margo Channing, Eve's mentor and victim.

(Need we add that she sang better than Lauren Bacall?)

As for Hilty, when she revived *Blondes* at Encores! she was portraying Ivy Lynn on the television series *Smash*—an actress who'd been endeavoring to portray Marilyn Monroe in the (mythical) musical *Bombshell*.

Now she was playing one of Monroe's most iconic roles for real, and doing it well.

And that, sad to say, is just about it for good stunt casting.

What Performer was the Best at Stopping the Show?

As soon as the marvelous song ends, those in attendance applaud wildly. Once their handclapping begins to abate, they realize that they really haven't given the performer or the song its entire due.

So they re-applaud. This time, though, they not only bring the applause back to the previous level, but they also ensure that this round is even stronger and louder than it was the first time.

It happened to the following.

Dorothy Loudon (*The Fig Leaves Are Falling*, 1969). It's the one and only Saturday matinee of Allan Sherman and Albert Hague's new musical. That evening, it will close as a four-performance flop.

Yet in her torch song that afternoon, trouper Dorothy Loudon gives her all in "All of My Laughter." Whatever theatergoers feel about the rest of the show, they sure respond to Loudon.

Cries of "More!" and "Encore!" fill the Broadhurst. Loudon has never received an ovation such as this, but as one who's always willing to please an audience, she does it again.

Were there any members of the Tony committee in the house? Probably, because Loudon received a nomination as Best Actress in a Musical. That doesn't often happen to those who appear in a show that runs three days.

Debbie Shapiro (*Perfectly Frank*, 1980). Broadway audiences had only seen the future Debbie Gravitte if they were looking carefully during *They're Playing Our Song*, where Shapiro was one of Sonia Wolsk's "Voices."

(Not in the Joan of Arc sense; Shapiro played one of Wolsk's three back-up singers.)

At the first preview of this Frank Loesser revue, Shapiro entered through the vertical opening of the front curtain and delivered "Junk Man," a 1937 song for which Loesser had provided lyrics. Shapiro did such a dynamic rendition that the applause would have sent a needle to six or seven on the Richter scale. She smiled and exited through that slit in the curtain.

Her leaving was not what the attendees wanted. They let her know that they greatly appreciated what she did by applauding very much longer than usual. It lasted long enough for Shapiro to return center stage and take a bow. The audience was oh so grateful that she did.

Alix Korey (*The Wild Party*, 2000). With a brassy voice in the tradition of Merman and Morrow (Karen, in case you're wondering), Korey blasted out Madeline True's lusty and unapologetic song about surveying party guests and picking out possible lesbians for late-night liaisons. Theatergoers could have applauded her and songwriter Andrew Lippa late into the night.

Author's Choice: Gwen Verdon (*Can-Can*, 1953). Whenever Cy Feuer, co-producer of this Cole Porter hit, spoke of that opening night, he'd get a deadly serious look on his face.

"People are always saying such-and-such a number stopped the show," he'd say with a disgusted look. "What they mean is a performer and a song got plenty of applause, more than was expected. But that's not the same thing as what happened to Gwen Verdon that night."

No, Verdon in "The Garden of Eden Ballet" made the first-nighters feel as if they'd been readmitted to paradise. She actually had enough time to reach her dressing room while the applause was still roaring through the theater. It continued as she was fetched to return to the stage where, needless to say, it then continued for some time more.

Yes, *that's* stopping the show . . .

WHO MADE THE BIGGEST MISTAKE IN DECLINING A ROLE IN A BROADWAY MUSICAL?

Robert Shaw was first announced to play Julius Caesar in *Her First Roman*, the 1968 musical version of George Bernard Shaw's *Caesar and Cleopatra*. He liked to joke that the reason he decided against it was "because they wouldn't call it *His First Egyptian*."

(Frankly, what probably happened is that he heard the score.)

So Richard Kiley took the role, endured painful tryouts in Boston and Philadelphia, and was employed for all of seventeen performances in New York.

So Robert Shaw *didn't* make a mistake. But some stars did.

Vivian Vance (*Leave It to Me!*, 1939). Getting cast in a chorus is never a great tribute to one's talent. Even understudying an important role isn't much of a compliment.

Nevertheless, a job is a job, so Vance agreed to join the ensemble of the 1937 musical *Hooray for What!* and cover Kay Thompson.

When Thompson was fired during the Boston tryout, Vance was offered her role but only on an interim basis. She turned it down, mostly because she felt bad for Thompson.

Then the star told Vance to take it, for "they'll just get someone else."

Vance did, and as the weeks went on, no one who auditioned was thought to be better than she. Finally, two days before the December 1 opening, Vance was officially awarded the role.

She received good notices, although John Mason Brown and other critics judged her overly vulgar in one song. So when producer Vinton Freedley was preparing his next musical, he offered Vance a role that included a striptease. Vance rejected it, fearing that her second such assignment would forever typecast her in "naughty" roles.

The show was *Leave It to Me*; the song was "My Heart Belongs to Daddy" which jump-started Mary Martin's rise to stardom.

As discouraging as that must have been, Vance would become more famous than Martin after she became Lucy and Ricky Ricardo's landlady.

Ray Bolger, Art Carney, Dan Dailey, Danny Kaye, Gene Kelly, Bert Parks, and Jason Robards, Jr. as Harold Hill (*The Music Man*). There, in alphabetical order, are the stars who turned down the opportunity to headline this new musical.

Why would any of them accept? It was written by that never-had-a-show-on-Broadway orchestra leader who had the presumption to think that he could write music, lyrics, *and* book all by himself.

Well, who else can they get to play the lead?

As it turns out, their worries were over after Robert Preston said yes.

Milton Berle as Pseudolus in *A Funny Thing Happened on the Way to the Forum*. Berle, known as "Mr. Television" in the early 1950s, was obviously close to doing it, for early newspaper ads sported his name and likeness in the logo. But he eventually said "Pshaw!" to Pseudolus.

Well, it's not as if he needed the money. In 1951, NBC signed Berle to a one million dollar a year contract, which they must have deeply regretted when they canceled his show only five years later.

Still, what Berle probably did need was a success that would have restored his pride. Pseudolus would have provided it.

Alfred Drake as Old Deuteronomy in *Cats*. When Cameron Mackintosh was readying the next Andrew Lloyd Webber musical, he sought this Tony winner.

"Alfred turned it down," recalls Broadway producer Max Weitzenhoffer. "He didn't want to spend intermission with people from the audience crawling all over him."

At this point, Drake hadn't appeared on Broadway in eight years, since his 1975 seven-performance stint in *The Skin of Our Teeth*. That turned out to be the legend's final appearance. Would that he could have ended his career with a smash-hit musical.

Author's Choice: Mary Martin (*Oklahoma!*). Martin wasn't afraid to do that striptease in "My Heart Belongs to Daddy." Now that she was the talk of Broadway, she was wooed by the managements of two musicals that would open in 1943. She claimed that she flipped a coin to decide which one she'd take: *Dancing in the Streets* or *Away We Go!*

We've all listened enough times to the cast album of the musical that had changed its title from *Away We Go!* to *Oklahoma!* to know that Martin isn't on it.

No, she wasn't fired or quit during tryouts. The coin that made the decision was a bad penny. *Dancing in the Streets* and *Oklahoma!* both played Boston, but only one of them came to New York.

Worse, this was the second consecutive out-of-town closing for Martin, whose previous disaster was called *Nice Goin'*.

Nice goin', Mary.

WHO WAS THE BEST REPLACEMENT IN A LEADING ROLE?

Some years back, the Tonys decided to bestow a prize for Best Replacement Performer.

In theory, it's a fine idea. However, accommodating hundreds of voters who have been accustomed to receiving two seats to every performance would cut into a show's gross and profits. If these voters started spreading bad word of mouth, productions that were struggling financially could close as soon as Sunday afternoon.

So the Best Replacement award was dropped without a single one ever dispensed.

Tony committees are occasionally impressed enough by replacements that they give Special Awards: John Cameron Mitchell, *Hedwig and the Angry Inch* (2015); Pearl Bailey, *Hello, Dolly!* (1969); and—stretching the definition a little—Mary Martin in 1948 for taking *Annie Get Your Gun* on the road.

But who *else* would have won if the committee hadn't changed its mind or if Best Replacement had been a category from the outset?

Herschel Bernardi (*Fiddler on the Roof*, 1965). Sheldon Harnick tells of the going-away party for Zero Mostel, who'd won a Tony as Tevye in the Tony-winning musical.

Although Harnick hadn't been happy with Mostel's recent anything-for-a-laugh improvisations, he thought he'd be gracious and tell the actor "We're sorry to see you go."

To which Mostel snappily said, "You'll just be sorry to see the grosses go down."

But they didn't fall perceptibly. Luther Adler played Tevye for three months until Bernardi arrived. For the next two years (save a month's vacation), he gave a memorable and honest performance.

In the scene where Tevye is holding his infant grandchild, Bernardi beautifully conveyed Tevye's heartbreak at realizing this was probably the last time he'd ever hold the boy in his arms.

That's quite a difference from Mostel's pretending that the child had urinated on him.

Bernardi was such an effective Tevye that Columbia Records had him do an album with ten songs from the score. His playing a full 25 percent of the run helped *Fiddler* become Broadway's longest-running show.

In 1981, Bernardi returned as Tevye in a revival that played the New York State Theatre. Despite its not being a conventional Broadway house, he nevertheless received a Tony nomination as Best Actor in a Musical. True, there wasn't much competition that season, but some finicky parliamentarian could have insisted he not be recognized for a role he'd played hundreds of times more than a decade earlier.

In a way, Herschel Bernardi was receiving a Lifetime Achievement Award.

Pearl Bailey (*Hello, Dolly!*, 1967). Nearly four years into the run, that train that rumbled on during "Put on Your Sunday Clothes" wasn't running out of steam, but the show certainly was. Betty Grable just wasn't selling.

Merrick's idea to bring in Bailey—but with an all-Black cast—doesn't much please us today. (It didn't please Carol Channing, either, who called the new iteration "a minstrel show.") Alas, non-traditional, colorblind casting was still some time away.

Suddenly, Bailey was on the cover of *Life* and *Dolly* had new life.

While we're at it, let's give an honorable mention to Phyllis Diller, who began playing Dolly in 1969.

Here was the nation's foremost female stand-up who made a career from her sardonic comments.

On her husband: "When we get up in the morning, we don't kiss; we touch gloves."

On her appearance: "I spent seven hours in a beauty shop—and that was just for the estimate."

On life in general: "I flew an airline so cheap that instead of showing a movie they put on a high school play."

She punctuated such lines with a wild laugh that could awaken David Belasco's ghost.

And yet, ask anyone who saw Diller in *Hello, Dolly!* and chances are you'll hear that she was excellent. Diller played Dolly 100 percent straight without adding any of her famous persona.

Bette Midler could have learned a lot from her.

Reba McEntire in *Annie Get Your Gun* (2001). Irving Berlin's classic received a big boost when this country superstar opted to visit Broadway.

By the time that she succeeded Bernadette Peters, McEntire had seen seven of her albums reach number one on the country charts and three settle at number two. Four went gold, seven platinum, two double platinum, three triple platinum, and one quadruple platinum.

Although Peters was expert is calibrating Annie's growth, showing her ever-increasing education in each successive scene, many preferred McEntire's McAlester, Oklahoma country twang. They considered it more natively right to New York native Peters'.

Frankly, Annie came from Grenville, Ohio, more than nine hundred miles northwest of McEntire's birthplace. But that's another story.

Mimi Hines in *Funny Girl* (1965). Broadway savants were surprised that producer Ray Stark even bothered to seek a replacement for seemingly irreplaceable Barbra Streisand.

Not only had she scored a personal triumph ("Everyone knew that Barbra Streisand would be a star and now she is one," Kerr, *New York Herald Tribune*), but she also had had a hit record with *Funny Girl*'s "People," reaching number four on the singles' charts when the Beatles were dominating it.

And yet, although Streisand had ended her stint as Fanny Brice after twenty-one months, Hines was able to add a year and a half to the run. Indeed, many who returned to the musical insisted that Hines was the better fit for Fanny.

(Of course, on their previous trips to see Streisand, they may have seen one of her infamous walk-through-it performances.)

Author's Choice: Liza Minnelli (*Chicago*). Gwen Verdon was injured, so Bob Fosse called his *Cabaret* leading lady and asked her to become *Chicago*'s leading lady.

Given that Fosse is the one who made Minnelli a true superstar (with *Liza with a "Z"* as well), how could she say no?

Minnelli started rehearsals on Tuesday and miraculously began performances on Friday. Suddenly the musical that had been doing good but not exceptional business was rivaling *A Chorus Line* as Broadway's most impossible-to-get ticket.

It wasn't simply a case of her reputation preceding her. Minnelli was the right age for Roxie Hart and had songs that fit her style ("He *LOVES* me so, that funny honey . . .").

No, Minnelli wasn't a replacement in the true sense: someone who's signed in advance, has ample rehearsal time, and plans to be there for the foreseeable future. Just try, though, to find a better replacement than she was here.

Whose Premature Death Represented the Greatest Loss to Broadway Musicals?

Jerry Ross. The co-composer and co-lyricist for *The Pajama Game* and *Damn Yankees* died at twenty-nine. That was devastating both to his collaborator Richard Adler and to Broadway.

No composer-lyricist before or since Adler and Ross—not even Stephen Sondheim—has written two shows that have won Best Musical Tonys in consecutive years. What's more, both *The Pajama Game* and *Damn Yankees* yielded two songs that most everyone in the country came to know. The former had "Hey There" and "Hernando's Hideaway" and the latter sported "(You've Gotta Have) Heart" and "Whatever Lola Wants."

In the twenty-one years after Ross' death, Adler went solo and wrote music and lyrics for three Broadway productions. *Kwamina*, even at thirty-two performances, turned out to be his longest runner of the trio. *A Mother's Kisses* (1968) closed in Baltimore and *Music Is* (1975) might as well have slept in Seattle, for it lasted but a week at the St. James.

What musicals we might have had if Adler and Ross had been able to continue their collaboration.

Judy Tyler. She garnered a Tony nomination for playing Suzy, an aimless lass who rued that "Everybody's Got a Home but Me" in Rodgers and Hammerstein's *Pipe Dream* (1955). That performance landed her on the cover of *Life* magazine as one of five "Shining Young Broadway Stars."

Even before then, Tyler was the idol of Baby Boomers, for she was Princess Summerfall Winterspring in the wildly successful children's television show *Howdy Doody*.

After *Pipe Dream*, Tyler played Elvis Presley's leading lady in *Jailhouse Rock*. It finished shooting on June 17, 1957. Only seventeen days later, Tyler and her husband were killed in a car accident in Wyoming.

Rodgers and Hammerstein, *Howdy Doody*, Elvis Presley: all household names. Che in *Evita* sings of Argentina's First Lady "A shame you did it all at 26." Tyler did it all by twenty-four.

Jonathan Larson. In *tick, tick . . . BOOM!*, the biomusical of the future auteur of *Rent*, Larson rues that he's turning thirty. Everyone does that, of course, but dramatic irony here is that Larson died unexpectedly days before he'd turn thirty-six. Most of us who hit thirty don't have lives that are five-sixths over.

Given that he died before *Rent* could start previews for its two-month run at New York Theatre Workshop, Larson would undoubtedly

Conventional wisdom decreed that the puppeteers should be totally clad in black so that the puppets themselves could be the stars. *Avenue Q* discarded that notion; as a result, the audience enjoyed both person and puppet (in this case, Tony nominee Stephanie D'Abruzzo). Photofest

Judy Holliday shone in her Tony-winning role of Ella Peterson, a switchboard operator for an answering service, in *Bells Are Ringing*. Although she's nice to all her clients, Ella's big smile here suggests that she's talking to Jeffrey Moss, whose voice alone has made her fall in love. Photofest

Rosie (Chita Rivera) has been waiting eight years for Albert (Dick Van Dyke) to marry her, which causes her to figuratively lose her head by wanting him to literally lose his. This dream ballet is now almost always omitted from *Bye Bye Birdie* revivals—probably because finding as deft a dancer as Chita Rivera isn't easy. Photofest

If Ray Bolger looks fey, well, that's the character he was playing in *By Jupiter*, set in an ancient Greece society where the women went to war and the men stayed home. When Bolger himself decided in 1942 that he wanted to go to war, management deemed him irreplaceable and the show closed (but not before it became Rodgers and Hart's longest-running hit). Photofest

Ethel Waters, when envisioning the hereafter, doesn't need all of heaven to be happy—just a little "Cabin in the Sky," she sings in the title song of this 1940 classic. As her husband Joe, Dooley Wilson (admittedly more famous as Sam in *Casablanca*) is very willing to see what she sees. Photofest

If there's any doubt that the red dress is the most valuable costume in Broadway history (Anastasia, Annie, Desiree Armfeldt, "Little" Edie Beale, Dolly Levi, Ella Peterson, Phyllis Rogers Stone and the unsinkable Molly Brown will all attest to it), this picture settles the argument. And yet, Katharine Hepburn as Coco Chanel in her trademark basic black stands out (although Ms. H. would in any dress). Photofest

Aren't we glad that in *The Drowsy Chaperone* that Sutton Foster's character was the one who was retiring from show business and that she herself wasn't? I'm afraid Janet Van de Graaff made a grammatical error—well, 20 double negatives, actually, starting with "I don't wanna show off no more." Foster, though, made no mistakes at all in another winning performance. Photofest

She'd just turned 19 when rehearsals began for *Flora, the Red Menace*—which she had to carry on her shoulders and learn "Sing Happy," her dynamic eleven o'clock number, at the last minute. No, the show itself wasn't a winner, but Liza Minnelli was, becoming the youngest to secure a Best Actress in a Musical Tony (a title she still holds more than a half-century later). Photofest

Do these two appear to be members of high society? Ah, but they once were, in the days when they entertained the likes of Joseph Kennedy, Jr. and Jacqueline Bouvier. But that was once upon a time, very long ago before "Big" Edie Beale (Mary Louise Wilson) and "Little" Edie Beale (Christine Ebersole) showed that their lives at Grey Gardens had turned pitch black. Photofest

No, this isn't the finale of *A Chorus Line* (although the configuration is markedly similar) and that's not director-choreographer Zach in front but Yul Brynner. This musical version of Homer's epic was originally titled *Odyssey* when it began its pre-Broadway tour, but en route saw it changed to the most embarrassing title a Broadway musical has ever had to endure: *Home, Sweet Homer*. Photofest

That's Elizabeth Seal as Irma
La Douce in her one and only
appearance in a Broadway musical.
Her expression, paired with her
arms akimbo, suggest that she's
thinking "Did you really believe
that Julie Andrews in *Camelot* could
beat me out for the Tony?" (In fact,
Andrews didn't.) Photofest

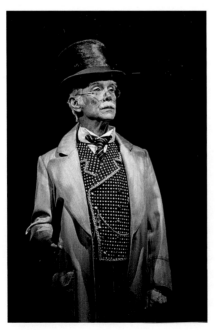

Pay great attention to that man
behind the curtain at *Wicked* once
it's raised and the show begins. Joel
Grey, with a look in his eye that
suggests that Oz's most famous resident also believes there's no place
like home, was the first of what will
be dozens upon dozens of wizards
to call the Gershwin Theatre home.
Photofest

Nobody was going to beat Gertrude Lawrence's Mrs. Anna in *The King and I* as 1951–52's Best Actress in a Musical, but if the Tonys would tell us how many votes each nominee received, Shirley Booth would have to have finished second for her stint as Cissy in *A Tree Grows in Brooklyn*. With apologies to Frank Loesser, Vivian Blaine, and "Adelaide's Lament," but Booth got the funniest song in all Broadway musical history via Arthur Schwartz and Dorothy Fields' "He Had Refinement." Photofest

As the starcrossed lovers in *The Apple Tree*, Barbara Harris received the Best Actress in a Musical Tony, while Alan Alda had to settle for a Best Actor in a Musical nomination. However, Alda had the consolation of having no less than Stephen Sondheim say his performance was one of the greatest he'd ever seen in a musical (and he saw quite a few). Photofest

Producer Alexander H. Cohen certainly thought big, as is proved by his spring 1963 rental of this block-long sign that dominated Broadway until The Marriott Marquis eradicated it. The sign displays that Cohen's track record as producer, though, wasn't big: *Beyond the Fringe* was the only hit of the eight; *Man and Boy, The Doctor's Dilemma, Baker Street,* and *Rugantino* were financial failures; two others went to different producers (*The Owl and the Pussycat,* a hit, and *Next Time I'll Sing to You,* a flop); and *Barnum* was a show by different authors that was never produced and not the one in the '80s that sported a song called "Bigger Isn't Better." Photofest have worked on his book, music, and lyrics. He might well have made a great musical even better.

Nick Cordero. He'd played characters outside the law in *Bullets over Broadway* (2014) and *A Bronx Tale* (2016); he'd received nominations from various organizations for both. In between, he played a nicer guy in *Waitress* (2016).

Then Cordero contracted COVID-19 in March 2020. Mid-April, he endured a leg amputation and then died eleven weeks later at the age of forty-one.

Cordero had proved in all three musicals that between his talent and rugged good looks, he could have justifiably been described by a term we don't encounter much anymore: a Matinee Idol.

How awful that it wasn't to be.

Author's Choice: Michael Bennett. In fifteen years of Tony races from 1967 to 1982, he was always nominated for the ten musicals he'd choreographed as well as for the four he'd directed and the one he'd codirected: *Follies.*

Let's reiterate that: Bennett was *never* denied a nomination whenever he created dances or direction for a Broadway musical—not once. He also won twice for direction and five times for choreography.

His first nomination came for *A Joyful Noise* (1966), which lasted twelve performances. More experienced choreographer Joe Layton couldn't get one for *Sherry!* that season.

Remember, too, that Bennett was originally set to direct *Chess* in London. You can bet that if he had, it would have enjoyed a Broadway run substantially longer than sixty-eight performances.

WHOSE ABANDONMENT OF BROADWAY HAS BEEN THE GREATEST LOSS?

We're not talking about death, but choice.

Julie Andrews and Carol Burnett. We'll link them together because they did two television specials together and have had a long-lasting friendship.

You might say "But both did return to the stage!" Indeed, Burnett even played the track on Broadway that Andrews had off-Broadway in *Putting It Together*. Besides, you'll argue, Burnett did *Moon over Buffalo* and Andrews *Victor/Victoria*.

Yes—when Hollywood and television weren't as interested as they once had been. The real factor is that Burnett was gone for thirty years and Andrews for more than a third of a century.

Those stats qualify as abandonment.

The Marx Brothers. Groucho, Chico, Harpo, and Zeppo gave 100 percent abandonment. They were such big hits in *Coconuts* (1927) and *Animal Crackers* (1928) that they were asked to film those musicals. The lure of the camera and Hollywood proved stronger than live audience approval, curtain calls, and *Playbill* bios.

Barbra Streisand. "For me, being a star is being a movie star." So is Streisand quoted in the liner notes of the soundtrack album of *Funny Girl* (1968).

At the time, William Goldman was writing *The Season*, about the 1967–1968 semester. He made an easy prediction: "Streisand will return to Broadway when Hollywood comes to Dunsinane."

Hollywood hasn't, but Streisand has returned to Broadway—for a few minutes at two Tony Awards. She appeared in 2016 to present the Best Musical Tony to *Hamilton*. A full thirty-five years earlier in 1970, she received a Special "Performer of the Decade" award.

To be frank, the Tonys were atoning for not giving her a prize for either *I Can Get It for You Wholesale* or *Funny Girl*.

Burt Bacharach and Hal David: *Promises, Promises* (1968). Paul Simon worked hard on *The Capeman* (1998) which endured an inordinately long period of fifty-nine previews, received unenthusiastic reviews, and limped through sixty-eight performances. No wonder that he took his melodies and went home.

But Bacharach and David's reviews included "a brilliantly modernistic score" (Watts, *New York Post*), "songs, one better than the other"

(Gottfried, *Women's Wear Daily*), and "the music excitingly reflects today" (Barnes, *New York Times*).

Promises, Promises became the longest-running show of its season. At 1,281 performances, it even eclipsed the musical that bested it for the Tony: *1776.* Sherman Edwards, its composer-lyricist, couldn't produce any famous songs, but Bacharach and David certainly could: "Knowing When to Leave," the title tune and the hastily written out-of-town hit "I'll Never Fall in Love Again."

With a critical and popular reception such as this, one would think that the team would immediately start work on a new musical. Bacharach didn't like having less control than he had in a recording studio. He and David also found the making of a musical too much trouble.

Little did they know that they'd experience much more trouble when they tried a musical for Hollywood: *Lost Horizon* landed on an inordinate number of lists of The Worst Films of 1973.

Author's Choice: Jerry Bock. Who would have expected that a seventeen-perfomance flop would sow the seeds for the eventual destruction of the Bock and Harnick team?

After *Her First Roman* received terrible reviews during its Boston and Philadelphia tryouts, director Michael Benthall left and Derek Goldby succeeded him.

Although Goldby's previous Broadway effort—Joe Orton's *Loot*—had been a quick 1968 flop, he was still esteemed for his much-heralded production of *Rosencrantz and Guildenstern Are Dead* that had opened a few months earlier.

Bock and Harnick were called in to buttress Ervin Drake's terribly out-of-period score. Says Harnick, "I soon realized that there were problems that new songs were not going to solve. I thought we were wasting our time. After a week and a half, I decided to go back to New York. Although we didn't have a verbal argument over it, I know how unhappy and angry Jerry was with me because he felt we were abandoning Derek, whom he'd come to like very much."

Two years later, Goldby was hired to direct Bock and Harnick's *The Rothschilds.* Says Harnick, "I remember being in the hotel out of town, getting up at ten after working till four, and looking out my window to see Derek sitting by the pool sunning himself. Why wasn't he working? We had a staff meeting where the producers said they thought that Derek had lost control of the show and wanted him fired."

Harnick did as well. "Jerry didn't. He felt that we were doing Derek a terrible wrong."

Meanwhile, audiences were disappointed that Hal Linden, who played paterfamilias Mayer Rothschild, died at the end of Act One, which took place in 1812. That was historically accurate, but everyone felt that Mayer should live at least until the middle of Act Two.

Says Harnick, "We agreed to write a song for him: 'In My Own Lifetime.' Up till then, whenever we'd finished a new song on the road, we'd always bring it in together to let everybody hear it. Jerry would accompany me on the piano as I sang it. The day when I expected we'd do that, people from the show were already coming up to me and saying 'Hey, we love the new song that Jerry played for us!' And that's when I knew our partnership was in serious trouble."

The Rothschilds would be the finale for the songwriting team that had won a Pulitzer Prize for *Fiorello!* as well as a Best Musical Tony for that one and *Fiddler on the Roof.* The two had also given Broadway one of its most admired musicals: *She Loves Me.* Who know what could have been? Neither Bock nor Harnick would ever again remotely reach the success they'd had with each other. Harnick got a few shows to Broadway that are barely remembered, and Bock wrote a few that never saw the lights of Broadway at all.

Who Best Captured the Real-Life Character that He or She Played?

Tom Bosley, Fiorello in *Fiorello!* (1959). How effective was he in playing the man who was mayor of New York from 1934 to 1945? Seriously: New York's mayoral election of 1961 saw Bosley receive more than two hundred write-in votes.

Howard Da Silva, Benjamin Franklin in *1776*. Have you ever noticed that in the first scene of the musical, Benjamin Franklin isn't in Congress? In every other scene that takes place there, he's a potent presence. Why isn't he in the opening?

He'd pull focus. We have a specific image in our heads of Franklin, even if we don't have many one hundred dollar bills in our wallets. Yes, we see Thomas Jefferson more often in our billfolds, but with so many men on stage around his age, any actor playing Jefferson wouldn't stand out as Franklin, the oldest man in congress, would have.

Da Silva had to do more than just resemble the icon. He was required to convey the wisdom, wit, and fierceness that we attribute to and expect from Benjamin Franklin.

Both in the original production and the 1972 film, he proved that he did.

Lewis J. Stadlen as Groucho Marx in *Minnie's Boys* (1970). He had the demeanor, the walk, the sound, and the perfect way with a cigar. Groucho's response after seeing him was "He does me better than I do." Not only that, Marx insisted that no other actor be allowed to play him but Stadlen (a directive that stayed in place right until the legend's death in 1977).

Stadlen was a delight in "The Four Nightingales." Julius, Leonard, Adolph, and Herbert—eventually known as Groucho, Chico, Harpo, and Zeppo—were about to go on stage. Then Leonard saw a backstage card game and joined it without letting his brothers know.

When Julius noticed the empty space, he endeavored to fill it by playing his role and Leonard's, too. Stadlen was marvelous in doing double duty, moving from one side of his other two brothers to the other side.

And yet, when the Tony nominations were announced, Stadlen was absent from Best Featured Actor in a Musical list. The bigger insult was that three performers were nominated instead of the traditional four. That Stadlen was snubbed caused so much commotion that *Minnie's* cast took out an ad in *Variety* to protest the decision.

Was the Tony committee too heavily influenced by what Clive Barnes had written in the *New York Times*? "Stadlen is remarkably good. Whether he has any skills other than playing Groucho Marx, I hesitate to say."

That may have put the idea in people's heads that Stadlen was limited. His subsequent roles in *The Sunshine Boys, Candide,* and plenty of other productions have certainly proved otherwise.

Adrienne Warren as Tina Turner in *Tina* (2019). For her singing, dancing, and acting, this was a well-deserved Tony win. What made the performance extra special, however, was Warren's conveying the former Anna Mae Bullock's astonishment and gratitude that she was able to hit the heights that she could have never possibly imagined.

Author's Choice: Stephanie J. Block. Not many (if any) performers have a Broadway resume that boasts that he or she portrayed not one but two Oscar winners on Broadway.

Block can. First, she was a very convincing Liza Minnelli in *The Boy from Oz* (2003) and then a superb Cher in *The Cher Show* (2018), for which she won her Tony. Block has proved herself so good at impersonations that you'd swear that she'd spent years in *Forbidden Broadway.*

No. Her only previous experience in portraying a legend occurred in commercials, when she provided the voice of Mattel's Barbie. Not that that was so hard, for who knows what Ken's inamorata sounds like? With Liza and Cher, we knew.

WHAT MUSICAL HAS OFFERED THE BEST AUDIENCE PARTICIPATION?

"Once in Love with Amy," *Where's Charley?* (1948). Frank Loesser's musical has opened to mixed reviews and isn't doing well. Co-producer Cy Feuer brings his little son to see a matinee, and the child, who's heard one of the songs on demos at home, can sing along with it.

And he does, right then and there as Bolger sings that out loud.

Usually in such a situation, people around the kid would shush him. But star Ray Bolger knows enough to make a thing of it, and encourages the audience to sing along, too.

This sequence eventually spurs *Where's Charley?* to a two-year run. A musical that also includes a song called "Make a Miracle" made one of its very own.

"No Time at All," *Pippin* **(1972).** When people complain about musicals that don't have "a tune you can hum," they certainly don't mean this one. All the audience had to hear was Pippin's grandmother Berthe sing it a few times, and they were able to join in when the sheet music (in Gregorian chant, yet) flew in and made the audience fly high.

The Mystery of Edwin Drood **(1985).** Here was a different type of showstopper. Rupert Holmes' musical simply stopped because Charles Dickens, who was writing the novel on which the musical was based, had died.

Everyone then had the chance to vote for the person either they thought was the murderer or the person Dickens thought was the murderer. Holmes reported that in both the original production and the 2012 revival Helena Landless, the Ceylonese immigrant, and Rosa Bud, Drood's fiancé, were most often chosen but strangely enough, at matinees, loveable Princess Puffer was found guilty by an audience of her peers.

Holmes also recalled that in the initial Broadway run, Neville Landless was an obvious suspect who constantly threatened Drood, so he was least frequently found guilty:

> *However, when the mesmerizing Tony Azito took over the role of Durdles the drunken gravedigger, he begged me to add Durdles to the list of suspects. I pleaded with Tony that I couldn't think of any reason why Durdles would have murdered Drood, but I was such a fan of Tony that I wrote a far-fetched confession for him.*
>
> *For the remaining year on Broadway and for the first national tour, I can report with chagrin that Tony was never voted the murderer—not even once. But in the Broadway revival, the charismatic Robert Creighton won for Durdles on two occasions. I got to see that confession for the first time on a Broadway stage nearly thirty years after the show had premiered at the Imperial.*

The 25th Annual Putnam County Spelling Bee **(2005).** The audience members who were brought up to succeed or fail at spelling made for great fun. Those who succeed joined the genuine cast members in the bleachers; those who failed would have the cast tauntingly sing "Goodbye! You were good, but not good enough!"

Was there ever a performance where some audience member had already learned the lyrics to "Goodbye" before attending the show, and when he or she successful spelled and joined the cast, and sang the "Goodbye" song along with them whenever a subsequent speller flunked?

Better still, was there ever an audience member who, after given the word to spell, first semi-danced all over the stage and used his or her own "magic foot" to spell out the word? Wouldn't *that* have stolen William Barfee's thunder?

Author's Choice: *The Rocky Horror Show* **(2001).** Before the performance, the cast entered and clapped hands over heads, signaling to the audience "C'mon! Clap along with us!" They then insisted "Gimme an R!" The audience did, only to hear it didn't measure up. "I can't hear you!" the performers taunted.

For those who'd wondered, "Will they let me participate in *The Rocky Horror Show* as I did at *The Rocky Horror Picture Show?*" director Christopher Ashley and the cast answered with a resounding "If you want to be a part of it, we'd love to have you."

Circle in the Square's T-shaped configuration allowed Jarrod Emick and Alice Ripley to play Brad and Janet on a proscenium stage while the other cast members sat in front of them in a tiny version of a movie theater to play most devoted *Rocky* fans. At the appointed times, they flung the rice, covered their heads with newspapers, and flicked their lighters. They represented everyone who'd ever participated in a midnight showing of film.

The production essentially and sincerely acknowledged, "Fans, we're nothing without you. This musical had played Broadway before, but nobody came. You're the ones who made a revival possible by making *The Rocky Horror Picture Show* a cultural phenomenon. We're deeply grateful and want you to know it."

Who Was a Musical's Most Irreplaceable Performer?

Poet Saxon White Kessinger titled her 1959 poem "The Indispensable Man." It ended with her coming to the conclusion that "There's no indispensable man."

Not necessarily, as was proved by some Broadway musicals and the stars who left them.

How tempting to put Nathan Lane's Max Bialystock and Matthew Broderick's Leo Bloom on the list. When they opened *The Producers*, it immediately became one of Broadway's all-time hottest tickets, even after management had raised prices to the first-ever one hundred dollar ticket.

When Lane and Broderick left, grosses fell; when they returned, the theater was selling standing room again.

Still, Lane and Broderick's two engagements represented only fifteen months out of the seventy-two that the musical played. So we can't call them irreplaceable.

We can, however, use that adjective for others.

Ray Bolger (*By Jupiter*, 1942). We all know Bolger as the Scarecrow, although he almost played the Tin Man. (You don't require the name of the film, do you?)

Soon after, Bolger moved from Oz to Ancient Greece in a story with gender roles reversed. Bolger portrayed an effeminate househusband while his Amazonian wife went to war.

Rodgers and Hart saw their musical become their longest-runner at 427 performances. It would have lasted substantially longer had Bolger not felt duty-bound to go to war. He'd become so identified with the role that no serious thought was given to replacing him.

Katharine Hepburn (*Coco*, 1969). How do you replace a star who's been in thirty-seven films?

Well, what about someone who's been in eighty-eight films?

However, we're talking about *Katharine Hepburn* who'd received eleven Academy Award nominations which had resulted in three

Oscars—one of which, for *The Lion in Winter*, she had secured only eight months before *Coco* would open.

When Hepburn left *Coco* after twenty months, producer Frederick Brisson opted for Danielle Darrieux, who was a big star—in France. Of those aforementioned eighty-eight films, thirty-one had French-language titles (including six with *Le*, four with *L'*, and three with *La*). So although Darrieux was the right nationality for Coco Chanel, she didn't have the box office power of Hepburn (who, ironically enough, had once been considered box office poison).

Darrieux preferred making movies. She famously said "The stage takes more from your life in three hours of work than one whole day in the film studio. On stage, you are a prisoner, even though it is a lovely prison."

Coco paroled her after merely two months.

The heyday of original cast albums had passed by 1970, so we couldn't expect that Darrieux would make a new one. However, the recordings she made of *Coco*'s title song and "Always Mademoiselle," the eleven o'clock number, displayed a pleasant soprano.

It was a marked contrast to Hepburn's voice. At the time, the joke around Broadway was that Hepburn should appropriate as her theme song the Beatles hit that begins "What would you do if I sang out of tune? Would you stand up and walk out on me?"

In actuality, Katharine Hepburn probably didn't endure many walkouts.

Hugh Jackman (*The Boy from Oz*, 2003). In 1964, when Carol Burnett needed a week off to recover from an injury during her stint in *Fade Out–Fade In*, Betty Hutton spelled her for eight performances. Around the same time, Steve Lawrence wanted a week's vacation from *What Makes Sammy Run?* The producer hired pop singer Paul Anka to sub for him.

And when Hugh Jackman went on a week's vacation from *The Boy from Oz*, the producers shut down the show.

Rosalind Russell (*Wonderful Town*, 1953). Let's face it: Betty Hutton was well on her way down when offered *Fade Out–Fade In*. Paul Anka in 1964 had seen his previous five singles reach no higher than number eighty-nine on the charts.

On the other hand, when Carol Channing took over for Russell as Ruth Sherwood, she was on her way up. If the Tonys had a category for Best Featured Actress in a Musical in the 1948–1949 season, Channing would have at least received a nomination for her cavorting in *Lend an Ear* (1948).

Is there any doubt that Channing would have received a Best Actress in a Musical nomination for bringing Lorelei Lee to the musical stage in *Gentlemen Prefer Blondes* (1949)? No, she wouldn't have bested Mary Martin in *South Pacific*, but she probably would have finished second in the voting.

Channing stayed with *Blondes* for the entire length of the run, which brought her to 1951. Seventeen months later, when she took over for Russell, she could only get three months out of the Tony-winning hit.

Perhaps Russell, who had starred in the film version of *My Sister Eileen*—the source material for *Wonderful Town*—was too associated with the role. Still, one would have expected that Channing would have done better box office.

And here's a sentence you probably never expected to read: Carol Channing probably sang it better.

Author's Choice: Gwen Verdon (*New Girl in Town*, 1957). The two-time Tony winner (soon to be three as a result of this performance as Anna Christie) would sometimes miss a show. That's when the understudies went on.

Yes, understud*ies*. Plural. One performer would sing the songs. Another would act the book scenes. A third danced the choreography.

Now *that's* irreplaceable.

Who Should Have Done Broadway Musicals but Didn't?
Zeppo Marx. He played the straight man in the first five movies that he and brothers Groucho, Chico, and Harpo made between 1929 and 1933. But after *Duck Soup*, he quit, because he didn't have the distinctiveness of his three siblings.

After he'd resigned, a studio executive told the remaining Marx Brothers that they should now demand one-quarter less money with only three of them on hand.

To which Groucho accurately quipped, "Without Zeppo, we're worth twice as much."

Still, Broadway would have welcomed Zeppo, who had a pleasant way with a song. By most eyewitness accounts of 1930s musicals, many leading men of the day were most lackluster, even go-to stars Oscar Shaw and William Gaxton. Zeppo would have done just as well or better.

Kathryn Grayson. On screen, she did many adaptations of Broadway musicals: *Rio Rita, Show Boat, The Desert Song,* and *Kiss Me, Kate.* Yet she did only one musical on Broadway: *Camelot,* and only for its final three months in late 1962.

Did anyone suggest that Kathryn succeed Katharine in *Coco?* With that Hollywood pedigree, Grayson had better marquee value than Danielle Darrieux.

Tommy Kirk. In the mid-1950s, Walt Disney was a big fan of his Hardy Boy and *Old Yeller* star. In the mid-1960s, not long after Kirk made *The Misadventures of Merlin Jones,* Disney was outraged by what he considered his star's misadventures with members of the male sex. Kirk's career was effectively over.

Why didn't Kirk come to New York, where even in the pre-Stonewall 1960s, being gay was hardly a barrier? If you remember Kirk, can't you see him as Snoopy?

Mama Cass. Although casting a role in a Broadway musical from the world of pop is now a common occurrence, back in the late 1960s, producer Lawrence W. Fineberg was ahead of his time with an atypical notion: Mama Cass (née Ellen Cohen) was his choice to play pseudo-evangelist Babylove in *The Grass Harp.* Even *Newsweek* reported that she'd probably do it.

Cass was the lead singer of The Mamas and The Papas, a group that had a number of top ten hits during the late days of 1960s.

(This information is provided for those whose knowledge of Mamas and Papas is limited to the opening number of *Fiddler*.)

Author's Choice: Frank Sinatra, Jr. Because his uber-famous father never did a Broadway musical, Junior would have had less basis for comparison than he encountered whenever he recorded or appeared in nightclubs.

(Especially when he sang "That's Life," which indeed he did.)

Even if Junior didn't natively have acting chops, Senior certainly had the resources to hire the best teachers who could have helped.

Such wise instructors would have also advised Junior to decline any offers to star in revivals of *On the Town*, *Guys and Dolls*, *Pal Joey*, and *Can-Can*.

WHO'S THE MOST UNLIKELY PERSON ASSOCIATED WITH A MUSICAL?

Sidney Sheldon (*Redhead*, 1959). What, the best-selling novelist who wrote *The Other Side of Midnight* and *Bloodline* had something to do with a Gwen Verdon–Bob Fosse musical?

Indeed, he co-wrote the book and won a Tony for it.

On second thought, Sheldon's writing *Redhead* isn't so mysterious; the show was, after all, a murder mystery.

The real surprise is that in 1943, he co-wrote a new book for Franz Lehar's famous 1905 operetta *The Merry Widow*. Considering all the murders that occurred in Sheldon's books, we must wonder how the operetta's main character *became* a widow.

Joyce Jillson (*The Roar of the Greasepaint—The Smell of the Crowd*, 1965). Those who know astrology will be surprised to hear that Jillson once played Anthony Newley and Cyril Ritchard's love interest.

Eight years after the show closed, Jillson began her astrological career in earnest. She was eventually hired to make predictions for the Ford Motor Company and the Los Angeles Dodgers. For Twentieth Century Fox, she read the stars to predict the best day on which to open *Star Wars*; no one could say that *that* didn't work out.

Even the Reagans sought Jillson's opinions, and took her advice on having George H. W. Bush as vice president.

Her book *Astrology for Cats* was published in 2005, a year after her death. Perhaps if it had been published some years earlier, everyone involved in *Cats* might have learned something that would have kept it literally running now and forever.

Arthur Penn. Although we associate him as the director of films—*Bonnie and Clyde*, *The Miracle Worker*, and *Little Big Man*—Penn obviously had an interest in musicals. He even proposed one on Fiorello LaGuardia, but *Fiorello!* would eventually be directed by George Abbott.

Five years later, when *Golden Boy* was dying in Boston and William Gibson took over the bookwriting, he recommended that Penn, who'd directed both his *The Miracle Worker* and *Two for The Seesaw*, succeed Peter Coe in staging the musical; Penn immediately said yes.

Three years later, Penn received rave reviews for his direction of the ambitious *Bonnie and Clyde* (which had music by *Golden Boy* composer Charles Strouse). Six months later, Penn received a Best Director Oscar nomination.

You might not think that in between he'd be directing the commercial musical comedy *How Now, Dow Jones*, but he was—at least until the Philadelphia tryout. David Merrick fired him.

Hired in his stead was *Fiorello!* director George Abbott.

Francis Ford Coppola (*Finian's Rainbow*, 1968). Yes, the director who had done *Dementia 13* soon followed it with the film version of the only Broadway musical set in Missitucky.

Good thing Coppola later did all three *Godfathers* and *Apocalypse Now*, for if his reputation had to rely on this poorly received and barely profitable film, his name would be, as David Mamet says of Hollywood has-beens, a punchline.

Blame Warner Bros. for some of that. After Coppola shot the picture in thirty-five millimeter, the studio thought they had enough of a winner to make it a reserved-seat, big-deal attraction. That meant transferring it to seventy millimeter, which resulted in the excising of the top and bottom of the film. Fred Astaire, who played Finian, was furious and blamed the blameless Coppola for amputating his feet, his greatest asset.

Actually, Coppola did do one more musical in a manner of speaking. In 2000, when the film of *The Fantasticks* was marking its fifth year of lingering on the shelf, Coppola came in and eliminated twenty-three minutes from the 109-minute running time. See it, and try to remember what's missing from the stage show.

Author's Choice: Dolly Sharp. If the name doesn't ring a bell, it did to many in 1972, when she appeared in the semi-mainstream porno film *Deep Throat*.

Linda Lovelace was the star, but Sharp had the line that most people remember. While she was sitting on a table, she looked down at the gentleman who was performing cunnilingus on her.

"Do you mind if I smoke while you're eating?"

Twenty years earlier, she was Helen Wood, who had appeared in *Seventeen* (1951) and the 1952 revival of *Pal Joey*. Wood even won a Theatre World Award (as did Audrey Hepburn) as a "Most Promising Personality."

This puts a different spin on "It's not where you start—it's where you finish."

WHO'S MUSICAL THEATER'S GREATEST UNSUNG HERO?

Charles Gilbert. He wrote a play called *Assassins*, whose script Stephen Sondheim saw on a desk; he was inspired by the title. Gilbert graciously assassinated his own work so Sondheim could write his.

Author's Choice: Samuel "Goatcart Sammy" Smalls. According to *DuBose Heyward*, James M. Hutchisson's 2000 biography of the writer, Heyward (1885–1940) had read a newspaper article about Smalls, who roamed around Charleston, South Carolina's, Cabbage (*sic*) Row on his little cart. Although Heyward's friends warned him that he'd make no money writing "a novel on Negro life," he spent much of 1924 writing *Porgy*.

(*Porgy*. Just *Porgy*. No *and Bess*.)

Hutchisson called the novel "the first psychologically true depiction of an African-American by a white Southerner." Did "Goatcart Sammy" ever know that he was responsible for inspiring what would become a major musical masterpiece? Here's a true example of "One person can make a difference."

CHAPTER THREE

Debating the Tonys

WHAT BEST MUSICAL LOSER SHOULD HAVE WON?
Gypsy **(1959–1960).** *The Sound of Music* has a multitude of fans who'll duel to the death to support its Best Musical Tony win. Would anyone really argue to any lengths that the musical that tied with the Rodgers and Hammerstein classic—*Fiorello!*—is better than *Gypsy?*

The Bock and Harnick musical hasn't even remotely had the afterlife of *Once upon a Mattress*, which it also beat.

At best, *Gypsy* finished *third?*

On the Twentieth Century **(1977–1978).** It happens every now and then. The show from which much was expected—Harold Prince, director; Betty Comden and Adolph Green, bookwriters-lyricists; Cy Coleman, composer; Madeline Kahn, star—doesn't quite live up to its promise. While a show that comes out of nowhere—the modest, five-character *Ain't Misbehavin'*—exceeds expectations.

Voters, who in their childhood read *The Little Engine That Could* chose the little show that could.

And Kahn's getting fired from *Twentieth Century* made it seem like damaged goods, too.

Dreamgirls **(1981–1982).** New York Mayor James J. Walker, sung about in both *Fiorello!* and *Jimmy* (which was all about him), co-wrote a song called "Will You Love Me in December as You Do in May?"

For *Dreamgirls*, the question for Tony voters was reversed: "Will you love me in May as you did in December?"

The answer was no, as more Tony voters chose *Nine*, which opened in May, as Best Musical over *Dreamgirls*, which opened in December. Did seeing it in only days before they voted make a difference?

Before that race, in the thirty-two-year history of Best Musical Tonys, only three times did a winning musical open so close to the deadline. After *Nine's* win, producers believed that familiarity would breed votes, and opening j-u-s-t before the deadline has become a coveted spot.

***Ragtime* (1997–1998).** When a musical wins Best Book and Best Score, shouldn't it win Best Musical, too?

It should have happened here, but the spectacle of *The Lion King* is what gave it the prize.

Perhaps the Best Musical Tony should be renamed Best Musical Production Tony. In the case of *The Lion King*, that's what this award meant.

Author's Choice: *Grand Hotel* (1989), which lost to *City of Angels* (1989). You had expected *Follies*, hadn't you? But that's a given.

Who Would Have Won Best Director of a Musical in the Years 1947 to 1959?

The Tonys have made many strange decisions in its long history. One of the most bizarre is that while Best Choreography was a category from day one, Best Director of a Musical wasn't.

From 1946–1947 through 1958–1959, the Tonys awarded a Best Director category that lumped together plays and musicals. George S. Kaufman was the first to win in 1950–1951 for *Guys and Dolls*, but no other director of a musical would win until 1959–1960, when Best Director of a Musical became a category.

If this had been in place since the first year, who would have won?

1946–1947: Charles Friedman probably had the harder task in directing *Street Scene*—a genuine opera—but the prize would have gone to

Bretaigne Windust for *Finian's Rainbow*. When it opened, his production of *Life with Father* was just about to break the long-run record, and this would have been a nice way of rewarding him.

1947–1948: George Abbott (*High Button Shoes*). Sure, it was a big hit and Jerome Robbins ran away with the reviews, but here too was a chance to reward the man who was already known as "Mr. Broadway" for having directed twelve musicals and many more plays.

1948–1949: Best Musical, Best Book, Best Score all go to *Kiss Me, Kate*. By many accounts, John C. Wilson's direction basically did the job—nothing more—but the show itself had enough coattails for him to ride on them.

1949–1950: Joshua Logan (*South Pacific*). He was the one who recommended the project to Rodgers and Hammerstein. More to the point, he realized that the audience wouldn't be aghast if they saw scenery flying in and out without a show curtain pulled in front while scenery was changed behind.

Indeed, audiences enjoyed seeing scenery appear and disappear. They still do.

1951–1952: Would it have been John Van Druten (*The King and I*) or David Alexander (*Pal Joey*)? The former musical was a hit that would run more than twice as long as the latter, but *Pal Joey* was an unexpected success that would become Broadway's longest-running revival.

No, it's Van Druten, because *Pal Joey* credits stated "Book Directed by David Alexander. Entire Production Supervised by Robert Alton." Alexander apparently needed help.

1952–1953: George Abbott for *Wonderful Town* or Joshua Logan for *Wish You Were Here?* The former opened to unanimous raves while the latter received almost all negative notices. But Logan didn't sit still; he returned to work on the musical (which a director seldom does) and turned it into a hit.

So would the voters say "Logan deserves the prize for improving it" or "Logan should have done that work initially"? The question alone puts Abbott in the winner's circle.

1953–1954: ***Can-Can*** **and** ***Kismet*** were splashy entertainments that received mediocre reviews. *Kismet* won the Best Musical Tony, but *Can-Can* would win for Best Direction, for Abe Burrows had become a Broadway favorite from *Guys and Dolls* which had recently closed. Albert Marre would have to wait until *Man of La Mancha* for his Tony.

1954–1955: Bob Fosse wins for Best Choreography for *The Pajama Game*, which also wins for Best Musical. Jerome Robbins, however, directs *and* choreographs *Peter Pan*, so he'd be rewarded for his staging.

1955–1956: Off-Broadway was such a new animal that the Tonys allowed it to compete this season. For *The Threepenny Opera*, Lotte Lenya and Scott Merrill received acting nominations, so Carmen Capalbo would, too, for Best Direction—which he'd actually win for rescuing and resuscitating what had been a twelve-performance Broadway flop.

1956–1957: Moss Hart (*My Fair Lady*). He might not have thought a Tony would be in his future as the musical unfurled on opening night on Broadway. Rex Harrison's "Why Can't the English?" didn't get the reaction it had been receiving during the tryout.

Hart rushed over to Lerner and Loewe and said, "I knew it! It's just a New Haven hit!"

No, it was also a hit in New York, New Jersey, New Hampshire, New Mexico, New Zealand, New Delhi, New Guinea . . .

1957–1958: Jerome Robbins (*West Side Story*). Morton Da Costa did splendidly by *The Music Man*, to be sure, but Robbins' hurdles were higher—and he and his cast jumped over every one.

1958–1959: Bob Fosse (*Redhead*). True, he got the job because his superstar wife Gwen Verdon said she wouldn't do it without him. After this, Verdon would never need make that threat again.

AND THE LUCKIEST TONY WINNER WAS . . . ?

The Wiz **(1974–1975).** This was the season that *Chicago* was to open, but Bob Fosse's heart attack postponed the show by a year—which, in 1975–1976, pitted him against *A Chorus Line*. Hence, he saw his show lose every award for which it was nominated.

Had Fosse been able to stick to his original 1974–1975 schedule, he would have won Best Director and Best Choreographer and *Chicago* would have won Best Musical.

And star Gwen Verdon? She would have been in competition with Angela Lansbury as Madame Rose in *Gypsy*. This would be a rematch, for nine years earlier, Lansbury's Mame bested Verdon's Sweet Charity. Would history have repeated itself?

(Frankly, in a word, yes.)

Fun Home **(2014–2015).** It received raves when it opened off-Broadway at the New York Shakespeare Festival's Newman Theatre in 2013. It planned an April 19, 2015, opening on Broadway.

Two months before that could happen, another musical opened off-Broadway at that same Newman Theatre: *Hamilton*.

There was time for it to transfer uptown, where it clearly would have won the Best Musical Tony. Lin-Manuel Miranda was in no hurry to get it uptown, to the relief of the *Fun Home* crowd.

"Wait till next year" is a frequent cry in sports when a team doesn't do well in one season and can only look to a hardly certain future. For *Hamilton*, waiting until next year wasn't a problem at all, and *Fun Home* will be forever grateful for its tardiness.

Author's Choice: Peg Murray (*Cabaret*, 1966–1967). She was named Best Featured Actress in a Musical for playing Fraulein Kost.

Do you even know who this character *is?*

She's the prostitute that rents from and does battle with Fraulein Schneider, that's who.

How did she win? *I Do! I Do!* had only one woman in the cast: Mary Martin, whose role was certainly not a supporting one.

The Apple Tree, three one-act musicals, only had one woman in the first act (Barbara Harris). The other two sections had four chorus women, only one of which even had a name.

Two of the other three nominees came from *A Joyful Noise*, which ran twelve performances, while the other could be found in *A Hand Is on the Gate*, which made it to twenty. Murray got a free ride—and a trophy—riding on *Cabaret*'s success.

WHAT WAS THE BIGGEST MISTAKE MADE ON THE TONY BROADCAST?

1969–1970. Jack Cassidy said "And the nominees for Best Supporting Actress in a Musical are Bonnie Franklin for *Applause*, Penny Fuller for *Applause*, Melissa Hart for *Georgy*, and Melba Moore for *Purlie*. And the winner is . . ."

He opened the envelope and glanced at its contents apparently too quickly: "Melissa Moore for *Purlie*."

No, that's *Melba* Moore, which he said after groaning at his mistake. Not only that, in rushing over to congratulate Moore, he forgot the Tony he was to give her and had to return to retrieve it.

Hart was later asked if she thought—even for a split second—that she, in her four-performance flop, had won.

"What I thought," Hart said, "was 'Jack is reading Melba Moore's name wrong.'"

1970–1971. During the fabulous twenty-fifth anniversary show when Angela Lansbury was on stage speaking and a flash bomb went off early (it was supposed to be for Gwen Verdon's entrance as Lola). It happened just as she'd said Marilyn Monroe. She gamely swam through the smoke and said, "Well, that's Marilyn!"

(Incidentally, has anyone noticed that if Marilyn Monroe had taken the surname of her third husband Arthur Miller, that she would have the same name as 1920s superstar Marilyn Miller?)

1978–1979. As Len Cariou accepts his Best Actor in a Musical Tony for *Sweeney Todd*, the cameraman shows "Mrs. Len Cariou," as the slate underneath identifies Glenn Close.

Friends of the two let out a sigh of happiness and squeal, "Oh, after all this time together, they finally got married! Good for them!"

Others snarled, "And we weren't invited to the wedding?"

No, because there was none. Although Cariou and Close had been close for some time, they hadn't married. They never have (at least as of this writing).

1981–1982. Robert Goulet gets it right the first time when he says, "The nominees for Best Book of a Musical are Tom Eyen for *Dreamgirls*" before naming three others.

But his attention span fails him when he announces the winner: "Tom Eyen for *Dreamfingers*."

Ah, yes, *Dreamfingers*! The musical about those machines in motels into which you put a quarter in order to make your bed massage you. Under those circumstances, *Dreamfingers* should have also been eligible for Best Choreography.

Author's Choice: 1981–1982. Many, many movie stars wend their way to Broadway after Hollywood has no use for them. Soon these faded celebrities are in New York giving interviews where they proclaim, "You know, theater was always my first love."

But many of these has-beens can't be bothered doing eight a week, so give Elizabeth Taylor credit for at least coming to town in *The Little Foxes* and bestowing the Best Musical prize at that year's Tonys.

Her entrance alone resulted in thirty-eight straight seconds of applause and a standing ovation. Taylor started by giving so many thanks that she eventually quipped, "This isn't an acceptance speech."

That spurred a generous laugh and twenty-one more seconds of applause.

She read the nominees and mangled the names Sondra Gilman, Louise Westergaard, and Richmond Crinkley; the audience stayed silent. Many in the Mark Hellinger Theatre probably didn't know these producers, anyway.

Taylor was aware that she was mispronouncing. "Forgive me. I can't read very well," she said, albeit with a semi-so-what demeanor.

Ah, but when she detailed the producers of *Woman of the Year* and said "Needleheimer" for Nederlander, the laughter poured through the house for a solid fourteen seconds, enhanced by applause that said "We forgive you."

No one was laughing harder than Taylor, who rallied when she announced another *Woman of the Year* producer: Warner Theatre Productions. "I can say that," she said assuredly.

Indeed she could, for at the time, she was married to Senator John Warner (R-VA). Had the Tonys invited her back any time between 1992 and 1996—and had there been a producer named Fortensky—she would have done well by that name, too.

IF THE TONYS USED A JANUARY-TO-DECEMBER CALENDAR, WHAT WOULD HAVE BEEN THE MOST DRAMATICALLY DIFFERENT RESULT?

She Loves Me versus *Oliver!* (1963). The former is, as its lyricist Sheldon Harnick will admit, "caviar" (which many people like as much as Tom Hanks did in *Big*).

And speaking of big, as 1963 was coming to a close, *Oliver!* was still doing big business after playing the entire year, while *She Loves Me*, which had opened more than three months after the British hit, only had eleven more days of life.

And the winner would have been . . . *She Loves Me*, often called "the perfect musical."

(Well, as Mary Poppins would say, *practically* perfect. Amalia and George are romantically involved pen pals who have no idea that they're co-workers, too. But while on the job, they've obviously had chances to see each other's handwriting; wouldn't they have recognized it?)

And yet, *She Loves Me* would win because Harold Prince had produced it while David Merrick had done the same with *Oliver!* Despite the fact that at this point Merrick had raised money for fifteen musicals to Prince's eight, Merrick hadn't yet won the Best Musical prize while Prince had already secured four.

Indeed, in Merrick's entire career, which saw his name on eighteen nominated musicals, he'd only win Best Musical twice: *Hello, Dolly!*

(1964) and *42nd Street* (1981). Broadway wasn't fond of this man who had proclaimed, "It is not enough for me to succeed; my enemies must fail."

Company versus *Applause* (1970). The first of many Sondheim masterpieces opened a mere twenty-seven days after the debut of the musical *All about Eve.* That amount of time, though, was enough to push *Company* into the following season.

If the two had gone head to head when the Tonys were actually dispensed on April 19, 1970, *Company*, the adventurous state-of-the-art soft hit, would have lost to *Applause*, the commercial and conventional big hit, partly because *Company*'s original cast album wouldn't be released for twenty-four more days.

However, had voting instead taken place at the end of 1970, those casting ballots would have had eight solid months to repeatedly listen to Sondheim's sophisticated score and catch up with Furth's contemporary worldview. *Company* would have won.

A Gentleman's Guide to Love & Murder versus *Kinky Boots* (2013). As events played out, *Guide* won Best Musical in 2014, a year after *Kinky* had won the same prize. Tonys tend to go to the bigger, splashier shows, so *Boots* would have booted *Guide* into the loser's column.

Come from Away versus *SpongeBob Square Pants* (2017). With *Dear Evan Hansen* out of the way, it would have been clear sailing for this small earnest and heartwarming musical about 9/11 victims and its saviors.

Author's Choice: *Fiddler on the Roof* versus *Hello, Dolly!* (1964). Prince would have emerged victorious over Merrick once again. *Fiddler* made its audiences emotionally involved in a way that *Dolly*, excellent as it was, couldn't quite match.

Paupers whose religion was the reason they were forced out of their homes into the unknown offered far more drama than people who left Yonkers for a spree in Manhattan.

There's a metaphor here too: *Dolly!* would become the longest-running musical in Broadway history for a mere eight months, when *Fiddler* surpassed it. No long-run champion has ever held the crown for so short a time; chances are, no other musical ever will.

WHAT DECISION BY THE TONYS DOES THE ORGANIZATION WISH IT COULD TAKE BACK?

Frank Loesser (*Guys and Dolls*) for 1950–1951 Best Score instead of **Irving Berlin (*Call Me Madam*).** Compare *Madam*'s big ballad ("Marrying for Love"), comedy song ("Can You Use Any Money Today?"), and eleven o'clock number ("You're Just in Love") with *Guys and Dolls*' "I've Never Been in Love Before," "Adelaide's Lament," and "Sit down, You're Rockin' the Boat."

Because many of Berlin's past successes had predated the Tonys (including the relatively recent *Annie Get Your Gun*), the sixty-two-year-old was essentially receiving a Lifetime Achievement Award for having his name on forty-eight musicals since 1910.

Conversely, *Guys and Dolls* was only the forty-year-old Loesser's second musical. Voters reasoned that he'd have plenty of chances to win Tony after Tony for Best Score.

Loesser never did win that prize, even with his Pulitzer- and Tony-winning *How to Succeed* in 1962. Still, voters assumed even then, the fifty-one-year-old would have more opportunities.

Alas, his next musical closed in Detroit and the one after that he never quite finished. Frank Loesser would die by the end of the decade and Irving Berlin—although twenty-three years his senior—would outlive him by literally two decades.

Julie Andrews (*Camelot*) as the 1960–1961 Best Actress in a Musical instead of **Elizabeth Seal (*Irma La Douce*).** That a performer so associated with musicals has never received a Tony is as much a surprise as an embarrassment. While we can castigate Andrews for abandoning Broadway, well, so did Seal; each made only one return visit.

Of course, Andrews would have easily won that next time around had she stayed in contention for *Victor/Victoria* (1995). Even Donna Murphy, who won in her stead (for *The King and I*) would readily admit to that.

Bravo Giovanni for Best Score instead of ***A Funny Thing Happened on the Way to the Forum*** **(1963).** The first time that people alleged that Sondheim couldn't write "a tune you can hum." Did they arrive late and miss "Comedy Tonight"? Were they in the restrooms when "Everybody Ought to Have a Maid" delighted not once but three times?

Falsettos for the 1991–1992 Best Musical instead of ***Crazy for You.*** The Tonys were much criticized for giving Best Book and Best Score to the gay-centric *Falsettos* while denying it Best Musical. Note, though, that thirteen years later, the 2005 Oscar voters proved they, too, didn't have the integrity and fortitude to give the Best Picture prize to gay-centric *Brokeback Mountain* but played it safe with *Crash*.

Author's Choice: You know you're about to read a sentence with the words ***Follies, Two, Gentlemen,*** **and** ***Verona,*** don't you?

What Was the Greatest Snub in Tony History?
We're not talking about those who were nominated and lost; we're talking about those who weren't even invited to the party.

Camelot **(1960–1961).** And that season there were only three nominees for Best Musical. Can we really say that this Lerner and Loewe show with their second-greatest score wasn't in the same league as *Do Re Mi*, *Irma La Douce*, and winner *Bye Bye Birdie*?

Kaye Ballard (*Carnival*, **1961–1962).** It would be a race between Barbra Streisand (*I Can Get It for You Wholesale*) and Phyllis Newman (*Subways Are for Sleeping*)—you may have forgotten that the latter won. Elizabeth Allen must have been very good to get a nod for the 113-performance flop *The Gay Life*, but Barbara Harris did far more sketch comedy than singing in *From the Second City*.

Ballard was in a musical that ran more than all four of their musicals *combined*. To be sure, that in itself doesn't entitle her to a Best Featured Actress in a Musical nomination, but the adjective given to her character—"The Incomparable Rosalie"—is one that Ballard had earned and delivered. A listen to the cast album reveals her terrific comic timing in "Humming" and "It Was Always You."

Shirley Booth as Mother Maria (*Look to the Lilies*, 1969–1970). There were only three nominees here, too. Including the Oscar winner and three-time Tony winner, Booth would have made that category with Katharine Hepburn (*Coco*) and winner Lauren Bacall (*Applause*) appear even stronger.

The other nomination, incidentally, went to Dilys Watling (*Georgy*). Was she really better than Booth?

(No.)

Claibe Richardson and Kenward Elmslie (*The Grass Harp*, 1971–1972). Truth to tell: Elmslie's adaptation of Truman Capote's novella about two sisters who need each other more than they realize, meandered.

What a score, though. Still, Broadway was entering the era when fine scores in the Golden Age tradition weren't appreciated as much.

A seven-performance flop—mostly because the producers didn't even have enough money to print a window card—usually doesn't get a major artist to record a song forty-seven years after the fact. But Audra MacDonald did "Chain of Love" on her 2018 *Sing Happy* album. In the Broadway production, Barbara Cook sang it superbly in what was, sadly enough, her last role in a book musical.

Karen Morrow savored a piece of material that, at a dozen minutes in length, could almost be called a song cycle. Opera star Carol Brice had two comedy numbers and one thrilling ballad. Try to find even one song that doesn't hit a bull's eye.

Author's Choice: Lonny Price as Charley Kringas (*Merrily We Roll Along*, 1981–1982). And the nominees were David Alan Grier (*The*

First), Bill Hutton (*Joseph and the Amazing Technicolor Dreamcoat*), and Obba Babatunde and Cleavant Derricks, both for *Dreamgirls*.

None of them had a piece of material that got the cheers Price received each night after he'd performed "Franklin Shepard, Inc."

WHO GAVE THE BEST TONY ACCEPTANCE SPEECH?
Well, we know who gave the best *non*-acceptance speech.

"I have searched my conscience and my heart and I am afraid I cannot accept this nomination. I prefer to stand with the egregiously overlooked cast and crew."

So spoke Julie Andrews from the stage of the Marquis Theatre after she took her curtain call after the May 8, 1996, matinee. She took umbrage that she was the only nominee for *Victor/Victoria*.

Others took their compliments where they could get them.

Kelly Bishop (*A Chorus Line*). Priscilla Lopez, as Diana Morales, was expected to win, for she had two songs to herself: "Nothing" and, the show's most famous song, "What I Did for Love."

In comparison, Bishop, as Sheila Bryant, had a third of "At the Ballet." Nevertheless, she won and said, "This is one of those dreams and it's come true. I have to accept this along with the rest of the cast because it's impossible without them," before adding "I'll keep it at my house, though."

Dorothy Loudon (*Annie*). She thought herself unwanted and retired when Mike Nichols called out of the blue and asked her to join *Annie*.

Loudon rebutted that she was too old to play Ethel Merman's role in the Irving Berlin classic.

(Actually, Loudon at fifty-one was seven years younger than Merman was in 1966 when she did the product semi-affectionately known as *Granny Get Your Gun*.)

No, Nichols wanted her to succeed Maggie Task as Miss Hannigan. Loudon did, jump-started a second career, and won a Best Actress in a Musical Tony.

After bounding onto the stage of the Shubert, Loudon exclaimed, "I can play this room!"

Ruth Brown (*Black and Blue*, 1988–1989). "It took me forty-two years to walk up those eight steps."

The entertainer, far better known as "The Queen of R&B," loved to relate that after she gave her speech, Broadway royalty Angela Lansbury rushed over to say, "That's the best acceptance speech I've ever heard."

Michael Jeter (*Grand Hotel*). In 1979, Jeter had a small role in the film of *Hair*, as a young man who was being evaluated for the draft.

He was in his late twenties then and looked younger. Ten years later in *Grand Hotel*, he was in his late thirties and looked older—substantially older.

In his acceptance speech for his well-deserved Tony as Best Featured Actor in a Musical, we learned what had happened.

"If you've got a problem with alcohol or drugs, you can't stop, you think life can't change, and that dreams can't come true, then I stand here as living proof that you can stop. It changes a day at a time and dreams come true."

Here's hoping that it made a difference in the lives of people who needed to hear it.

Author's Choice: Marilyn Cooper (*Woman of the Year*, 1980). After Arthur Laurents was signed to direct *I Can Get It for You Wholesale*, he had Cooper in mind for long-suffering secretary Miss Marmelstein.

And then Barbra Streisand arrived to audition.

Laurents had had a history with Cooper—she was in his *West Side Story* and *Gypsy*—so he thought of what seemed an ideal solution: Cooper would play romantic lead Ruthie Rivkin, who's desperately in love with Harry Bogen, who's just not that into her.

Streisand stole the show (and even Harry Bogen; she married Elliot Gould, who'd played him). Cooper's career stalled, and by 1979, she was grateful when Michael Bennett cast her in the ensemble of *Ballroom*.

After its premature closing, Cooper was absent from Broadway for two years until *Woman of the Year*. In "The Grass Is Always Greener," Anchorwoman Tess Harding (Lauren Bacall) and Housewife Jan Donovan (Cooper) traded notes on their lives and displayed more than a little envy.

Cooper was only in one scene, but it was enough to get her the Tony. At the podium she said, "I'm a poker player, and I say if you stay at the table long enough, you're bound to come up with a winner."

We're glad she did.

What Was the most Unexpected Result of Any Tony Race?

We're not talking about a *Two Gentlemen of Verona* over *Follies* type of injustice. The most unexpected result of any Tony race would have to be a tie, for we always expect one and only one winner.

1958–1959 Best Actress in a Musical. Gwen Verdon and Thelma Ritter both won for *New Girl in Town* in yet another example of billing issues. Verdon was clearly the leading lady, playing that new girl in town. She was involved in twice as many songs as Ritter (six to three), who clearly should have been in the Featured category.

Perhaps the voters wanted to appreciate Ritter for returning to Broadway after a more than quarter-century absence. A Tony would show their esteem, certainly in contrast to Hollywood, which had nominated Ritter four times for an Academy Award but never gave her a statuette.

(Ritter wouldn't get one in her next two Oscar contests, either.)

Barbara Cook had to be happy that Ritter was in that category, for that allowed her to win Best Featured Actress in a Musical for her Marian the Librarian in *The Music Man*.

Or perhaps she wasn't happy at all. She might well have felt that if she weren't the leading lady of *The Music Man*, who was?

1959–1960 Best Musical. Celeste Holm had the job of announcing the Best Musical—not as the evening's ultimate prize, strangely enough, but at 44:44 of the sixty-minute commercial-free local broadcast.

"It's a tie," Holm gleefully announced, before adding that one winner was *Fiorello!* but not mentioning the other.

So onto the stage bounded Bock, Harnick, bookwriter Jerome Weidman, director George Abbott, and producers Robert E. Griffith and Harold S. Prince (who wasn't yet wearing his trademark glasses on his head).

Abbott spoke for all for a full three minutes and thirty-eight seconds. Only after that did Holm divulge that *The Sound of Music* was the other winner.

Think of those 218 torturous seconds for the other nominees: *Gypsy*, *Once upon a Mattress*, and *Take Me Along*. And what was the evening like for Mary Rodgers, who saw her *Mattress* lose, but had to accept the award for her father Richard? (He was vacationing in Italy and couldn't be bothered to come to the ceremony.)

Author's Choice: And here we have *another* tie, thanks to two very different results.

1967–1968 Best Actress in a Musical. That Patricia Routledge (*Darling of the Day*) and Leslie Uggams (*Hallelujah, Baby!*) tied isn't the only quiddity; that Jule Styne wrote the music for *both* shows makes the situation even more unlikely.

1992–1993 Best Score. Who would have expected this? Broadway old guard John Kander and Fred Ebb (of *Kiss of the Spider Woman*) would stand on the same stage holding the same award as Pete Townshend, co-founder, lead guitarist, secondary lead vocalist, and principal songwriter of The Who, for the stage version of *Tommy*.

IF THE TONYS HAD A CATEGORY FOR BEST SONG, WHAT WOULD HAVE WON?

The Oscars established a Best Song category soon after the advent of talkies. Why didn't those who created the Tonys in 1946 make this category as well?

The winners would probably be songs that stepped out of the shows and into the public consciousness. The stirring and exciting "One Day

More" may be the song that you put on "Repeat" after you got your *Les Miserables* CD, but "I Dreamed a Dream," recorded by many singers, probably would have won.

So just as Hollywood has awarded its Oscar to many more pop-oriented songs than book ones, Tony voters would have chosen in similar fashion whenever they could.

1946–1947: "Almost Like Being in Love" (*Brigadoon*). The song owes a good deal to Oscar Hammerstein's penchant for having men and women who are attracted to each other proceed cautiously: "Make Believe (I love you)," "People Will Say We're in Love," and "If I Loved You," with the emphasis on "If." Alan Jay Lerner gave it his own special slant with the word "almost."

1947–1948: "I Still Get Jealous" (*High Button Shoes*). Soft-shoe was still a viable entertainment entity.

1948–1949: "Once in Love with Amy" (*Where's Charley?*). The show had opened in October, so by Tony time, enough voters would have experienced Ray Bolger's sing-a-long with the audience to put it over the top.

1949–1950: "Some Enchanted Evening" (*South Pacific*). Producer Joe Josephson, seen in *Merrily We Roll Along*, used it as the quintessential example of a tune you can hum (although he couldn't quite hum it correctly).

1950–1951: "A Bushel and a Peck" (*Guys and Dolls*). Maybe a win here would have kept it in the film version, where it was inexplicably dropped.

1951–1952: "Getting to Know You" (*The King and I*). However, what did Anna mean when she sang that she was "putting it my way, but nicely"? Was she implying that "nice" isn't her default mode and that she was usually a witch with a capital B?

1952–1953: "Wish You Were Here" (*Wish You Were Here*). Eddie Fisher's number one gold record often received credit for immeasurably helping the musical. Many have claimed, however, that his millions of teenage female fans bought the record not so much for the song, but for the picture sleeve (RCA Victor's first) of the handsome singer.

1953–1954: "Stranger in Paradise" (*Kismet*). Not "I Love Paris" from *Can-Can*? Actually, that song took a while to catch on; "Stranger" was no stranger to the charts, where it reached number two.

That was close to seventy years ago, but its singer wasn't one who faded away: Tony Bennett.

1954–1955: "Hey, There" (*The Pajama Game*). Even without the then-state-of-the-art Dictaphone repeating what Sid Sorokin had said into it as it did in the musical, this song had three recordings that reached the top forty: Johnny Ray's (twenty-seven), Sammy Davis, Jr's. (sixteen), and Rosemary Clooney's (one).

1955–1956: "(You've Gotta Have) Heart" (*Damn Yankees*). The 1950s were still a time when musicals proudly offered optimistic songs.

1956–1957: "I Could Have Danced All Night" (*My Fair Lady*). Although we must wonder why Eliza sang "I'll never know what made it so exciting," she should have been able to discern that it was her finally being able to properly recite "The rain in Spain falls mainly on the plain."

1957–1958: "Till There Was You" (*The Music Man*). Remember, *West Side Story*'s "Tonight" and "Maria" didn't really score until the film became a sensation.

1958–1959: "I Enjoy Being a Girl" (*Flower Drum Song*). Those were simpler times . . .

1959–1960: "Small World" (*Gypsy*). Johnny Mathis' top twenty hit would have helped *Gypsy* to win its one and only Tony.

1960–1961: "If Ever I Would Leave You" (*Camelot*). Robert Goulet's crisp recording would have helped it edge out *Bye Bye Birdie*'s "Put on a Happy Face" and *Do Re Mi*'s "Make Someone Happy."

1961–1962: "The Sweetest Sounds" (*No Strings*). A nice companion piece to Richard Rodgers' win for Best Score.

1962–1963: "What Kind of Fool Am I?" (*Stop the World—I Want to Get Off*). Although in the context of the show, the uneducated Littlechap would not be grammatically aware enough to sing "A lonely cell *in which* an empty heart must dwell."

1963–1964: "Hello, Dolly!" (*Hello, Dolly!*). Louis Armstrong's unexpected hit that leapt to number one on Leap Year Day would allow it to eclipse Barbra Streisand's "People" (*Funny Girl*).

1964–1965: "A Quiet Thing?" (*Flora, the Red Menace*). The first great Kander and Ebb song was one of the reasons that Liza Minnelli won her Tony as Best Actress in a Musical.

1965–1966: "The Impossible Dream" (*Man of La Mancha*) would have bettered the title song from *On a Clear Day You Can See Forever.*

1966–1967: "Cabaret" (*Cabaret*). Sally Bowles was another character who wasn't likely to put a preposition in front of a pronoun. But is the C-section in which she mused about Elsie—"*with whom* I shared four sordid rooms in Chelsea"—part of the actual song she was singing to the Kit Kat Klub audience or was it her own internal monologue? The lyrics don't register as the type that would be found in a cabaret song.

1967–1968: "I've Gotta Be Me" (*Golden Rainbow*) was released a few weeks after the show had closed. Had it been available while the musical was still running, it not only would have won, but it might have also helped the show.

1968–1969: "Aquarius" (*Hair*). All those Bacharach-David *Promises, Promises* hits would have succumbed to the song that The Fifth Dimension made the number two record of the year. (Only the immortal "Sugar, Sugar" bested it.)

1969–1970: "Mama, a Rainbow" (*Minnie's Boys*). This is arguably the most beloved song from a musical that couldn't crack one hundred performances.

1970–1971: "I Do Not Know a Day I Did Not Love You" (*Two by Two*). Richard Rodgers' final burst of glory, although some have accused it of sounding like a musical ping-pong match.

1971–1972: "Losing My Mind" (*Follies*). Dorothy Collins was the first to stand center stage and deliver this ballad; thousands of singers have since done the same.

1972–1973: "Corner of the Sky" (*Pippin*). Only later did "Send in the Clowns" make an impact.

1973–1974: "Over Here!" (*Over Here!*). Patty and Maxene, the two surviving Andrews Sisters, did the work of three in this raucous 1940s boogie-woogie that didn't sound like the Sherman Brothers we knew from *Mary Poppins*.

There was a reason for that: the Shermans fully admitted in the published script the "creative contributions of Walter Wechsler"—who just happened to be Patty Andrews' husband and pianist.

1974–1975: "Ease on Down the Road" (*The Wiz*). With the entire score of Jerry Herman's *Mack & Mabel* dismissed, "I Won't Send Roses" probably would have been, too.

1975–1976: "What I Did for Love" (*A Chorus Line*). Edward Kleban, who wrote its lyrics, detested it. If he'd been given a ballot for Best Song that season, before choosing this he'd have voted for "The Rosencrantz and Guildenstern Boogie" from *Rockabye Hamlet*.

Kleban even insisted that it not be sung at his memorial service, as his excellent biomusical *A Class Act* reiterated.

And it wasn't.

1976–1977: "Tomorrow" (*Annie*). Broadway's most famous song that was never recorded by anyone who could get a hit record out of it.

1977–1978: "City Lights" (*The Act*). Songwriters love to love New York, and who more than Kander and Ebb? Granted, this one finishes a distant second to the New York song they had written a year earlier for a film.

1978–1979: "Pretty Women" (*Sweeney Todd*). So much for Sondheim's supposed inability to write a beautiful melody.

1979–1980: "Don't Cry for Me, Argentina" (*Evita*). However, Eva's claim that "although she's dressed up to the nines" and that she's "at sixes and sevens with you" sound more like Tim Rice than Ms. Peron.

1980–1981: Considering that the three of the four Best Musical Nominees were *42nd Street*, *Sophisticated Ladies*, and *Tintypes*—all shows without original scores—the category would have been eliminated.

1981–1982: Of the two "Going" songs, "And I Am Telling You I Am Not Going" (*Dreamgirls*) would beat "Good Thing Going" (*Merrily We Roll Along*), clever and glorious as it is.

1982–1983: "Memory" (*Cats*). The song that's said to have calmed Donald Trump when he became angry may be one you're sick of hearing, but it would have won.

1983–1984: "The Best of Times" (*La Cage aux Folles*). This might have had a different outcome if "Putting It Together" from *Sunday in the Park* *with George* had been used at the time as its eventual much-aired television commercial.

1984–1985: The nominators eliminated Best Actor and Actress in a Musical, so they'd eliminate Best Song.

1985–1986: Same sad story as 1980–1981. Three of the four nominees for Best Musical don't have new scores: *Big Deal, Song and Dance,* and *Tango Argentino.* Category eliminated.

Urinetown referred to "The Stink Years." For Broadway, these were they.

1986–1987: "I Dreamed a Dream" (*Les Miserables*). It would have won even without Susan Boyle's help.

1987–1988: "The Music of the Night" (*The Phantom of the Opera*). Voters would have ignored how much it resembled *Brigadoon*'s "Come to Me, Bend to Me." (Too bad that they wouldn't have opted for the superior "All I Ask of You.")

1988–1989: Here we'd have a conundrum: Irving Berlin wrote "Mr. Monotony" for *Easter Parade* (1948), where it was cut, and then put it in *Miss Liberty,* where it had a sex change to "Mrs. Monotony." The operation was reversed the following year when Ethel Merman sang "Mr. Monotony" during the tryout of *Call Me Madam*—but not on Broadway.

As monotonous as all this sounds, "Mr. Monotony" finally reached Broadway this season, thanks to *Jerome Robbins' Broadway.* Considering that *Gigi* had plenty of existing songs when it won Best Score in 1973–1974, would this song have been allowed to compete in the Best Song category?

(Now nobody's saying that it would have won *had* it been eligible ...)

1989–1990: "With Every Breath I Take" (*City of Angels*). A song that goes up, down, and all over the scale made us wonder how Cy Coleman could have ever found those notes on the piano. Voters would have been glad that he did.

1990–1991: "The Human Heart" (*Once on This Island*). There are so many other worthies in the excellent Ahrens-Flaherty score that the nominators would have had a difficult time choosing one.

1991–1992: "Unlikely Lovers" (*Falsettos*). Do you prefer "The Games I Play"? You've got a point.

1992–1993: "Tell Me It's Not True" (*Blood Brothers*). By the very nature of its heading for a long run, it would have bested the flavorful title song from the too-short-running *My Favorite Year*.

1993–1994: "Loving You" (*Passion*). Perhaps it's all for the best that there's no Best Song Tony. How many more statues could Sondheim's West 49th Street townhouse have accommodated?

1994–1995: "As If We Never Said Goodbye" (*Sunset Boulevard*). It would win in a walk, despite the fact that Andrew Lloyd Webber stole the B-section from another song. Don't call the cops; the theft came from his own B-section of "Half a Moment" from his 1975 London musical *Jeeves*.

1995–1996: "Seasons of Love" (*Rent*). It really doesn't have anything to do with the show, but its vamp, melody, simplicity, and the musical's juggernaut would win over the voters.

1996–1997: The Tony voters wouldn't give *Jekyll & Hyde* a Best Score or Best Musical nomination. Would they have thrown a bone to "This is the Moment"?

1997–1998: "Wheels of a Dream" (*Ragtime*). Ahrens and Flaherty did their part; Brian Stokes Mitchell and Audra MacDonald did theirs, too.

1998–1999: "Sons of Dixie" (*The Civil War*). That wonderful "wrong note" on the syllable "Dix" was as pleasing as bittersweet dark chocolate.

1999–2000: "A Little Mmm" (*The Wild Party*). Between this musical and *Marie Christine*, composer-lyricist Michael John LaChiusa racked up an even dozen Tony nominations. He won none, but would have scored if this category had existed.

2000–2001: "The Next Best Thing to Love" (*A Class Act*). Sophie described her friendship with Ed before coming to the oh-so-valid conclusion that that great friendship is love, too.

2001–2002: "Follow Your Heart" (*Urinetown*) proved that melodies can be simple without being simplistic (and beautiful to boot).

2002–2003: "Welcome to the '60s" and "You Can't Stop the Beat" (*Hairspray*) would have battled it out. Would this have been the first tie in the Best Song category?

2003–2004: "For Good" (*Wicked*). And Stephen Schwartz would finally win a Tony.

2004–2005: "Nothing Is Too Wonderful to Be True" (*Dirty Rotten Scoundrels*). David Yazbek succumbed to Adam Guettel's *The Light in the Piazza* for Best Score, but he would have won for Best Song.

2005–2006: "The Color Purple" (*The Color Purple*). Did you know that this particular color is associated with luxury, royalty, nobility, ambition, power, and creativity? Allee Willis, Brenda Russell, and Stephen Bray conveyed that in this solid and stirring anthem.

2006–2007: "The Song of Purple Summer" (*Spring Awakening*). For the second consecutive year, the color purple would have been mentioned when the Best Song winner was announced.

2007–2008: "When You're Home" (*In the Heights*). Nina and Sonny remembered and traded their childhood memories, just as we all like to do with old friends.

2008–2009: "Shine!" (*Billy Elliot*). The second most famous song to include the expression "Give 'em the old razzle-dazzle."

2009–2010: Dare we say "God" (*Sondheim on Sondheim*)? It was Sondheim's tongue-in-cheek tribute to himself, acknowledging that he'd been called by that name by many musical theater enthusiasts.

(They *did* have a point . . .)

2010–2011: "Butter Outta Cream" (*Catch Me If You Can*). The musical, which started in the era of the Rat Pack (meaning Frank Sinatra, Dean Martin, Sammy Davis, Jr., et al.), gave us one rat (Frank Abagnale, Sr.) and one rat-to-be (Frank Abagnale, Jr.) warbling in the swingin' style of these singers whom they (understandably) admired.

2011–2012: "How 'Bout a Dance?" (*Bonnie & Clyde*). Frank Wildhorn has always wanted pop music and theater musical to intersect as they once did. This award would have suggested he was succeeding.

2012–2013: "Ralphie to the Rescue" (*A Christmas Story*). And Pasek and Paul were officially on their way.

2013–2014: "Babkak, Omar, Aladdin, Kassim" (*Aladdin*). Despite Chad Beguelin's anachronisms of "Let's boogie!" and the even more regrettable "Tough noogie!" Alan Menken's music would get the song over the finish line.

2014–2015: "Changing My Major" (*Fun Home*). Not long after Alison left home for college, she met the young woman who'll be her first official girlfriend. "I'm changing my major to Joan," she exclaimed, in a delightful Lisa Kron–Jeanine Tesori waltz. Voters gay or straight remembered their own college days when they fell in love and nothing but *nothing* else in the world existed or mattered.

2015–2016: "You'll Be Back" (*Hamilton*). Many Tony voters were now Baby Boomers who spent their teen years savoring songs with a bubble-gum sound.

2016–2017: "One of the Great Ones" (*A Bronx Tale*). Alan Menken, whose heart is more on Broadway than in Hollywood, deserves more Tonys.

2017–2018: "Do the Work" (*Prince of Broadway*). Jason Robert Brown's lyrics captured Hal Prince's philosophy: "Do the work. Get it done. When you finish, start the next one." Shouldn't we all?

2018–2019: "I Only Want to Dance with You" (*The Prom*). Matthew Sklar's beautiful melody set to Chad Beguelin's lovely lyric that underlined that a young woman taking a young woman to a dance shouldn't be the cause of a town-wide panic. "All it takes is you and me and a song," sang Emma to Alyssa—and that *is* what it all comes down to, doesn't it? The damn thing is a dance—so let the kids dance.

2019–2020: Given that no musical was nominated for Best Score, this category would have undoubtedly been dropped. Kiss that year goodbye, and point us to tomorrow.

If the Tonys Had a Category for Best Production Number, What Would Have Won?

1946–1947: "The Sword Dance" (*Brigadoon*). And nobody ever got cut while doing it.

1947–1948: "On a Sunday by the Sea" (*High Button Shoes*). Those unborn or too young to see what was better known as "The Bathing Beauties Ballet" had a second chance when Jerome Robbins revived the showstopper in his 1989 eponymous revue.

1948–1949: "Too Darn Hot" (*Kiss Me, Kate*). On the surface, seeing people frenetically dance "when the thermometer goes way up" makes no sense. Let's think of it in the context of those scenes in summer movies where someone inadvertently falls into a swimming pool followed by someone else, which leads to everyone jumping in just for the fun of it.

Still, what would someone as inventive as Tommy Tune have brought to this number?

1949–1950: "I'm Gonna Wash That Man Right outa My Hair" (*South Pacific*). Investors may have balked at how much the production was spending in shampoo each week, but in the long run, the long run paid for itself.

1950–1951: "Sit Down, You're Rockin' the Boat" (*Guys and Dolls*). If there were a prize for Best Eleven o'clock Number of All Time, this would hold the title for eleven more years.

What would eventually beat it? Stay tuned.

1951–1952: "The Small House of Uncle Thomas" (*The King and I*). Mrs. Anna has taught her Siamese students *Uncle Tom's Cabin*—spurring Tuptim to write her Asian-centric version and make a statement on slavery while she's at it. Whether Buddha made a miracle or Oscar Hammerstein, dance composer Trude Rittman, and choreographer Jerome Robbins did, it was a stunning and imaginative showpiece.

1952–1953: "Lizzie Borden" (*New Faces of 1952*). Here was a delicious spoof of the Crime of the *Previous* Century, which had only eight more years to go.

1953–1954: "The Garden of Eden Ballet" (*Can-Can*). But wouldn't you think that the winner would be a can-can?

1954–1955: "Once a Year Day" (*The Pajama Game*). After every picnicker fell to the grass utterly exhausted, the music ended and the number was over.

Not quite: one dancer still had enough life in her to stretch her legs up and wiggle them.

And we smiled.

1955–1956: "Shoeless Joe from Hannibal, Mo" (*Damn Yankees*). When veteran outfielders catch a ball, they purposely make it look casual, as if they've done nothing special. It's called "nonchalanting." Whether Bob Fosse was an inveterate baseball fan or if he went to a single game and had excellent powers of observation, he was astute enough to notice it and have his dancers replicate it here.

1956–1957: "Sadie Hawkins Day" (Li'l Abner). In actuality, it offered more running than actual choreography, but it was still the talk of Broadway.

1957–1958: "76 Trombones" (*The Music Man*). When seen-it-all first-nighters spontaneously clap in rhythm during the number, it's the hands-down winner in this category.

1958–1959: "The Uncle Sam Rag" (*Redhead*). Is there any style of music that makes people happier than ragtime?

1959–1960: "All I Need Is the Girl" (*Gypsy*). A production number with the fewest people ever but with more heart than many others. How happy we were that Louise found a beau—until, the next scene, when her hopes and ours were dashed.

1960–1961: "The Telephone Hour" (*Bye Bye Birdie*). With the Sweet Apple teenagers all encased in boxes, this would probably be the winning production number with the least choreography. Producer Edward Padula could have said, "You want me to pay for a bulky and elaborate set that'll only be used *once*?!" Give him credit for spending the money.

1961–1962: "Brotherhood of Man" (*How to Succeed in Business without Really Trying*). Here's the one that supplants "Sit Down, You're Rockin' the Boat" as the Best Eleven o'clock Number Ever.

Thanks again, Frank Loesser.

1962–1963: "Deep Down Inside" (*Little Me*). Star Sid Caesar just sat in his wheelchair but everyone else had plenty to do around him.

1963–1964: "Hello, Dolly!" (*Hello, Dolly!*). Gower Champion spent the first two weeks of rehearsal refining and defining this number. As exorbitant and even unnecessary as that sounds, it turned out to be time well spent.

1964–1965: "The Tailor Motel Kamzoil" (*Fiddler on the Roof*). Here was a very different kind of dream ballet: it didn't solely offer music, but contained important dialogue and funny lyrics, too. The result was a dream for everyone except Lazar Wolf.

1965–1966: "Rich Man's Frug" (*Sweet Charity*). A close contest between this and "Mame" from you-know-what. Remember, Bob Fosse bested Onna White in the Best Choreography race, so he would have emerged victorious here with his parodies of the dance crazes that were then ubiquitous in the city's discotheques.

1966–1967: "Willkommen" (*Cabaret*). Yes, it would have easily won, but as we saw, it set up the show in the wrong way.

1967–1968: "Step to the Rear" (*How Now, Dow Jones*). Now how would Michael Bennett feel about this number narrowly beating out "I Wonder How It Is to Dance with a Boy" from *Henry, Sweet Henry*?

That one was his own special creation; for "Step to the Rear," he only dance-doctored Gillian Lynne's original choreography. Because her name was retained and his wasn't listed, she would have won the prize.

1968–1969: "Turkey-Lurkey Time" (*Promises, Promises*). This year, Bennett wins outright for having put his dancers in a figure-eight configuration, keeping them moving, and turning them into a Mobius Strip.

In case you've forgotten your high-school science, it goes on into infinity. Audiences would have been happy if this number had, too.

1969–1970: "Applause" (*Applause*). There was more to this number than the cast album reveals. Midway through, the chorus boys did excerpts from *Rose-Marie, Dolly, Fiddler, Cabaret, West Side Story, Oklahoma!*, and the then-notorious-but-now-forgotten nude revue *Oh! Calcutta!* In tribute, each dancer bared his gluteus maximus.

1970–1971: "I Want to Be Happy" (*No, No, Nanette*). Ruby Keeler, who hadn't tap-danced professionally in decades, kicked up her heels and made her contemporaries in the audience feel young again.

1971–1972: "Who's That Woman?" (*Follies*). Frankly, the greatest production number that Broadway has seen in the last half-century (and maybe earlier).

Those who experienced the first ten minutes of the show wouldn't have believed that the opening number could possibly have been bettered, but that was the fate of "Beautiful Girls." As poignant as it was to see these once glorious young women make their entrance down the staircase that they once owned all these decades later, seeing them dance aside their earlier selves was even better.

1972–1973: "With You" (*Pippin*). Our young hero discovered women, who slithered around his shirtless body as only Bob Fosse could make his dancers slither. The *piece de resistance*, though, was having chorus members pick up Pippin by the arms and legs, hoist him horizontally over the stage, lower him onto the woman who had just rolled in place under him, pick him up again, have another woman roll beneath him, bring him back down, and repeat. The mechanical nature that rather resembled a pants-pressing machine was a perfect way to illustrate mindless, promiscuous sex.

1973–1974: "It's Not Where You Start" (*Seesaw*). Did the exorbitant budget for the balloons that engulfed Tommy Tune keep the show from returning its investment?

1974–1975: "Hundreds of Girls" (*Mack & Mabel*). Not nearly that many, to be sure, but Gower Champion effectively created the illusion by having one chorine after another slide down a circular slide and return to the top to slide down again.

1975–1976: "Hello Twelve, Hello Thirteen, Hello Love" (*A Chorus Line*). The obvious choice is "One," a great finale, to be sure. However, its staging was inherently conventional in order to resemble a Broadway eleven o'clock number.

Far more challenging for Michael Bennett was finding a way to maintain this stream-of-consciousness piece that ran close to twenty minutes.

Of course he did.

1976–1977: "You're Never Fully Dressed without a Smile" (*Annie*). Needless to say, the first part of the number that was set in a radio studio would not be the reason why this would win.

1977–1978: "She's a Nut" (*On the Twentieth Century*). This one's impact can't be gleaned from the cast album. Although the lyrics repeat themselves and few new ones are heard, wonderful chaos ensued as one person spread the bad news to another from train compartment to train compartment—culminating with Mrs. Primrose, the song's titular unbalanced creature, riding on the train's cowcatcher.

1978–1979: "The Ballroom Montage" (*Ballroom*). A cha-cha segued into a meringue which morphed into a waltz before finishing with a fox-trot. If this had been a Gershwin musical, at least one critic would have said, "Who could ask for anything more?"

1979–1980: "Famous Feet" (*A Day in Hollywood, a Night in the Ukraine*). Tommy Tune, on a little stage-above-the-stage, only showed us dancers from mid-calf to toe. And yet, we recognized each one.

1980–1981: "Lullaby of Broadway" (*42nd Street*). Broadway loves to celebrate itself—and why shouldn't it?

1981–1982: "Steppin' to the Bad Side" (*Dreamgirls*). Michael Bennett dropped out of high school when he was sixteen. However, he must have stayed around long enough to study geometry, for the geometric patterns he made in this number would have made Sir Isaac Newton flip his wig.

1982–1983: "'S' Wonderful" (*My One and Only*). Less is more won again. Instead of a stage-filling swimming pool, there was a strip of water shorter and more narrow than your bathtub.

It was, however, long and wide enough for both Tommy Tune and Twiggy to cavort in it.

1983–1984: "The Best of Times" (*La Cage aux Folles*). Jerry Herman's best eleven o'clock number—and the last of his that Broadway would ever see.

1984–1985: Same story as Best Song: The Tony committee eliminated Best Actor and Actress in a Musical, so they would have eliminated Best Production Number, too.

1985–1986: "Beat Me, Daddy, Eight to the Bar" (*Big Deal*). It opened the Tony broadcast that Sunday night in June, which is always a good indication that it's the best number of the season.

1986–1987: "One More Day" (*Les Miserables*). But *Me and My Girl's* "Lambeth Walk" received some votes, too.

1987–1988: "Anything Goes" (*Anything Goes*). Songs are made the titles of their show for a reason—but the privilege must be earned. Revivals are required to keep the flame burning, and this hot number did.

1988–1989: "On a Sunday by the Sea" (*Jerome Robbins' Broadway*). Should this "Bathing Beauties Ballet" have been eligible, given that it was a replication of what had come before? Even Robbins admitted that he wasn't quite sure if it was what he did forty-one years earlier, so the Tony nominators would have allowed it to compete—and win.

1989–1990: "We'll Take a Glass Together" (*Grand Hotel*). But if this brilliant number hadn't existed—heaven forfend!—the show's "Who Wouldn't Dance with You?" would have won.

1990–1991: "Our Favorite Son" (*The Will Rogers Follies*). Although this number owed a great deal to "I Like to Do Things for You" from the 1930 film *King of Jazz*, the asymmetrical handclapping and coordinated leg movement that all the chorus girls were required to learn and perform were quite remarkable.

1991–1992: "I Got Rhythm" (*Crazy for You*). In this new version of *Girl Crazy*, no one noticed that this was a reasonably close replication of the same number in the 1965 film *When the Boys Meet the Girls*—itself a loose adaptation of *Girl Crazy*.

1992–1993: "Where You Are" (*Kiss of the Spider Woman*). This song wasn't in the ill-fated tryout at Purchase, New York, when Lauren Mitchell was playing the title role. Once Chita Rivera was on board, Kander and Ebb knew what to write for their star.

1993–1994: "Twelve Days to Christmas" (*She Loves Me*). As the days dwindle down to a precious few—from a dozen to nine to four to one—choreographer Rob Marshall showed how increasingly panicked people get when they haven't yet done their shopping before that big day.

1994–1995: "Can't Help Lovin' Dat Man" (*Show Boat*). Susan Stroman made a cakewalk a most delicious piece of cake. One of the goals of the number is having Julie be fully exuberant at the start and then lose a little for a moment when a salient piece of information is divulged. (More on that later.)

1995–1996: "Bring in 'Da Noise, Bring in 'Da Funk" (*Bring in 'Da Noise, Bring in 'Da Funk*). Savion Glover, his four dancers, bucket drummers, and two vocalists (Jeffrey Wright and Ann Duquesnay) provided music just right for tap.

The lyrics also took time to remember the African American past, including entrepreneur Madam C. J. Walker, musician Robert Johnson, author Zora Neale Hurston, and singer Billie Holiday.

Glover's choreography made good on the script's stage direction: "The number builds to an explosive ending."

1996–1997: "Montage I, II, and III" (*Steel Pier*). Yes, the award goes not to one single number, but three different phases of the dance marathons of the 1930s. Susan Stroman had to calibrate the dancers' exuberance when they were starting out, when they tired, and when they were exhausted. The contrast would have secured the Tony win.

1997–1998: "Ragtime" (*Ragtime*). Actually, the best-case scenario would be a Tony for this number at both the start and end of the show. They're variations on a theme, for Blacks, WASPs, and Jews start out wary of each other, which choreographer Graciela Daniele conveyed. At the end, they're not nearly as distrustful, and Daniele allowed us to feel that, too.

1998–1999: "Pas de Deux" (*Swan Lake*). Balletomanes will tell you that the dance in which the prince is misled into abandoning the love of his life is the highlight of Tchaikowsky's 1877 masterpiece. It was here as well in Matthew Bourne's production.

1999–2000: "The Curtain Call" (*The Music Man*). For anyone who's wondered if River City ever got it together to form that boys' band, Susan Stroman wittily answered the question. She actually had her performers learn as best they could to play the instruments found in a marching band.

Were they any good? Well, as good as a band would be headed by someone who couldn't teach them a thing.

Best touch: Charlie Cowell, the anvil salesman, got into the act as well playing—what else?—that nineteenth-century novelty instrument: the anvil.

2000–2001: "Springtime for Hitler" (*The Producers*). The original 1968 film only showed us the title song. Here was much more of the musical that was supposed to close on page four. Aren't we glad it didn't?

2001–2002: "Forget about the Boy" (*Thoroughly Modern Millie*). Millie's co-workers supported their friend who was disappointed in love. What would happen, though, when no-nonsense, all-business harridan boss Miss Flannery came around?

Why, she joined, of course, in that time-honored convention of the repressed person who loosens up if the song is right.

This one was.

2002–2003: "You Can't Stop the Beat" (*Hairspray*). A number so exciting that it didn't even need the cannons shooting off at the end to spray confetti over everyone.

2003–2004: "Waltz in Swing Time" (*Never Gonna Dance*). This was definitely the right title for the song, but certainly not the right title for the show, what with Jerry Mitchell's generous amounts of Tony-nominated choreography.

2004–2005: "Always Look at the Bright Side of Life" (*Monty Python's Spamalot*). It was a spoof, to be sure, but Casey Nicholaw replicated a Golden Age number so winningly that nothing else that season would have bettered it for the win.

2005–2006: "Show Off" (*The Drowsy Chaperone*). The lady—superstar Janet Van De Graaff—doth protested too much, wethinks, as her claims of retirement were greatly exaggerated. Otherwise, why would she keep plate-spinning, hoop-jumping, and water-drinking while ventriloquizing?

2006–2007: "Supercalifragilisticexpialidocious" (*Mary Poppins*). Choreographer Matthew Bourne took advantage of the song's inordinate number of syllables by creating a gesture for each one.

2007–2008: "In the Heights" (*In the Heights*). The cast stood as tall as the George Washington Bridge behind them.

2008–2009: "Freak Flag" (*Shrek*). Did you know that this phrase actually originated in 1967 by Jimi Hendrix? Although it's more than five decades old, it's been adopted as a mantra by the current generation of theater kids.

2009–2010: "I Got the Feeling" (*Fela!*). The song's always been associated with James Brown, but even he might have abdicated his title as "The Hardest Working Man in Show Business" when he saw what Ismael Kouyate and the rest of the cast did with this number.

2010–2011: "Anything Goes" (*Anything Goes*). Kathleen Marshall incorporated some yo-ho-ho sailor moves for her boatload of passengers and yielded a boatload of smiles from the audience.

2011–2012: "Rise Up!" (*Leap of Faith*). A Broadway musical can never go wrong by starting with a gospel-inspired rave-up. Sergio Trujillo provided enough voltage to make the title truth in advertising.

2012–2013: "Magic to Do" (*Pippin*). Diane Paulus took Fosse's original, turned it into a circus (that's not a criticism), and gave it a new spin.
   (Pun not intended, but now noticed.)

2013–2014: "Friend like Me" (*Aladdin*). We can assume that Casey Nicholaw didn't receive any help from a genuine genie, but he certainly got it from the genie played by James Monroe Iglehart as well as his stage-filling cast.

2014–2015: "A Musical" (*Something Rotten!*). Thomas Nostradamus doesn't have quite the abilities of his illustrious forebears, so when predicting that musicals will come into being, he can only see and hear bits and pieces of what's to come. They were enough for Casey Nicholaw to make a marvelous mosaic of musical theater history.

2015–2016: "The Room Where It Happens" (*Hamilton*). Joy usually propels a great production number, but anger can, too. This is where Aaron Burr's fury at being excluded put him on a trajectory that would make him eligible for *Assassins*.

2016–2017: "The Hollywood Wiz" (*Paramour*). "Crazy visuals you won't believe," went the lyric. That was only true for those who had never witnessed a Cirque du Soleil show; others became believers there and then.

2017–2018: "We Dance" (*Once on This Island*). As exciting as it was in the original production at the Booth on a proscenium stage, it was that much better in the environmental oval setting that Circle in the Square afforded it.

2018–2019: "I Can't Get Next to You" (*Ain't Too Proud*). Every great musical must have a great finale. As all The Temptations we'd met—from the distant to recent—paraded and celebrated on stage as we celebrated with them.

2019–2020: Same old story we had with Best Song: Given that no musical was nominated for Score, this category would have undoubtedly been dropped. Kiss that year goodbye, and point us to tomorrow.

CHAPTER FOUR

Debating the Songs

WHAT HIT MUSICAL HAS THE BEST OVERTURE?

The candidates for this question won't involve many twenty-first-century musicals, for precious few contemporary shows bother with overtures.

These days, many theatergoers prefer to arrive home five minutes earlier so they'll get that three hundred seconds of extra sleep before rising for work the next morning.

(Maybe musicals could have overtures on weekends . . .)

But we still have the following.

Gypsy. It's the default answer, isn't it? Sure, it's terrific, but would we think as highly of it if Dick Perry and his trumpet didn't emulate the world of burlesque? Talk about a big finish!

What's interesting is that the two songs that begin this overture are secondhand ones. Jule Styne's melody for "Everything's Coming up Roses" was originally found in his 1947 hit *High Button Shoes*. Sammy Cahn's title was "I'm Betwixt! I'm Between!" until director George Abbott cut the song.

The second, "You'll Never Get Away from Me," originally had a Leo Robin lyric and was called "I'm in Pursuit of Happiness" for a 1957 television special *Ruggles of Red Gap*. Later, Sammy Cahn, for a planned but unmade film called *Pink Tights*, turned it into "Why Did You Have to Wait So Long?"

So that one is really a *third*-hand song.

Fiorello! The overture starts and ends with the sound of a fire siren. Audiences laughed in recognition, for New York City Mayor Fiorello H. La Guardia was well known for rushing to the site of a fire whenever he could get away from City Hall.

Jerry Bock's music then set the overture ablaze. "The Name's La Guardia" segued into a few seconds of "I Love a Cop" before it got to the big ballad: "When Did I Fall in Love?"

Then came the spirited Charleston "Gentlemen Jimmy" to signal that much of the musical would take place in the Roaring 1920s (and to suggest that the show would offer a roaring good time). Another ballad, "Till Tomorrow," offered some golden trumpeting of its own before the tubas introduced "Home Again," a thumping march that returned to "The Name's La Guardia" before the siren once more blared to a big finish.

My Fair Lady. In a score that certainly provided more than its share of hits, we're a little surprised that this overture began with more than a half-minute of the far-lesser-known book song "You Did It!"

"On the Street Where You Live" and "I Could Have Danced All Night," the latter replete with fluttering flutes, received their due. Yet we must wonder what the overture would have sported if "On the Street Where You Live" had been dropped during the tryout.

There was serious talk of that, for, after an intermission, audiences couldn't place the dapper gentleman who arrived at Eliza's residence. Alan Jay Lerner then wisely wrote a verse that reminded theatergoers of Freddy Eynsford-Hill's previous interaction with her, and the overture could proceed on its merry way.

The Roar of the Greasepaint—The Smell of the Crowd (1965). This was a hit if we use the classic definition of a show that returns its investment. Granted, if the musical had had to depend on Broadway alone, its 232-performance run wouldn't have been enough to put it in the black. A lengthy pre-Broadway tour did.

Songwriters Leslie Bricusse and Anthony Newley obviously believed that "Who Can I Turn To?" would be the big song, for more than one-

and-a-half minutes of the three-minute-and-twenty-two-second over-ture is devoted to it.

"Feeling Good," however, the song that has passed the test of time, mostly comes from its enhancing dozens of television commercials, from Volvos to Weight Watchers.

And it isn't in the overture at all.

Author's Choice: *Funny Girl* **(1964).** It started by quoting what wasn't quite a song: "Nicky Arnstein, Nicky Arnstein," which Fanny Brice sang about the man whom she initially judged as too far above her but who had "The Music That Makes Me Dance."

"I'm the Greatest Star" showed what Fanny thought of herself just before the biggest ballad of the year: "People," a bigger hit than its equiv-alent in *Gypsy*: "Small World."

By the time it built to a boil with "Don't Rain on My Parade," you may have noticed that this overture and *Gypsy*'s have something in com-mon that's a phenomenon: each contains songs that are solely sung by its over-the-title female star.

WHAT MUSICAL FLOP HAS THE BEST OVERTURE?

Play the first track on the cast album of the sixty-four-performance *Mack & Mabel*, and you'll want to put it on this list.

It's ineligible. Although it starts every recording of Jerry Herman's score, it was actually the show's Entr'acte. Director-choreographer Gower Champion wanted to start on a serious note: Mack Sennett, silent movie legend, would return to the studio he built and owned on the night before a new owner took over.

But we still have the following.

Candide **(1956).** Those who appreciate opera bouffe love this one, which, for much of it length, is its own animal with melodies that aren't heard in the musical. We're all glad that "Glitter and Be Gay" was well repre-sented. (Those who remember *The Dick Cavett Show* in the 1970s will notice that his theme song was inspired by it.)

Tenderloin (1960). Another winner for those who take to opera bouffe. It did, however, reveal what has often been cited as the reason the musical didn't succeed: the minister's religious campaign against irreligious prostitution wasn't much fun. So in the overture, the minister's songs showed up far less than the ones sung by the so-called bad guys and women. "Little Old New York" and "Picture of Happiness," whose titles alone suggested good times, were well represented.

This overture also sported trumpet licks that may not have impressed as much as the burlesque-centric ones in *Gypsy*'s overture, but they were still as choice as tenderloin steak.

Dude (1972). Don't laugh: Galt MacDermot was a terrific composer. The opening salvos of *Dude* will surprise many who wouldn't expect such a—yes—*majestic* sound from a sixteen-performance disaster.

What people most remember about *Dude* is that it removed the seats from the Broadway Theatre so that the audience could surround a "stage" on which dirt was strewn. Water was needed to keep the dirt from rising, which resulted in mud.

Mud was the show's name after it opened, too. But, oh, that overture . . .

Cyrano (1973). The word always used to describe Cyrano de Bergerac is *panache*. That's what's required of an overture to a musical of Rostand's play.

Michael Lewis' music certainly provided that, but he didn't neglect one of the most glorious unknown ballads in the entire musical theater canon: "You Have Made Me Love," which Roxana sang to her lover Christian.

(Or so she thought.)

Author's Choice: *Merrily We Roll Along* (1981). Of Stephen Sondheim's five put-him-on-the-map musicals of the 1970s, only one (*A Little Night Music*) stated in the *Playbill* that it had an overture—and that one, in fact, was unconventional (Sondheim's lifelong inclination) in that it was mostly sung.

Because *Merrily* often had the sound of musical comedies of yore, its overture reflected that: "Rich and Happy" was made to sound like non-stop fun; "Good Thing Going" provided the beautiful ballad and even the semi-sardonic "Now You Know" sounded unabashedly upbeat.

Note, too, that none of the subsequent Sondheim musicals had overtures. It seemed as if he'd saved it all for this one.

WHAT MUSICAL HAS THE GREATEST OPENING ENSEMBLE NUMBER?

"Another Op'nin', Another Show" (*Kiss Me, Kate*). But wouldn't you like to know what happened during that second week of rehearsals?

"Comedy Tonight" (*A Funny Thing Happened on the Way to the Forum*, 1962). The best opening number ever added during a pre-Broadway try-out. Yes, work takes as long as the time you have to do it.

"Beautiful Girls" (*Follies*). Watching the once young and beautiful Weismann Girls walking down that somewhat shabby staircase was the essence of poignancy. While they descended the staircase, they looked as if they were ascending into heaven.

Sondheim's Irving Berlin-tinged melody had lyrics that only he could have written: "Beauty celestial; the best, you'll agree . . . Faced with these Loreleis, what man could moralize?"

"Magic to Do" (*Pippin*). Jazz hands were seen emerging from a smoky darkness before a leading player pulled scenery right out of the stage—stage-magically, of course.

Author's Choice: "The Circle of Life" (*The Lion King*, 1997). Its music and lyrics aren't extraordinary. The idea of having a parade come down the aisles of the house was close to threadbare by 1997, too, for countless entrances from the back of the house had long been witnessed by one and all.

Julie Taymor's unique costumes made the difference. If we must have premium seats, for this show they should be the ones on each aisle, rows

B through ZZZ, so those seated in them could be just inches away from these masterpieces.

What Musical Has the Greatest Opening Solo?
"Why Can't The English?" (*My Fair Lady*). And yet, this song would have been even better if it *weren't* a solo and musicalized the exchange between Higgins and Pickering about Eliza, leading to the bet—all in the cause of moving the action forward.

"Hurry! It's Lovely Up Here!" (*On a Clear Day You Can See Forever*, **1965**). Shy Daisy Gamble blossoms and blooms when telling Dr. Mark Bruckner how she talks to her flowers to encourage their growth: "Push up, azalea! Don't be a fail-ya!"

Alan Jay Lerner made Daisy smart and inventive when she sang but not when she spoke. Perhaps his point was that singing elevated her to a new level. Whatever the case, after Mark heard this paean to peonies, et al., he should have fallen in love with her on the spot.

"Heaven on Their Minds" (*Jesus Christ Superstar*, **1971**). Matters get off to a thought-provoking start when Judas tells Jesus "I've been your right-hand man all along."

Christians have always been taught that Peter had that role, but Judas' thinking he was number one—and then eventually feeling that he'd been shunted to second place—could be one reason for his betrayal.

For the 2012 revival, director Des McAnuff devised such a good idea that one might suspect divine intervention.

Previous directors had simply put Judas alone on stage to deliver a musical interior monologue in which he imagined what he'd say to Jesus if He were there.

McAnuff instead shrewdly brought Jesus on stage mid-number and had Judas directly state, "Listen, Jesus, I don't like what I see" en route to listing his complaints, advice, and demands.

This gave the song added urgency and made Judas stronger. Haven't you told off your boss in the privacy of your own home? Such a harangue stayed in the room where it *didn't* happen.

Here, Judas dared.

"Movies Were Movies" (*Mack & Mabel*). Mack Sennett remembered the days of silent movies: Keystone Kops, Westerns, Charlie Chaplin, and, of course, a mustachioed villain who tied a poor miss to the railroad tracks. Jerry Herman's ricky-tick music sounded as if it had been taken from the soundtrack of one of those turn-of-the-century films.

Author's Choice: "A Terrific Band and a Real Nice Crowd" (*Ballroom*, **1978**). Widowed Bea Asher (the magnificent Dorothy Loudon), who's been wasting away since her husband's death, has finally been convinced by her best friend Angie to visit the Stardust Ballroom.

She's now at the entrance, but does she dare go in? Finally she decides, "That's not the Matterhorn—it's just a flight of stairs" in one of Marilyn *or* Alan Bergman's best lyrics. We were so glad when she made the climb and took us with her.

WHAT'S THE GREATEST SOLO THAT ENDS ACT ONE?
"Everything's Coming Up Roses" (*Gypsy*, **1959**). Does this woman want to stay in show business, or what?

"Dear Friend" (*She Loves Me*, **1963**). "Don't break my heart," sang Barbara Cook, speaking for us all who have ever been *this close* to love and yet saw it somehow slip away.

"And I Am Telling You, I Am Not Going" (*Dreamgirls*, **1981**). Oh, but you are, Effie, and you know it, too, even before you recede upstage and out of sight as the reconfigured Dreams confidently storm the stage.

"Defying Gravity" (*Wicked*, **2003**). No, nothing was going to bring her down until the blackout. Even if Elphaba's return to the stage were noisy, no theatergoer would notice, for each was saying some variation of "Wow!"

Author's Choice: "Soliloquy" (*Carousel*). Billy's thrilled that Billy, Jr. will soon be on the scene—until he realizes that the child might need to be named Wilhelmina.

A man's joy at the prospect of being a father is soon tempered by the need to be responsible and rich. Billy's plans to make money do include a redundancy: "steal it," after all, is the same thing as "take it." Let's just assume that Billy was so nervous that it was his awkward mistake and not Oscar Hammerstein's.

WHAT'S THE GREATEST DUET THAT ENDS ACT ONE?

"My Own Best Friend" (*Chicago*, 1975). Roxie Hart and Velma Kelly each have the same worldview: you'd better look out for yourself. By the end of the show, however, they see that they can best succeed by being each other's best friend (at least on stage).

"You're Nothing without Me" (*City of Angels*). Everyone's a critic! This time, however, screenwriter Stine is stunned when Stone, the private eye he's created, pans what Stine is making him say and do. Stine rebuts though David Zippel's on-target lyrics: "I'm still your creator . . . your private dic-tator" to which Stone re-rebuts "I'm a famous shamus and most people don't know your name."

Them's fightin' words, and Stine makes certain that Stone gets quite the pummeling as the Act One curtain falls.

"Who Will Love Me as I Am?" (*Side Show*, 1998). Musical theater enthusiasts, that's who. They may have come to a show about conjoined twins expecting a spoof; after all, nine years earlier, an off-Broadway musical called *Twenty Fingers, Twenty Toes* had its twins sing that they possessed "two tushes; two bushes."

In *Side Show*, Bill Russell and Henry Krieger instead wanted us to care about these women with their literally inextricable problem. Indeed we did.

Author's Choice: "A Little Priest" (*Sweeney Todd*, 1979). Many musicals show their characters having a great time only to see them followed by disaster. Sondheim, as always, reversed musical theater expectations. After Sweeney showed us his darkest side in "Epiphany," then came the funny number, in which Mrs. Lovett and Sweeney played word games to minimize what they'd really do to build a business. Both are very good at it, too, *locksmith* notwithstanding.

WHAT'S THE GREATEST ACT TWO OPENING NUMBER?
"You're Never Fully Dressed without a Smile" (*Annie*, **1977**). We've all done it: aped our favorite stars by learning their trademark songs and moves. In the days of radio, aping the songs wasn't hard, but what about their movies? That didn't stop the girls in Miss Hannigan's orphanage from doing what people did in the days of radio: used their imaginations.

"Don't Cry for Me, Argentina" (*Evita*, **1979**). Sure, some of its power came from the gown that Mrs. Peron wore. Andrew Lloyd Webber's melody was stirring, though, and Tim Rice wisely made sure at the end that Evita acted meek and mild in an expert example of crowd manipulation.

"The Ladies Singing Their Song" (*Baby*, **1983**). Lizzie's pregnant. And if morning sickness, itchy skin, and swollen ankles aren't enough, what about those *im*perfect strangers who come up to her, ask to touch her belly, and, as they do, tell their own war stories? Their tales of woe about their deliveries make Lizzie wish that hers could be returned to sender.

"King of New York" (*Newsies*, **2012**). The young boys who've been trumpeting so many other peoples' names in newspapers finally see their own names on the front page. If that's not a reason to dance for joy, what is?

The number would have been even better if strike leader Jack Kelly interrupted the celebration to remind his colleagues that a name in a newspaper is glory that only lasts a day and that they mustn't lose sight of the fight ahead. Then we'd see that Jack has really earned the title of leader.

Author's Choice: "Come Follow the Band" (*Barnum*, **1980**). And who can resist with this Pied Piper of a melody that celebrates the circus?

To say it's a toe-tapper cheats it by 90 percent; you'll be using all ten toes with this *toes*-tapper.

Another term that doesn't do it justice, either, is *earworm*. This is much too celebratory a song for a word that sounds more apt for an unfortunate malady in one's Eustachian tubes.

Keep this one in mind whenever you feel down and out. Listening to this joyous celebration will pull you out of your funk for at least ten or twenty minutes.

No, the song isn't nearly that long, but you'll be playing it again and again for at least that length of time.

What's the Best Eleven O'clock Solo Ballad?

"Best Production Number" elsewhere in the book covers the ones that involve ensembles. So let's concentrate on solos.

"I've Grown Accustomed to Her Face" (*My Fair Lady*). How smart of Alan Jay Lerner to know that this was the only way that Henry Higgins could possibly say "I love Eliza."

Yes, there's a frenetic section in the middle where Henry becomes as angry as Henry VIII. But it returns to ballad status in short order.

"I Never Know When" (*Goldilocks*, 1958). Those who become fans of Broadway musicals quickly learn three things: 1) tickets are expensive, 2) the seats nearest the stage are called orchestra seats, and 3) Elaine Stritch could be a handful.

And yet, in this song, the acerbic Stritch proved that she could be tender when the occasion called for a lament to lost love.

"The Music That Makes Me Dance" (*Funny Girl*, 1964). By the way, the version one hears on the original cast album doesn't really reflect what Jule Styne wrote. He saw the melody in a series of quarter notes; Streisand was the one who added the stylization and the pauses between the notes (and improved it).

Author's Choice: "If He Walked into My Life" (*Mame*, 1966). During the entire show, Mame has been a free spirit and has sought to make her young nephew Patrick one, too. Now that he's turned out much differently from what she expected, she turns introspective and questions the decisions she made from the first day she met him, when the nephew she had loved at first sight has become the type of person she doesn't want to love at all.

WHAT'S THE BEST COMIC ELEVEN O'CLOCK SOLO?
"I'm Goin' Back" (*Bells Are Ringing*). And to think that this was hastily written out of town. Judy Holliday told her old friends Betty Comden and Adolph Green that if she didn't get a great number in the final scene, she just might quit the show.

After they wrote this, she stayed for the entire 924 performances.

"Reviewing the Situation" (*Oliver!*). Now that Fagin's in trouble, he wonders how he can reinvent himself. "Better settle down and get myself a wife," he sings, before realizing seconds later that she'd "go for me and nag at me; the fingers, she will wag at me; the money she will take me. A misery, she'll make from me."

After careful review, Fagin decides that as a husband, he might turn out to be far more sorry than grateful.

"Suppertime" (*You're a Good Man, Charlie Brown*). As the Charles Schulz comic strip went on, an argument could be made that Snoopy actually eclipsed Charlie Brown in popularity. This hilarious number might have tipped the scales in the beagle's favor.

"I'm Glad I'm Not Young Anymore" (*Gigi*). Honore, seeing Gaston suffering over Gigi, sings this better-him-than-me song. "How lovely to sit here in the shade," he muses, "with none of the woes of man and maid . . . the rivals that don't exist at all; the feeling you're only two feet tall" have all gone by the wayside with the wisdom of aging.

Author's Choice: "Why Do the Wrong People Travel?" (*Sail Away*). The song insists that "the right people stay at home," but those who did during the show's 167 performances missed quite a song from Noel Coward and performance by Elaine Stritch.

(If you don't know the song, get the London cast album rather than the Broadway one; it fearlessly retains a "profane" word that the American one didn't dare put on vinyl.)

What's the Most Dynamic Eleven O'clock Solo?

"Fifty Percent" (*Ballroom*, **1979**). Alan and Marilyn Bergman's lyric seems to have been inspired by the old saw "50 percent of something is better than 100 percent of nothing." Dorothy Loudon gave it 100 percent of everything. In a non–*Sweeney Todd* year, she would have had her second Tony.

"What Would I Do?" (*Falsettos*). Fanny Brice wasn't the only one to feel "Oh, my man, I love him so." Marvin did, too. And just as Fanny's relationship wasn't a perfect one, Marvin's wasn't as well, for it went even worse than hers. Those who ever loved the wrong people but couldn't help themselves—and would still enter the relationship knowing the consequences—would weep during this one.

"Back to Before" (*Ragtime*). Think of it this way: World War II saw the men go to war and the women replace them at their jobs. Once the men came home, they returned to the kitchen.

Compare this to Mother. As we discussed, once her husband had left home for an extended period of time, she found herself in charge. When he returned, she wouldn't go meekly back into the kitchen. We're proud of her for taking her happiness where she can find it.

"Lot's Wife" (*Caroline, or Change*). The saddest, albeit brilliant, eleven o'clock number. Caroline releases her frustration in a prayer to God, not for better times or mercy, but to kill her. Thank God He doesn't.

Author's Choice: "Rose's Turn" (*Gypsy*). Sure, Merman and the others have made it a forceful tour de force, but let's not overlook Stephen Sondheim's great lyric when Rose details the sacrifices she'd made for her daughters.

"It wasn't for me, Herbie," she notes, before adding, "and if it wasn't for me, then where would you be, Miss Gypsy Rose Lee?"

The first phrase means that "My efforts weren't for me and me alone" while the second means "I'm responsible for your success." It's one of Sondheim's greatest early career achievements.

WHAT'S THE MOST CLEVER SONG IN A BROADWAY MUSICAL?
"Do-Re-Mi" (*The Sound of Music*, 1959). No brilliant production number in the Broadway canon is as taken for granted. But take a good look at this Rodgers and Hammerstein classic. Really, what could have been a better teaching tool to learn the scale than a description of each note with a visual image?

(We can only begin to feel Hammerstein's pain in not being able to do better than "La, a note to follow so.")

"Useful Phrases" (*Sail Away*, 1961). Noel Coward spoofed those guidebooks for foreign travel where our every need has been anticipated—overanticipated, in fact. Coward was exaggerating when he had Elaine Stritch wonder why her book included "Does your child have convulsions?" or "Kindly bring me a hatchet."

But he wasn't exaggerating by much.

"Backstage Babble" (*Applause*, 1970). Friends and acquaintances come to Margo Channing's dressing room after opening night. What can they say? "It's a bomb." "It's a hit." "If you want entertainment, this is it."

Lyricist Lee Adams chose those precise words as well as plenty of other clichés in an earlier version of the song. Then he came to the conclusion that he might just as well have everyone say nonsense syllables—which contain about as much content as the heard-it-all comments that well-wishers would say under the circumstances.

"Mix-Tape" (*Avenue Q*, 2003). Princeton brings Kate Monster a cassette of songs he's specifically made for her. She wonders if this present means that he's interested in her. When she reads the list of songs, she becomes hopeful, for the titles are romantic—at least for a while. Suddenly they get very generic, and when Princeton says that he plans to make a similar tape for each of his new neighbors, Kate is utterly discouraged. So the tape doesn't mean he's interested in her.

In fact, he is, as he proves when he asks her for a date. (That he's clueless in being able to glean what just went on makes us question how bright he is, but we still wish them both much happiness.)

Author's Choice: "Can't Help Lovin' Dat Man" (*Show Boat*, 1927). When Julie sings this, Queenie, the Black maid, mentions that she'd never heard anyone but someone from her race sing this. What a subtle way of suggesting to us that Julie has an enormous secret and is passing for white.

And this in an era when musicals didn't give a thought to subtext, but merely wanted their songs to entertain.

WHAT'S THE BEST SONG ADDED TO A SCORE WHEN A FILM MUSICAL BECAME A BROADWAY MUSICAL?

"Practically Perfect" (*Mary Poppins*, 2004). The scene in the 1964 film when Mary makes this declaration practically begs for a song.

That the Sherman Brothers didn't seize the opportunity may have been a blessing in disguise. We could have been saddled with a song called "Practiperfilictious."

Credit George Stiles and Anthony Drewe, recruited by Cameron Mackintosh to buttress the score for its London stage premiere. They seized the "Practically Perfect" opportunity, to which they contributed to an appropriately charming and elegant melody.

As for Drewe, he had Mary sing about her "forte" and pronounce it "for-tay." Etymologists prefer "fort." But if Mary's erring, that does make her *practically* perfect as opposed to perfect.

(Years later, when Drewe was congratulated on his clever in-joke, he blinked and said "Oh, it's supposed to be pronounced 'fort'?")

"She's in Love" (*The Little Mermaid*, 2008). Nice to know that mermaids, just like those human teenage girls, can lovingly mock a friend who's just discovered what first love is.

Author's Choice: "The Contract" (*Gigi*, 1973). This musical is often thought of as a light-hearted and delicious bon-bon.

At its core, it's about selling a young girl to an older man.

So Lerner took one of Loewe's orchestral melodies from their Oscar-winning film and gave it magnificently funny lyrics that showed the negotiators coming down to the brassiest of tacks.

Honore is representing Gaston in his offer to marry Gigi, and tells her Aunt Alicia, "Such are his feelings for your niece that he's provided for her as Louis for DuBarry in Versailles did . . . a Taj Mahal where love may thrive, the rooms of which will number five."

Aunt Alicia's response? "Monsieur's idea of splendor is my idea of jail." She demands that Gigi has seven rooms, a staff, a chauffeur, and the deed to the house.

Then there's cold hard cash to be considered. Honore offers seven thousand francs a year, and while she approves of the sum, she wants them dispensed each month.

He counters with twenty thousand, and she counterpunches with fifty thousand. Seven more parries continues until each realizes the other has said "Thirty-five!" Now they can all sing "Little Gigi has fallen in love!"

(Oh, she has?)

WHAT'S THE FUNNIEST SONG IN A MUSICAL?

"To Keep My Love Alive" (*A Connecticut Yankee*, 1943). Morgan le Fay was said to have both a good and bad side.

(Don't we all?)

Lorenz Hart took advantage of the latter by having her tell us why her first marriage didn't last: "Sir Paul was frail; he looked a wreck to me. At night, he was a horse's neck to me, so I performed an appendectomy."

The merry murderess continued this plan with Sirs Thomas, Philip, George, Charles, Francis, and Athelstane: "I bumped off every one of them" before their love could turn sour, as Hart turned one good phrase after another.

"Adelaide's Lament" (*Guys and Dolls*, 1950). W. Somerset Maugham said that the only love that lasts is unrequited love. Perhaps that's true of fourteen years of unrequited marriage, too.

Best line: "When she's tired of getting the fish-eye from the hotel clerk." Where else do you hear the word "fish-eye"?

"I'd Rather Wake up by Myself" (*By the Beautiful Sea*, **1954**). The musical took place in the early 1900s, when women wanted husbands as much as fresh air. Lyricist Dorothy Fields had Lottie Gibson (Shirley Booth) realize that marriage, as Katharine Hepburn once said, wasn't a word but a sentence.

Lottie told of all the men she could have married, but just in time realized that they just weren't good enough for her: "Joe made big dough; his business, he said, was printin'. What Joe was printin' got him San Quintin."

Actually, that's a so-near-yet-so-far rhyme, but we wouldn't trade it for all the buttons on the first-act finale costumes of *Me and My Girl*.

Author's Choice: "He Had Refinement" (*A Tree Grows in Brooklyn*, **1951**). Actually, he had nothing of the kind, which is what makes this song the funniest ever. Cissie (Shirley Booth again) gives as evidence that her long-lost love was a classy guy by quoting him "May I suggest you call a lady's chest a chest instead of her 'points of interest'?"

Before you balk, take into consideration that this was written by a woman: Dorothy Fields, again.

What's the Best Reprise?

"Adelaide's Lament" (*Guys and Dolls*). When Adelaide first tells us of her plight, we laugh, but later, at a slower tempo, we empathize at how truly unhappy she is. Nathan, it's been fourteen years. You know you love her. Marry the miss today.

"Comedy Tonight" (*A Funny Thing Happened on the Way to the Forum*). You could simply call it a finale, but it counts. For all the talk of how Sondheim had to come up with a new opening number in a hurry, he also had to write new lyrics that would delightfully sum up the show.

And he did.

"Somewhere That's Green" (*Little Shop of Horrors,* **1982**). When Audrey initially yearns for greenery, she means the suburbs: "A picture out of *Better Homes and Gardens* magazine."

Attendees couldn't guess that lyricist Howard Ashman was setting them up for a reprise where, Audrey, now weary of life, decides that the ideal "somewhere that's green" is inside the very green Audrey II.

"I'll Cover You" (*Rent,* **1996**). Angel proclaims his love, and Tom answers in kind. The next time we hear it, Tom must sing it alone, for Angel has died.

Suddenly Joanne joins in and covers him, reminding us of what Sondheim had insisted nine years earlier: "No One Is Alone."

Author's Choice: "Staying Young" (*Take Me Along,* **1959**). Nat Miller is more forward-thinking than his blue-nosed neighbor. "I'm staying young! I'm staying young!" he insists. "But ev'ryone around me's growin' old but me."

In Act Two, after a couple of family crises, he sings the same melody: "'Cause everybody else is growing old," he sings before pausing, giving out a little sigh and admitting "Like me."

Throughout Broadway history, reprises have been employed mostly to remind audiences that the song they'd heard in Act One was worth hearing again (and buying the sheet music and/or recording of it). Often the lyrics were simply repeated.

Not here. The musical theater playbook says that the best show songs take you to a different place by song's end than you were at the beginning. But how often does that happen in reprises? Bob Merrill starts Nat as a man in denial about his age to one who acknowledges it. This doesn't negate what he'd said earlier; he's still young at heart. But he can no longer deny that whatever youthful beliefs he keeps in his head aren't commensurate with what's happening to the rest of him.

WHAT'S THE BEST SONG FROM A REVUE?

As wondrous as so many Gerard Alessandrini lyrics for *Forbidden Broadway* have been, let's only make eligible the best songs with original lyrics *and* melodies.

"Crossword Puzzle" (*Starting Here, Starting Now*, **1977**). A woman rues that those *Sunday Times* puzzles, which she and her beau loved to do, weren't enough to keep him.

"I'd let him hold the pencil; he could write in the word," she notes. Is there any greater gift than that?

Who else but Richard Maltby, Jr.—who's devised thousands of such puzzles in his time—could have written such a song?

But a note to auditionees: Casting directors say that those powers-that-be sitting behind the table are mighty tired of hearing this one.

"Something" (*Upstairs at O'Neal's*, **1982**). Really, was Mr. Karp's directive that Morales do improvs such an outrageous one? Here we get his side of the story. As director, Martin Charnin said, "People use the expression 'I fell on the floor laughing' when they mean they really laughed a lot. Well, when I heard 'Something,' I literally fell on the floor laughing."

"One of the Good Guys" (*Closer Than Ever*, **1989**). Richard Maltby, Jr.'s lyrics and David Shire's music gives us a long-married husband who has never cheated on his wife and has been an excellent father to boot. Now he takes stock of his life; you decide if he's more sorry than grateful.

"Ninas" (*Showing Off*, **1999**). A tribute to Al Hirschfeld, who inserted his daughter's name in his caricatures—"on the foot of Edith Head and the head of Horton Foote," as one of Denis Markell and Douglas Bernstein's sharp lyric goes.

They save the best for last: "David Mamet has a Nina; it's a fucking piece of shit."

Author's Choice: "Just One Step" (*Songs for a New World*, **1995**). Talk about "Miss Velma Kelly in an act of desperation." What about this mafioso's wife who threatens to jump off the ledge of her apartment building because he won't buy her a new fur coat?

She knows she's losing her man so this suicide ruse is to "get him back" in both senses of the phrase.

Jason Robert Brown brilliantly characterizes a woman who's argued with her husband so many times that he long ago stopped loving her.

She knows it, so, after trying everything else, she has nothing left but this dramatic "step."

And she will inadvertently take it, right into the night air.

WHAT'S THE BEST SCENE FROM A MUSICAL THAT WASN'T IN THE PROPERTY FROM WHICH IT WAS ADAPTED?

"A Little More Mascara" (*La Cage aux Folles*). Neither the original play nor the famous film showed Albin's transformation into Zaza.

Of course not. How boring that would have been for an audience to just sit there watch his paint dry.

But in a musical, Albin can sing to himself during the transformation, making for an absolutely fabulous five minutes.

"Carry a Tune" (*The Human Comedy*, 1984). Homer Macauley is a four-teen-year-old whose father has died and whose older brother is fighting in World War II. Now the responsibility falls on the teen to support the three people at home.

In the film version of William Saroyan's novel, Homer lands a job at a telegraph office, but questions his ability with singing telegrams. His boss says that it's no big deal to deliver one, immediately assuming that the boy has a good voice. He does say, "Let's see how you'd do it," and Homer then delivers a perfect rendition of the famous "Happy Birthday" song. "That's fine," says the satisfied boss.

It's a nice scene, but not nearly as good as what William Dumaresq and composer Galt MacDermot created for the musical. Here, Homer hasn't yet won the job. One of his two would-be bosses says, "You're a little bit young," making us worry for him. Then another boss notes, "Sometimes we have a telegram requiring you to sing. Can you carry a tune, or do you sing flat?"

So now Homer must audition, and if he doesn't come through, he and his family will suffer. The boy then goes into one of MacDermot's most felicitous melodies, "I can carry a tune," he insists, "at the drop of a hat, at weddings or funerals, just like that."

Then one of the prospective employers asks, "Do you know how to sing 'Happy Birthday'?" Homer then sings the famous song—God-awfully, nowhere near the melody (which smartly saved the production for paying royalties to the tune's composer). But how the boy throws his heart and soul into it! When he gets to the name of the birthday boy—"Methuselah" (!)—he sings with such amazing zeal, knocking himself out, stretching the name over literally dozens of measures of music, always atrocious, never on-pitch, which is the fun of it.

Yet while we're laughing, we're also concerned that he won't get the job. But the moment he finishes, the bosses look at each other and, knowing that the kid wants it so bad, say in tandem, "That's good!" Homer's hired, and we're happy for him and happy that we had such a good time listening to him crucify a melody.

Carrie (1988). This has been the go-to title for musical disasters since Ken Mandelbaum chose to title his excellent study of musical flops *Not Since Carrie*. Had he named it *Not Since Home, Sweet Homer*, that would have become the idiom for ultimate musical incompetence.

Give *Carrie* credit for providing at least one innovation. Once theatergoers were seated—some chatting with their friends, some reading their *Playbills*, some simply waiting for the show to begin—the house lights did not dim and fade to black; they simply snapped off the way we shut off lights in our homes.

The audience was in the light one second and in the dark the next. Attendees yelped in fright and then laughed in amusement. Many suddenly realized why the walls of the theater had been painted black. All the better *not* to see you with, my dear.

Many who saw the five-performance flop have joked that they would have been better off if they'd stayed in the darkness for the next two hours. *Carrie* at least deserves credit for doing what it wanted to do for the rest of the show: startle and scare us.

Author's Choice: "Sounds While Selling" (*She Loves Me*, 1963). Women shoppers enter Maraczek's Parfumerie to shop. Most lyricists would have written a list song with clever rhymes for various soaps and beauty products. Sheldon Harnick instead came up with the inspired notion of cutting from one conversation between clerk and customer to another. This resulted in some non-sequiturs and extra jokes: "I would like an eyebrow . . . under my chin."

Thank you, Sheldon; please call again; do call again, Sheldon.

WHAT WAS THE BEST SONG THAT WAS ADDED EN ROUTE TO A BROADWAY OPENING?

"Before the Parade Passes By" (*Hello, Dolly!*). But if Dolly has now resolutely decided to "rejoin the human race," why does she want "an *old* trombone" and "an *old* baton"?

Considering that she repeats the lyric, she should correct herself the second time. A *new* trombone and a *new* baton would be more appropriate for someone who plans to start her life anew.

"Miracles of Miracles" (*Fiddler on the Roof*). After Tevye granted permission for Motel to marry Tzeitel, the betrothed man originally sang "Now I Have Everything" when the show began its pre-Broadway tryout. Eventually the powers-that-be decided that it'd be a better song for Perchik to sing in Act Two, so Bock and Harnick went to work.

Harnick's Detroit hotel room, like all others in the nation, included a Gideon Bible. The lyricist perused it for miracles, found the ones involving Jericho, Pharaoh, and David and Goliath, and used them in his lyrics.

Fiddler was a show about breaking traditions, but there was one that it slavishly followed. Back then, after a blackout, a musical's orchestra would reprise the song that the audience had just heard as the next set was moved into place. But if you see a production of *Fiddler* today, after "Miracle of Miracles" ends, the orchestra will play "Now I Have Everything." Nobody ever bothered to change the scene-shift music.

"I Got Love" (*Purlie*, 1970). The song that cemented Melba Moore's Tony was added so quickly before the opening that it wasn't even listed in the *Playbills* that the first-nighters received.

"Someone Else's Story" (*Chess*, 1988). The song written after the 1984 concept album is one of the most glorious ballads we've had in recent decades. Too bad that the original cast album is out of print, for Judy Kuhn's rendition should be heard more and more.

Author's Choice: "I'm Still Here" (*Follies*, 1971). Even in a list song, Sondheim could be incisive. He had faded star Carlotta Campion sing, "First, you're another sloe-eyed vamp; then someone's mother—then you're camp." That distills Shakespeare's Seven Ages of Man into Three Stages of Actress.

Carlotta's calling her child "someone" reveals that she's a less-than-devoted mom. First and foremost comes the career; motherhood comes in second (if it even ranks that high).

"I'm almost through my memoirs" is perceptive, too. Granted, people use the singular and plural of "memoir" interchangeably, yet would one be surprised if Carlotta Campion felt that her life deserved more than one measly volume?

WHAT WAS THE BEST SONG TO BE CUT FROM A MUSICAL?

"The End of the Party" (*Cabaret*, 1966). And the celebration for the engagement of Fraulein Schneider and Herr Schultz was going so nicely—until Nazi sympathizers smash the front window of his store. Nevertheless, the ever myopic Sally Bowles sang that "It's the end of the party—not the end of the world."

Yes and no.

"When Messiah Comes" (*Fiddler on the Roof*). Sheldon Harnick has said that this song received a great response at backers' auditions and helped raise the $376,000 that got *Fiddler* produced.

And yet, "When Messiah Comes" wasn't landing during the Detroit tryout, it was cut during the second tryout in Washington, DC. This surprised and disappointed everyone connected with the show, but especially star Zero Mostel, who said it was his favorite song in the show.

Assuming where it was isn't hard. Near show's end, after Mendel said, "Rabbi, we've been waiting for the Messiah to come all our lives. Wouldn't this be a good time for him to come?" Tevye had stepped forward and sung the song.

Listen to the song on the Broadway Deluxe Collectors Edition CD and you won't immediately know why it was dropped. "When Messiah comes, He will say to us 'I apologize that I took so long'" is a very funny concept. So is "But I had a little trouble finding you; over here a few, and over there a few. You were hard to reunite, but everything is going to be all right."

Still funny, yes. And yet, Alisa Solomon, in *Wonder of Wonders*, her magnificent study of the musical, noted that the lyrics referred, albeit "obliquely, to the Holocaust . . . the song had to go, the authors understood, because at a moment of pathos the audience could not accept a wry comic number."

So to answer Mendel's question—"Rabbi, wouldn't this be a good time for the Messiah to come?"—the answer is "No, this is the time to end *Fiddler* on the appropriately serious note as Anatevkans must leave their homes for the unknown."

"That's How Young I Feel" (*Mame*). Before you write a letter to the editor to state that this book's author must mean the film version (which did indeed excise it), here's the story.

"That's How Young I Feel," which Mame sang when visiting Patrick in college, was dropped after the show's Philadelphia tryout. Composer-lyricist Jerry Herman replaced it with a new song called "Do You Call That Living?" When the musical opened its Boston tryout, that's what the audience heard.

However, during that leg of the tryout, Herman and his collaborators decided that "That's How Young I Feel" was actually the superior song. So it replaced its replacement.

"There's Gonna Be a Sweeping Change" (*Here's Where I Belong*, 1968). Many point to the 1980s as the decade that introduced super-duper effects into the musical: the barricade in *Les Misérables* and the falling chandelier in *The Phantom of the Opera* started the parade that continued with the helicopter in *Miss Saigon* and the floating mansion in *Sunset Boulevard*.

However, back in 1968, composer Robert Waldman and lyricist Alfred Uhry wrote an opening number in which a street-sweeping machine roared onto the stage as the chorus sang.

Alas, producer Mitch Miller (better known as a 1960s television host who asked us to sing along with him), decided the effect would be too expensive.

Perhaps, but producers Cameron Mackintosh and Andrew Lloyd Webber have validated the old belief that "To make money, you have to spend money." *Here's Where I Belong* closed after opening night.

Author's Choice: "Sweet River" (*110 in the Shade*). Somewhere during the gestation of this musical, someone had the idea that Lizzie Curry, a textbook Plain Jane, would have a glorious and lilting soprano voice to indicate her considerable inner beauty.

That decision cost the show this song where Lizzie muses on her recent vacation to another town; there, she had hoped to meet a man with whom she could begin a relationship.

"And when you're back from Sweet River," she mused, "You're happy for a minute or two. Then you suddenly realize your big vacation is through. Your dreams did not come true. You're still the same old you."

Having Lizzie try without success is a stronger and more poignant situation than having her be cautiously optimistic in the song that succeeded it: "Love, Don't Turn Away."

WHAT'S THE BEST LIST SONG?

"Brush Up Your Shakespeare" (*Kiss Me, Kate*). Cole Porter, you're the top in purveying list songs. His masterpiece is this eleven o'clock number.

However, why do two gangsters who arrive at Ford's Theatre in Baltimore to collect a gambling debt from Fred, get lost, wind up on stage—and in costumes yet. The orchestra plays the vamp and they start singing.

What got these guys on stage in *Taming of the Shrew* garb isn't the only question. How would these low-lifes know erudite references to thirteen of Shakespeare's plays (and his one narrative poem, yet)?

Bookwriters Sam and Bella Spewack would have done better to have these henchmen stage-struck individuals who have yearned to be in a show. They promise Fred that they'll go easy on him if he puts them in the musical. The desperate Fred does just that, and the showstopper is justified.

Still, what fun they and we have when they cite those Shakespearean plays and one of The Bard's poems ("Venus and Adonis"). Porter, who made ribaldry one of his trademarks, must have enjoyed inserting *Coriolanus* into the mix.

"The Name-Dropping Gavotte" (*Bells Are Ringing*). At least that's what the New Haven *Playbill* called the song before Comden and Green decided that just the *idea* of a gavotte might unnerve those who saw that title in the *Playbill*.

"Drop That Name" it became.

Switchboard operator Ella Peterson feels out of her league when attending a swank show-biz party. There everyone is gossiping and rolling off well-known names that she either doesn't know or can't place in context.

They include one golfer, financier, singer, producer, and radio personality. Also mentioned are ten actresses, eight actors, four authors, four directors, three fashion designers, two agents, two members of royalty, and a couple of animals: Rin-Tin-Tin and Lassie.

Those two, however, are mentioned by Ella, who, by the end of the number, triumphantly feels as if she belongs.

"I'm Still Here" (*Follies*, 1971). These reminiscences of an actress has had younger musical theater fans Googling to learn what Beebe's Bathysphere was and who the "five Dionne babies" were.

"I've been through Brenda Frazier" mystified quite a few, too. Older theatergoers at the time, however, well remember Brenda Diana Duff Frazier. For on December 27, 1938, this seventeen-year-old debutante had the biggest coming-out party of the century (and during the Great Depression, yet).

At New York City's Ritz-Carlton in New York, more than three dozen waiters served 1,249 guests. Diamonds weren't her only best friends that night; she sported emeralds and pearls, too.

Her escort, incidentally, was Curtis "Curt" Arnoux Peters, Jr., better known by his pen name Peter Arno; we know him from his logo for *The Pajama Game*.

After that, life for Frazier went very much downhill with the force of an avalanche. Sadly enough, the times her name was in the papers was relegated to suicide attempts (as many, some say, as thirty).

Eleven years after *Follies* opened Frazier died, and soon after the lyric went with her. Sondheim replaced her name with Shirley Temple.

"Napoleon" (*Jamaica*, 1957). Most list songs are just a sequence of rhymes. Here E. Y. Harburg also wanted to make the point that fame is indeed fleeting.

He noted that a luminary from the past will eventually be somewhat diminished by entrepreneurs who'll name their mundane products after these legends so they can attach themselves to greatness.

"Napoleon's a pastry; Bismarck is a herring; Alexander's a crème de cacao mixed with rum," Harburg wrote. He also had famous women of yore meet the same fate: "DuBarry is a lipstick; Pompadour's a hairdo; Good Queen Mary just floats along from pier to pier; Venus de Milo is a pink brassiere."

(Oh, such bras came in more shades than pink. But what do you do with that pesky extra syllable?)

"A Little Priest" (*Sweeney Todd*, 1979). Mrs. Lovett and Mr. Todd attempt—and succeed—at topping each other in punning how the various people they kill will land on their plates and palates.

What a playful way of making cold-blooded murder seem merry rather than macabre. That it becomes a challenge match of words also undercuts the horror of what these two crazies plan to do. What's more, in a musical that was turning increasingly serious and operatic, audiences needed this real ol' fashioned musical comedy number to laud during intermission.

Author's Choice: "Dead End" (*Hair*, 1967). Co-lyricists Gerome Ragni and James Rado's list song was in the Public Theatre production, dropped for Broadway, but was later brought back into the fold.

"Dead end," sings Sheila, "Don't walk, Keep out, red light." A litany of other demands are made: "Keep off the grass . . . Hands off . . . Loitering forbidden . . . All trespassers will be shot."

They're words that we've all seen on signs many times in our lives. After we hear Sheila list one banned directive after another, we suddenly realize how many actions we're not allowed to take.

Sheila eventually adds one other detail: "Claude loves Sheila: he better love her not." She's warning herself as much as she is cautioning him, for he could bring her heartache.

(And in fact, will.)

What Was the Most Unexpected Cover of a Broadway Show Song?

Frank Sinatra's "Oh, What a Beautiful Mornin'" (*Oklahoma!*). Twenty-seven-year-old Young Blue Eyes did a fine job in a perfectly decent if not particularly distinctive rendition.

What makes this a must-hear is what happens after he finishes. Unknown to listeners, Sinatra was singing to a group of teenage lasses who waited until he finished to punctuate the song with screams that girls usually give out for Elvis, the Beatles, David Cassidy, and Conrad Birdie. And who'd expect that reaction to a Rodgers and Hammerstein *waltz*?

Bobby Darin's "Artificial Flowers" (*Tenderloin*, 1960). In the musical, this is an art-song waltz that tells of a poor young girl who freezes to death while selling flowers. Once Darin found it, he made it a four-four up-tempo Vegas-styled lounge song and gave it his finger-snapping all. He wasn't above adding the line to "those dumb-dumb flowers"; as you may well have inferred, Sheldon Harnick didn't write for this song that's sung in the late nineteenth century.

The Beatles' "Till There Was You" (*The Music Man*). Baby Boomer husbands who'd been dragged by their wives to see this Meredith Willson hit, be it on stage or screen, must have suddenly awakened near show's end and cried out "Hey! That's a Beatles song!"

Yes, on their 1964 debut album for Capitol Records. Considering that the recording has since sold well over five million copies, Willson made much more in 1964 from this one song than he did for the film version of his *The Unsinkable Molly Brown* and his Broadway musical *Here's Love* that played to wan houses before ignominiously closing that July.

Jay-Z's "It's the Hard-Knock Life" (*Annie*). Who'd ever think that this future Rock & Roll Hall of Famer could be bothered with a song from this sentimental show?

Did the former Shawn Corey Carter actually sit and watch the 1982 film? Attend a community theater production? Play Daddy Warbucks in middle school?

No, he simply heard it after a performance when a DJ played it. It caught his attention as "a real special song" (which nobody can deny). That led to his recording on an album that sold five million.

One must wonder, however, what a DJ was doing playing a show song after a Jay-Z concert. Whatever the case, composer Charles Strouse and lyricist Martin Charnin are certainly glad that he did.

Less happy was Danielle Brisebois, the first voice heard on the sample. Brisebois, *Annie's* original Molly, was paid a flat fee to record the original cast album; thus, Jay-Z (the first hip-hop billionaire, incidentally) wasn't legally bound to reimburse her.

"I'm singing the lead vocal on a #1 song but not making a penny out of it," Brisebois told *Blender Magazine*.

It's the hard-knock life, Danielle . . .

Author's Choice: Bobby Sherman's "I'm in a Tree" (*Prettybelle*). At the Shubert Theatre in Boston, mentally unbalanced Prettybelle Sweet (Angela Lansbury) is literally perched on a branch of an elm. She tells us "My son John is what first triggered off my nerves because at the age of thirteen, John shot three men dead from the top of this tree."

Under those circumstances, you'd think that Prettybelle would go nowhere near it. She then explains "I'm in a tree . . . because life is too frightening down there."

Are you surprised to hear that the song was dropped in the only city that the musical ever played?

Two-year-old Metromedia Records bought the rights to record *Prettybelle*. To promote the album, they asked their biggest star, one Bobby Sherman, to record one of its songs. He chose this.

A full, violin-heavy orchestra begins. What Sherman says before singing is quite different from Lansbury's: "How the heck did I get myself up here? I'm so embarrassed! I hope nobody—oh, boy! Here comes somebody! Oh, no, I hope they don't look up here. Oh, please don't look up here!"

But someone apparently does, for Sherman affably says, "Hello! How are you?" and then he begins the song.

(If he wants out, why does he sing "Life is too frightening down there"?)

During the inevitable instrumental section that so many pop songs had at the time, Sherman returns to narration.

"Say, maybe you can get some help for me. Call the fire department or something. See, what happened is I went up to get this cat that was strung out on the limb here, and he got down and I got stuck. It's kinda strange."

(Not as strange as this take on the song . . .)

"Oh, here they come!" Sherman says with glee as we hear a fire siren. "Hello, officer, how are you? Yeah, see what happened is I was up here with—"

He doesn't get to finish because another problem arises. "Watch my foot! My foot, sir! My foot!" he exclaims before screaming as we hear his voice fade en route to the ground below (and not a moment too soon).

Sherman wasn't the only famous singer to record something from *Prettybelle*. Take a listen to the demo—short for "demonstration record," made in hopes to entice popular recording artists to hear the score and choose to record a song or two—and you'll hear a just-starting-out singer named Peter Allen.

What Song Has the Best Encore?

Although "Always leave 'em wanting more" has been a long-established and much-trusted show business policy, some showstoppers do indeed want to give them more.

Hence the encore, which makes audiences coo in approval when they glean that they'll be getting more.

The time-honored tradition has songwriters giving their encores new lyrics, which ideally will get an even better response this time around.

Good lyricists know enough to save their best jokes for last. And they did in the following.

"To Keep My Love Alive" (*A Connecticut Yankee*). Remember how we said that Morgan le Fay had seven husbands? Indeed she did—but that was before she returned for her encore.

She then told us about Sirs James, Frank, Alfred, Peter, Ethelbert, Curtis, Marmaduke, and Mark, as well as their untimely deaths.

Alas, Lorenz Hart died, too, at only forty-eight, a mere few weeks after he'd finished this masterpiece. And yet there must have been a part of Hart that died happy, for he proved to his previous collaborator Richard Rodgers—then riding high with Oscar Hammerstein and *Oklahoma!*—that he still could write great lyrics when he had a mind to.

"Diamonds Are a Girl's Best Friend" (*Gentlemen Prefer Blondes*, **1949**). The original cast album doesn't offer Carol Channing singing lyricist Leo Robin's most entertaining encore.

The official reason was that so-called long-playing records could only hold so much material; the real reason was what the encore stated: that men, be they "buyers or sighers, they're such goddamn liars."

In 1974, Channing opened in *Lorelei*, a revisal of her earlier hit. By then, audiences had since heard worse from Tennessee Williams and Edward Albee, so the unexpurgated encore was recorded on the new cast album. And by 2012, when Encores! decided to revive it, there it was again, for audiences had since heard much worse from David Mamet.

"I'm Glad I'm Not Young Anymore" (*Gigi*). In the Oscar-winning film, Honore didn't sing what he did on stage in this encore: "All others but you she may enchant. You feel that you should. You do. You can't."

Have you any doubt that Alan Jay Lerner wrote this many years later? Erectile dysfunction was not mentioned in songs in the 1950s.

"The Grass Is Always Greener" (*Woman of the Year*). Nationally famous Tess Harding yearns for the simpler life, while Jan Donovan, a housewife who had just that, feels stymied by it.

Lauren Bacall and Marilyn Cooper sang the song while sitting on stools. Once they finished, they rose and moved away until Bacall gave a swoop of the head as if to say, "Let's go back and continue." And who was going to argue will Lauren Bacall?

Author's Choice: "Old-Fashioned Wedding" (*Annie Get Your Gun*, 1966). This was the fourth jewel of Irving Berlin's quadruple crown of encores, joining the ones that scored in the original 1946 production: "Doin' What Comes Naturally," "You Can't Get a Man with a Gun," and "Anything You Can Do (I Can Do Better)."

Once again, Berlin would write a stunning quodlibet (where one person sings one part, another person another, and then they each sing what they'd sung before as the audience is delighted to find that their melodies perfectly dovetail).

Here Annie Oakley (Ethel Merman) and Frank Butler (Bruce Yarnell) told how they envisioned their impending nuptials. They're as far apart as Candide and Cunegonde are in "Oh, Happy We."

Those two are kids; Annie and Frank aren't. Frankly, with each of them having such different ideas of what the ceremony should be—with neither she nor he actually listening to what the other wants—anyone would give the marriage six months at best.

That said, the encores of "Old-Fashioned Wedding" seemed to warrant six months of applause. Ask those who saw this twentieth anniversary revival, and they'll tell you that at each performance, Merman and Yarnell did four, five, or six encores.

"Old-Fashioned Wedding" was so good that for this encore, Berlin didn't need to write a single new word. The audience was just happy—nay, *thrilled*—to hear the same ones again and again and again.

What's the Best Title Song from a Flop Musical?
Sure, many of us love the title songs from such hits as *Anything Goes, Guys and Dolls, Cabaret, They're Playing Our Song, Grand Hotel, Rent, In the Heights,* and *Fun Home.*

Now—what about the title songs in the musicals that didn't quite make it?

"Do I Hear a Waltz?" (1965). Sondheim wrote the lyric, gave it to Rodgers, and may not have been pleased, given that he had his own melody in his head while writing it. But Rodgers did give it "such lovely Blue Danube-y music."

"Sherry!" (1967). "Sherry" was the nickname of Sheridan Whiteside, Kaufman and Hart's man who came to dinner. And yet, as *Jersey Boys* would later reiterate, we think of it as a girl's name. So Andy Williams' cover recording made heterosexual sense. Yet Marilyn Maye, who didn't worry about the gender implications, had the more popular recording.

However, neither he nor she did the song justice. In the musical, actress Lorraine Sheldon visits Sherry and dishes enough dirt to fill one of Daisy Gamble's potted plants. The hilarious lyrics were by James Lipton—yes, the *Inside the Actors Studio* host.

The Christine Baranski-Jonathan Freeman recording on an *Unsung Musicals* album will convince you of its worth.

"The Happy Time" (1968). A swirling Kander and Ebb waltz that reminds us of the nice things that have happened in our lives. But don't expect non-stop sentimentality, not from Fred Ebb. "The compliment you once received" is followed by "The lie you told they all believed."

(Ebb's right, though, isn't he?)

"Smile" (1986). It's the night of the Young American Miss Pageant, and the contestants have the bounciest of Marvin Hamlisch's melodies to sell their stories and (let's face it) their bodies.

Hamlisch originally wrote the score for this musical version of the 1975 film with Carolyn Leigh. When that didn't work out, Howard Ashman became involved. What's remarkable is that he said that all the songs that Hamlisch had written with Leigh had to go, with the exception of this song.

Yes, in 1982, Ashman had a big hit with *Little Shop of Horrors*, but by that point, Hamlisch's *A Chorus Line* had been running seven years in a theater four times as large. And yet Hamlisch agreed.

He might have dueled to the death if Ashman had suggested dropping the title song. And if he had—and the jury had heard the song as exhibit A—he would have been found innocent.

Author's Choice: "A Broadway Musical" (1979). To hear this gem from a one-performance flop, you'll have to get the video of *A Visit with Charles Strouse*. He enthusiastically sings the song in which a producer is trying to convince a most serious playwright that his hard-hitting drama should be a musical.

"The ultimate dream! That sweet illusion! A Broadway musical!" the producer maintains. "You want to escape the world's illusion? A Broadway musical!"

The playwright rebuts, "It doesn't have one redeeming feature: a Broadway musical."

The producer gets the last words, and glorious ones they are: "And yet, when it works, forget the jerks who told you it would not go, 'cause there's nothing like a Broadway show."

WHAT SONG DROPPED DURING REHEARSALS WOULD YOU MOST LIKE TO HEAR?

"The Wonderful Plan" (*Here's Love*, 1963). In fact, this musical version of *Miracle on 34th Street* was originally called *The Wonderful Plan* because Willson had written a song by that name for *The Music Man*, where it was cut. He then put it into *The Unsinkable Molly Brown*, where it was also cut. Willson must have really loved it to give it yet another chance.

(Either that, or this native from the Hawkeye State was, to cite one of his previous songs, "Iowa Stubborn.")

Alas, "The Wonderful Plan" wasn't a case of "third time's the charm" but "three strikes and you're out." It never made the finished musical, and it lost its standing as the title tune long before Willson selected *Here's Love*.

Willson even tried to insert it in his final musical, *1491*, a 1969 effort about Columbus' plans to sail the ocean blue. But this plan turned out to be a not-so-wonderful plan after all. It closed without even daring to come to Broadway.

Under these circumstances, wouldn't you want to hear this song and see if you like it as much as Willson apparently did?

"Fred Astaire" (*Mame*, **1966**). In Patrick Dennis' bestselling novel *Auntie Mame*, our hero tells of going off to college and making friends. "Our only god was Fred Astaire," Dennis wrote. "He was everything we wanted to be: smooth, suave, debonair, dapper, intelligent, adult, witty and wise."

That was enough to spur Jerry Herman to write "Fred Astaire." As late as January 1966—only a matter of weeks before the show went into rehearsal—it was still in the script.

Whether or not it would have served the show, a Jerry Herman song about Fred Astaire sounds irresistible.

"Folk Song" (*70, Girls, 70*, **1971**). Senior citizens were the main event in this Kander and Ebb musical. In Act Two, one dowager came forward to say "Good evening. Y'know, we were afraid, y'know, because all of us are over 60, y'know, that the show wouldn't have any youthful views expressed in it, y'know. But fortunately, one of our cast members has a nephew—y'know, a yippie—who wrote the following song just for us."

And without further ado, the young man came forward and sang to atonal guitar chords, "You! Old! Bastards! You! Old! Bastards! Old! Old! Old! Old! Bastards! Bastards! We got something to tell you! Old! Bastards! Bastards! Bastards!"

Some won't find this funny. They're in a demographic called old bastards.

Author's Choice: "Going" (*The Act*, **1977**). Kander and Ebb had Michele Craig ruminate on a former relationship. It started out with "We've got a good thing going. . . . Let's keep the good thing going, but the going's going good."

Then came a section with Kurt Weillian melody as the relationship is ending: "Going? Well, I guess you're going. . . . Yes, you should be going."

The conclusion she reaches is, "We've got a good thing going," which she corrects to "We *had* a good thing going. . . . Now it's going, going—gone."

This may strike you as similar to a song written a few years later.

What's the Best Song to Receive a Standing Ovation?

Today's Broadway musicals usually receive standing ovations at the end of their performances or during curtain calls. But giving a standing ovation to a singer at the end of a song—or even the middle—doesn't happen very often.

Although it may not have happened at the performance you attended, it did occur at least once after or during the following tunes.

"I Hate Men" (*Kiss Me, Kate*, 1999). Actually, the fondly remembered Marin Mazzie did not hate men, especially not Jason Danieley, to whom she was married for nearly twenty-one years; only in death did they part.

Yet Mazzie certainly had the audience believing that her character hated anything and everything male. How funny she was when snarling out, "But don't forget 'tis he who'll have the fun and thee the baby!" as she spread her legs as wide as they could go while managing a tortured grimace worthy of a delivery of twins.

"Can't Take My Eyes off You" (*Jersey Boys*, 2005). Bookwriters Marshall Brickman and Rick Elice astounded theatergoers with the information that the song they were about to hear had a terribly hard time exciting record executives: "Can't Take My Eyes off You."

How could it have had this rocky beginning when it rocked the charts and reached second spot in 1967?

Theatergoers are even more astonished at how Tony winner John Lloyd Young performed it. Up they went.

"Totally Fucked" (*Spring Awakening*, 2006). This was Melchior's assessment of his life after he'd been unjustly accused and expelled from school.

Jonathan Groff's powerful rendition of equally powerful Steven Sater lyrics and Duncan Sheik's music were the main reason that audiences stood after the final note. Another explanation, though, was that everyone who stood could empathize with the situation. Who *hasn't* been totally fucked?

"You Oughta Know" (*Jagged Little Pill,* **2019).** Gay or straight, we all can relate to "You told me you'd hold me until you died,'til you died, but you're still alive." There's such sadness in saying "You oughta know" to someone who no longer has any interest in knowing; he or she has moved on and certainly without a hint of a forwarding address.

Lauren Patten's Tony was secure before she reached the second section of this cry of pain; the standing o soon followed.

Author's Choice: "And I Am Telling You, I Am Not Going" (*Dreamgirls,* **1981).** Was this the first one ever to get people to bolt out of their seats as if pierced with electric cattle prods? During the Boston tryout, they couldn't even wait until Jennifer Holliday finished; they were standing mid-song and didn't sit down until the first act ended.

WHAT'S THE BEST SONG THAT WAS DROPPED FROM A MUSICAL BUT THEN HAD A RENAISSANCE?

The famously trite question—"What comes first; the music or the lyrics?"—is sometimes easily answered.

Songwriters who find that their songs don't fit into a musical don't necessarily forget them. There could be another time and another place that would be ideal for them.

Stars on My Shoulder. In the 1920s, Irving Berlin wrote a song for this musical that went unproduced. After he was signed to write the 1942 film *Holiday Inn*—in which he was required to write songs about holidays—he remembered "White Christmas" and put it in the film.

Needless to say, it then went into phonographs, jukeboxes, automobile cassette players, CD units, Spotify, mp3s, and Americans' hearts and souls.

Everybody's Welcome **(1931).** This musical's plot sounds ahead of its time: Steve will stay home, tend house, and write his novel while wife Ann goes out and earns their daily bread.

She won't be the usual receptionist, secretary, teacher, or nurse. Ann auditions for musicals and is cast in one.

What she doesn't get is the most famous song that Herman Hupfeld ever wrote: "As Time Goes By"; it was sung by another actress.

It was one of musical's eleven songs; coincidentally, eleven years had to pass before it was genuinely appreciated, when Ilsa and then Rick demanded that Sam play it in *Casablanca.*

Softly. The Colonial Theatre was booked in Boston for a September 5, 1967, opening. Jason Robards would star in this musical with a book by Hugh Wheeler (based on a story by Santha Rama Rau), music by Harold Arlen, and lyrics by Martin Charnin.

When it didn't happen, Charnin didn't later reuse his entire lyric for "You're Never Fully Dressed without a Smile," but he certainly recycled the title.

"When I Get My Name in Lights" (*The Boy from Oz*, 2003). When enough people told composer-lyricist-star Peter Allen that a new opening number was needed for his 1988 musical *Legs Diamond*, this was the charmer that he concocted.

However, when Jack "Legs" Diamond sang it, he was a still-incarcerated criminal who gave no evidence of being innocent. As a result, audiences couldn't relate to an inmate who wasn't worth time or sympathy.

However, fifteen years later, when Allen's life was brought to the stage, eleven-year-old Mitchel David Federan, playing Young Peter, captured our fancy with the same song. Who doesn't enjoy hearing a child telling us what he wants to be when he grows up?

Author's Choice: "Witches' Brew" (*Hallelujah, Baby!*, 1967). After an event where Betty Comden and Adolph Green had been interviewed, the moderator asked for questions from the audience.

One young man stood and said, "There's your song 'Witches' Brew' in *Hallelujah, Baby!* But in your earlier show *Fade Out–Fade In*, there was a song called 'Call Me Savage'—"

He got no further. Comden interrupted by droning "It's the same song" before stretching out her arms in front of her, pushing her hands and wrists together as if preparing to be handcuffed and adding "Arrest me."

WHAT SONG HAS THE BEST DOUBLE ENTENDRES?

Yes, Broadway lyricists have been known to be naughty.

"My Handyman Ain't Handy No More" (*Blackbirds of 1930*). To a sultry Eubie Blake melody, lyricist Andy Razaf created what *The Brooklyn Daily Eagle* called "probably the dirtiest song that Broadway has had since the demise of burlesque."

A chanteuse rues that her employee is "not the man he was before" because "he doesn't perform his duties like he used to do"—when he'd "churn my butter" and "chop my meat." She recalled when "You used to get up at dawn, full of new ambition—and how you'd trim my lawn."

You get the point. Audiences in 1930 only had fifty-seven chances to hear the song. It had to wait until 1978 to make its 439-performance renaissance in *Eubie!*

What's remarkable is that it was written and inserted during the tryout in Boston, where even twenty years later the censor who saw Cole Porter's *Out of This World* asked that the term "sexual insecurity" be eliminated.

No doubt that "Handyman" went in the waning days of the Boston run when the censors were busy making "suggestions" for the next tryout that had recently opened.

"Humble Hollywood Executive" (dropped from *Mexican Hayride*, 1944). Of one studio higher-up, a young lass sang, "You talk about endurance? This guy is dynamite! Works at MGM in the daytime and Fox at night."

What's surprising is that the song was to be sung by Edith Meiser, an "If you saw her, you'd know her" performer. The Vassar graduate would eventually play unctuous, high-born, and snooty women; on *I Love Lucy* she twice portrayed Mrs. Phoebe Littlefield, whose name alone should give you an idea of her aristocratic nature. On Broadway, she was the future unsinkable Molly Brown's oh-so-uppity tormentor Mrs. McGlone.

Considering those roles, Meiser's singing this "naughty" ditty suggests a very different wayward youth.

"Can That Boy Foxtrot!" (dropped from *Follies*). During the Boston tryout, Yvonne De Carlo so enjoyed stretching out the "F" in "Foxtrot" that many first-timers wondered "Is she really going to sing what we think she's going to say?"

"The Tennis Song" (*City of Angels*). David Zippel was slightly more elegant than his fellow lyricists in delivering double entendres. He had private eye Stone have questions for the alluring Alaura, who's hired him to investigate a missing person.

He shows up just as Alaura's just finished a game of tennis. Now she'll play a game with him: "I like to work up a sweat. . . . I'm good for more than one set. . . . It's not exciting unless the competition is stiff."

And both sing, "It's time for someone to score."

Author's Choice: "I Never Do Anything Twice" (*Side by Side by Sondheim*, 1977). A madam ruminates on her past, when she was told by a customer that he didn't want her repeating herself sexually.

She quoted his view on the matter: "'Once, yes, once for a lark; twice, though, loses the spark. One must never deny it, but after you try it, you vary the diet,' said my handsome young guard. 'Yes, I know, that it's hard . . .'"

That was the first hint of a double entendre. Soon came a section about a baron "who came at my command and proffered me a riding crop and chains. . . . He took the most extraordinary pains . . . his cheeks were quite aglow."

The madam decided, "once is delicious, but twice would be vicious or just repetitious."

This is the song that Cole Porter wished he'd written. The sad part is that what Sondheim so meticulously crafted for the 1976 movie *The*

Seven-Per-Cent Solution was so mercilessly cut that you'd expect the credits to say "Film Editor: Sweeney Todd." So little remained that producer-director Herbert Ross might as well have thrown out the whole thing.

That Ross allowed the amputation is surprising, for he and Sondheim had had a history together; Ross had choreographed *Anyone Can Whistle* (and received the show's only Tony nomination), dance-doctored *Do I Hear a Waltz?*, and directed Sondheim and Anthony Perkins' great mystery film *The Last of Sheila.*

Even that wasn't enough to keep the song intact in the final film. Bless Ned Sherrin for creating a revue that allowed us to hear it in all its glory.

WHAT'S THE MOST HILARIOUS MONDEGREEN EVER "HEARD" IN A SONG FROM A MUSICAL?

Essayist Sylvia Wright coined the term "mondegreen" in 1954 when relating an incident from her childhood. At bedtime each night, her mother would read her the same poem. Although it ended with the words, "and laid him on the green," little Sylvia heard it as "and Lady Mondegreen."

"Mondegreen" is now included in the *Oxford English Dictionary*: "a misunderstood or misinterpreted word or phrase resulting from a mishearing of the lyrics of a song."

We've all made one or two while trying to decipher lyrics. Readers who have shared their mondegreens have asked that their names be withheld to save embarrassment. It's a deal.

"Mr. Snow" (*Carousel*). Reader One didn't hear Carrie sing, "He comes home every night in his round-bottomed boat with a net full of herring from the sea," but "He comes home every night in his round-bottomed boat with Annette Funicello from the sea."

(Well, Annette *did* spend a good deal of time in water with Frankie Avalon . . .)

"Sit Down, John" (*1776*). Reader Two said, "Because there were no women in the Congressional Chamber, I couldn't understand why John Adams was singing, 'I say gorgeous! gorgeous!' It took many listens before

I caught on that William Daniels was actually singing, 'I say, vote yes! Vote yes!'"

"The Ladies Who Lunch" (*Company*, 1970). Reader Three initially heard, "I'll drink to that! And one firm olive!"—thinking that the vodka stinger Joanne had mentioned earlier came with an olive on a toothpick. Only much later did he discover that the line was, "And one for Mahler!"

"I Am Changing" (*Dreamgirls*, 1981). Reader Four wrote, "At the end of the song, I thought Effie was singing 'I'll change my life, and oy Gevalt, nothing's gonna stop me now!' I couldn't fathom why this Black woman from Detroit would know that Yiddish term. It wasn't until years later that I realized that she was singing 'I'll make a vow!'"

Author's Choice: "Dice Are Rolling" (*Evita*). Reader Five stated, "I thought it was bad enough for Peron to blatantly sing to Eva 'You are dying' but then I was really outraged at what he sang next. When I told friends about it, they pointed out that what he actually sang was 'This talk of death is chilling,' not, as I had assumed, 'This taco tastes of chili.' And I'd been thinking that he was such a real boor for eating at such an emotional moment."

WHAT'S THE WORST SONG FROM A BROADWAY MUSICAL?
"Nothing Can Replace a Man" (*Ankles Aweigh*, 1955). Lyricist Dan Shapiro had Jane Kean acknowledge that oleomargarine could be an able substitute for butter and before making similar comparisons, including "Throughout the world of science, no one's found a new appliance that ever can replace a man."

Now *there's* a dated lyric. You can now go into any drug store and buy one for about $4.98.

"Puka, Puka Pants" (*13 Daughters*, 1961). The first two words of the title are each only one letter away from what you might do while hearing it.

Not only does the song stink, but the kid who sings it on the original Hawaiian cast album (yes, there is such a thing) is equally atrocious. She's even worse than the teen who ruins "Growing Pains" in *A Tree Grows in Brooklyn*.

"She Hadda Go Back" (*Here's Love,* **1963**). Here the musical version of *Miracle on 34th Street* takes a strange and wild turn. Meredith Willson gave his hero Fred this long patter song in which he predicted that Doris, whom he was expecting, wouldn't arrive until midnight.

The reasons? She'd forget her gloves and return to fetch them. She'd check herself in the mirror countless times. There'd be other such time-consuming irrelevancies, too.

What was genuinely irrelevant was that the film's plot doesn't contain this scene nor does it need one.

As it turned out, the doorbell indeed did ring just at the moment Fred predicted that it would. He opened the door in triumph only to find that Doris wasn't standing there; a Girl Scout selling cookies was.

(At midnight? Where's her mother?!)

"One Beating a Day" (*Peg,* **1983**). Miss Peggy Lee, in her biomusical, told of the physical abuse she received as a child.

"She hit me in the head with a frying pan, and she pushed my face in the garbage can. She kicked me in the stomach and she pulled my hair, but it made it grow, so I really don't care."

As atrocious as Lee's lyrics are, what places this in the worst-ever category is that composer Paul Horner set these grisly words to a happy-go-lucky samba beat.

Author's Choice: "Paris Makes Me Horny" (*Victor/Victoria,* **1996**). Many Broadway fans like to criticize composer Frank Wildhorn, but here his only crime was agreeing to put music to Leslie Bricusse's lyrics.

Just from the title, you'd have low expectations, but midway through the song, you'd see them go lower when Rachel York was forced to sing "When I see the Eiffel Tower, I have to go and take a shower." Worse still was "Been to Munich, where ev'ry guy's a eunuch." We've heard that Hitler had only had one testicle, but that's not the same thing.

CHAPTER FIVE

Debating the Recordings

WHAT CAST ALBUM PROVES THAT A COMPOSER COULD MEET A SEEMINGLY INSURMOUNTABLE CHALLENGE?

Charles Strouse (*Golden Boy*). After he'd composed the two upbeat commercial musical comedies, *Bye Bye Birdie* and *All-American*, who could have ever anticipated that he was capable of this sultry black-tinged masterpiece?

Jerry Herman (*Dear World*). After *Hello, Dolly!* and *Mame*, we expected Herman would give us another razz-ma-tazzer with a New York locale. Instead, he signed on to write a musical set in Paris. Most didn't know, though, that Herman in college had performed in *The Madwoman of Chaillot* and had plenty of time to absorb the atmosphere.

Yes, the title song has taken a great deal of criticism—much from Herman himself—but the rest is superb.

Stephen Schwartz (*The Baker's Wife*, 1976). Here was another composer who didn't seem natively right for a musical set in long ago France. After all, he'd established himself as one of Broadway's best purveyors of pop-rock via *Godspell*, *Pippin*, and *The Magic Show*.

Those who doubted had their skepticism disappear when they heard his luscious, traditional score that sounded just right for the region. The achievement was clear from the first song, appropriately called "Chanson."

As for lyrics, Schwartz met that challenge, too. This is the story of a wife who's never fallen in love with her aging and overweight husband.

When a handsome young stud comes along, off she goes. To what conclusion does she come after comparing him to her husband?

"The fire is there. But where is the warmth?"

And who suggested that Schwartz musicalize *The Baker's Wife* in the first place? No less than Neil Simon, who offered it as a project on which they might work together. Would that musical have avoided closing on the road had Simon continued with it?

Benj Pasek and Justin Paul (*A Christmas Story*, 2012). The famous Jean Shepherd story and film that's set in the 1930s was given to two novices who hadn't even *reached* their thirties. How could these two millennials write convincingly of the era?

They did so well that they seemed to be a Golden Age team. And yet, as their subsequent scores for *Dogfight* and *Dear Evan Hansen* have proved, they're very much members of their musical generation. So many of their contemporaries would have written anachronistically for a period property; they knew enough not to.

Author's Choice: Richard Adler (*Kwamina*). "A village in West Africa" was the setting, so Adler needed to merge Broadway with Bantu music. He certainly did. The trial songs are exquisite.

Despite the musical's running a mere month, the Tony committee nominated it as Best Score. Such fine work as Kander and Goldmans' *A Family Affair*, Harold Rome's *I Can Get It for You Wholesale*, Dietz and Schwartz's *The Gay Life*, Wright and Forrest's *Kean*, Noel Coward's *Sail Away*, and Styne, Comden, and Green's *Subways Are for Sleeping* all ran longer yet weren't nominated.

WHAT CAST ALBUM WAS THE LEAST EXPECTED?

Today, many obscure musicals receive cast albums, usually subsidized by the writers on a "label" that they created.

Before recording in a bedroom or a garage was an option, writers had to rely on genuine companies to record their shows. So wasn't Broadway surprised when cast albums were released for the following.

Anyone Can Whistle **(1964).** No cast album had ever been made of a musical that had run a mere nine performances. And yet Stephen Sondheim's second Broadway score has seldom been out of print in the ensuing six decades. It's been on LP, CD, cassette four-track, and even eight-track tape.

It also served to introduce Sondheim's new and ambitious sound that would dominate the musical theater in the 1970s. As *New York Times* theater critic Frank Rich would write twenty-three years later in his review of *Into the Woods*, "Time and second hearings always tell with a Sondheim score." We wouldn't have had those additional chances with *Anyone Can Whistle* had it not been preserved.

Since then, the score has even inspired two more recordings. Can any show boast of having as few as three pro-rated performances per recording?

Oh! Calcutta! **(1969).** A now-pretty-much-forgotten revue that prided itself in its nudity.

That wasn't possible to capture on a cast album.

It was enough for 7,273 Broadway audiences in two productions ranging from East 12th Street to West 46th, playing sixteen of the twenty years between June 1969 and August 1989.

Amazingly, Samuel Beckett, Jules Feiffer, Sam Shepard, Kenneth Tynan, and even John Lennon were among those who contributed sketches. However, never was any one of their names attached to a specific sketch. Were they ashamed?

In *Upstairs at O'Neal's*, a 1983 cabaret musical, Martin Charnin wrote a song that maintained, "You can do a revue without taste. I know of one that's been running for years." His not-so-veiled acknowledgment of *Oh!, Calcutta!* was quite accurate.

Author's Choice: *Mummenschanz* **(1977).** All right, this was a mime show, so there was neither speaking nor singing. But it's such an oddity it's worth mentioning.

All that one heard was the audience response—whatever it happened to be on the night of the recording. "It's a great party record," insisted Jeffrey Richards.

He was the show's press agent.

WHAT'S THE BEST REVIVAL CAST ALBUM?

A Party with Betty Comden and Adolph Green **(1977).** Wine could only hope to age as well as these two legends did.

As much as the illustrious duo savored the chance to revisit their 1958 revue and bring even more gusto and brio to it, those who bought the new album received much more, too.

The original recording abridged the revue to one record with sixteen songs. Nineteen years later, record producer Hugh Fordin afforded the pair a two-record set on which ten more songs could be added: three songs from when they were part of the comic troupe known as The Revuers—one each from *On the Town* and *Two on the Aisle* and two each from *Wonderful Town* and *Peter Pan*.

And of course the earlier recording couldn't include the songs that they'd yet to write: one each from *Do Re Mi* and *Subways Are for Sleeping* and—here's a bonus—two from *Straws in the Wind*, a 1975 off-Broadway revue to which they set lyrics to Cy Coleman's music. One's tender; the other's hilarious.

But that's Comden and Green for you.

The Most Happy Fella **(1992).** Of course it's no substitute for the magnificent original. But it has its place, for its two-piano orchestration makes for nice late-night listening when you just couldn't deal with the blaring *Lorelei*, which really makes you face the music.

St. Louis Woman **(1998).** This score provided Capitol Records with its first original cast album. That's no surprise, for Johnny Mercer, the musical's lyricist, was one of the company's three founders.

When the musical premiered in 1946, the 78 rpm record was the only recording medium. So eleven songs were put on five ten-inch records.

Missing were an overture, an Entr'acte, eight additional songs, one reprise of the big hit "Come Rain or Come Shine," and a finale.

All those were recorded when Vanessa Williams and twenty-six others revived the musical at Encores!

Both recordings offer "Cakewalk Your Lady," which, it's been said, was Stephen Sondheim's model for "Comedy Tonight" when he had to come up with a new opening number in a hurry for *A Funny Thing Happened*. Listen and decide if you agree with what many have alleged.

Tenderloin (2000). After Rex Harrison semi-sang his songs, many non-singers were suddenly populating Broadway musicals.

That includes noted Shakespearean actor Maurice Evans. He played the title role in the first uncut *Hamlet* that Broadway ever saw (in 1938). Many more saw him as warlock Maurice—Samantha's father—in the sitcom *Bewitched*.

In Weidman, Bock, and Harnick's *Tenderloin*, he played sobersided minister Doctor Brock and made him stodgier than he needed to be. David Ogden Stiers seems more human on the recording made at Encores! forty years later.

The 2000 album has Patrick Wilson bring both voice and character to Tommy, Brock's ostensible mentee. Ron Hussman, the original Tommy, was one of those performers who was intent on showing off his voice and didn't worry about character.

He should have gone into opera.

Author's Choice: *Follies in Concert* (1985). All right, for this "complete" recording, some of the dance music in "The Story of Lucy and Jessie" wasn't included. But considering what a disemboweled mess the oh-so-truncated original cast album was, hearing "Beautiful Girls" and "I'm Still Here" in all their lyrical glory made this the quintessential recording. After this one, listening to the original made us pine for what we knew we were missing.

WHAT MUSICAL THAT WASN'T RECORDED SHOULD HAVE BEEN?

Love Life (1948). Alan Jay Lerner and Kurt Weill's musical was scuttled by a musician's strike. Only after eleven months did the musicians see many of their demands met. A lyric in one of the score's jaunty songs turned out to be an inadvertent comment on the situation: "That's good economics, but awful bad for love"—love of a good score.

Call Me Madam. We're talking about a real original cast album, not the two hybrids that resulted from recording companies' restrictions and red tape.

RCA Victor had invested substantially to land the recording rights to the new Irving Berlin musical. Meanwhile, Ethel Merman was signed to Decca. Surely the company would let her make the cast album, wouldn't it?

No. So RCA went to its most popular female singer—Dinah Shore—to sub for Merman who in turn made her own album with a few recording artists of the day.

Merman's character, Mrs. Sally Adams, is a shark-out-of-water as the United States ambassador to a mythical small foreign country. She's brash, bold and, well, Merman.

Shore's nice and pleasant—all wrong for the character who has, to use a word from a non-mythical country, *cojones.* Alas, Merman's album comes across as just that: a Merman album.

We would have had a great recording if RCA had used Merman's understudy. Of course that wouldn't have happened, but a *Call Me Madam* starring Elaine Stritch would have hit the spot.

Foxy **(1964).** It opened a month to the day after *Hello, Dolly!* David Merrick—who'd produced both—had a smash hit, so he lost interest in this musical that had "only" received raves for star Bert ("The Cowardly Lion") Lahr.

RCA Victor had the rights to record it; without Merrick's prodding (and his actually selling to show to Billy Rose for literally a few dollars), the company had little incentive to bring the cast into Webster Hall.

After seventy-two performances, *Foxy* closed. Thirty-six days later, Lahr won the Tony as Best Actor in a Musical. Had Merrick or Rose kept it running, RCA might have recorded it after all.

Grovers Corners **(1987).** For a musical version of Thornton Wilder's unconventional masterpiece *Our Town,* no Broadway songwriters were more right for it than Tom Jones and Harvey Schmidt.

Sure, they could write fine Broadway-centric material when they needed to; *110 in the Shade* and *I Do! I Do!* proved that. Their true heart and spirit, however, were in the unconventional, as much of *The Fantasticks* and more of *Celebration* and *Philemon* had proved. No Broadway composer has had such a gentle minimalist touch as Schmidt, which was ideal for this gentle play.

Too bad that the Thornton Wilder estate lost faith in the project and withdrew the rights. A bigger pity: Mary Martin was set to play the Stage Manager, but then became too ill to perform.

Author's Choice: A tie among the eleven Rodgers and Hammerstein properties.

"What?!" you say. "We have dozens of those!"

No, let's hear the melodies that Oscar Hammerstein had in his head while he was writing lyrics before he handed them over to Richard Rodgers.

Hammerstein's family members who heard them said they were *terrible*. Wouldn't you like to know for sure?

WHAT ALBUMS SHOULD BE INCLUDED IN A BROADWAY MUSICAL TIME CAPSULE?

Time capsules are, by their very nature, small. So although there would be enough room for a cape as red as blood, hair as yellow as corn, and a slipper as pure as gold, just try getting a cow as white as milk in there.

Recordings are ideal for a time capsule because they don't appropriate much space. When the capsule is finally opened, those curating can see how cast albums looked and advanced from the 1940s onward.

Finian's Rainbow as a long-playing 33-1/3 rpm record. Columbia's first non-breakable twelve-inch vinyl was something sort of grandish both in its technology and its score.

Make a Wish (1951) in a box set of 45 rpm records. It wasn't a long-running hit, no, but much underrated composer-lyricist Hugh Martin should be remembered, even in a small seven-by-seven inch box.

South Pacific on a four-track, reel-to-reel tape full of some enchanted music—no, *all* enchanted music.

Darling of the Day (1968) on eight-track tape. And yes, this thirty-two-performance musical *did* make it to this short-lived medium.

Hair (1968) on cassette. Many of the little tapes helped its original Broadway cast album (as opposed to its original *off*-Broadway cast album) reach number one on the charts.

Grind (1985) on compact disc. That this unsuccessful musical made it to CD was the first indication that a show needn't be a smash to be digitally celebrated.

And would there be a way to include mp3s and Spotify links in a capsule?

Author's Choice: *Oklahoma!* as six 78 rpm very fragile records. This was the set to which the nation could not say no.

CHAPTER SIX

Debating the Movie Musicals

WHAT'S THE BEST FILM VERSION OF A MUSICAL?

West Side Story **(1961).** Few would believe that Tony, as played by Richard Beymer, could have ever been the leader of a street gang, but the rest of the casting is fine.

Choreographer and codirector Jerome Robbins had the toughest job in making juvenile delinquents not look silly when they danced. On stage, that was hard enough, but the harsh reality of film and actual city streets made the task seemingly impossible.

Robbins conquered the problem early on by having the Jets walk down the street, then glide, and then slowly break into dance. It was all perfectly calibrated.

There was, of course, another reason why it didn't look silly: Leonard Bernstein's music would make anyone want to dance.

Screenwriter Ernest Lehman made one mistake and one improvement to Arthur Laurents' script. On stage, the second act began with the audience knowing that Bernardo had been killed, so the dramatic irony in watching his unaware sister Maria be so joyous in "I Feel Pretty" was heartbreaking.

In the film, she sang it *before* his murder. The song seemed to be there just because enough time had passed that a new song should be introduced.

Credit, though, goes to Lehman for reversing the order of "Cool" and "Gee, Officer Krupke." In the stage version, the Jets sang the comic song after they saw their leader killed and their former leader murder their enemy.

273

They're not that callow. "Cool," which their new leader Ice urged them to be, was the right song for the moment.

There was also a change in "America," but it was a change back. Originally, Sondheim had written it so that the Sharks could sardonically criticize their new "homeland" while their girlfriends defended it. Robbins felt there was so much testosterone in the singing that the young women deserved a number all their own.

That's what Broadway audiences saw and heard.

For the film—especially after Robbins was fired because many felt that he was working too slowly—Sondheim was able to reinstate his original lyrics.

***West Side Story* (2021).** As extraordinary as the ten-Oscared 1961 film was, screenwriter Tony Kushner and director Steven Spielberg delivered a more powerful one.

These Jets made you wonder why the ones from sixty years earlier didn't sport tattoos and have sex in construction cranes. These punks even terrorize old men. To say that in a brawl one of them was nailed wouldn't just be a fanciful expression; Baby John actually did succumb to a Shark hammering a nail into his earlobe. Lieutenant Shrank is a more taunting enemy here, telling the Jets to their faces that they're "the last of the can't-make-it Caucasians." Candy store-owner Doc has now been supplanted by his widow Valentina, who recalls that she knew them as children and is aghast at what they've become.

Kushner gave Bernardo more depth. The Sharks' leader now has a career that in the 1950s offered one of the few opportunities for immigrants: boxing. Bernardo is a genuine mentor to an appreciative Chino, who nevertheless still has a need to be tough and join the Sharks. Bernardo wants more for him, and Chino is taking night school classes. These attempts at careers make both men's terrible fates much more tragic.

It's still Maria and Tony's story, of course. Once they meet at the dance (where Kushner was wise to add additional just-in-case police presence), Maria knows what she wants and impulsively kisses Tony. For their fire escape scene, a horizontal grate keeps them apart, symbolizing how difficult a time these two will have.

Making matters more dangerous is that Bernardo and his girlfriend Anita arrive home, only a few feet away from the clandestine lovers. The original stage show and film had Maria living with her parents; here her brother is the parent figure who'd be even less accepting of Maria's beau than her father would be.

Riff, who co-founded the Jets with Tony, virtually brags that he was "born to die young." Little does he know how accurate his prediction is. In one of the film's best masterstrokes, Tony now sings "Cool" to him. That makes sense, for Tony is the one—the only one of both gangs—who wants everyone to calm down.

Kushner wisely gave Tony and Maria a scene on a subway in which they frankly acknowledge the roadblocks they'll endure; this makes them less naïve and starry-eyed. They go to the peaceful Cloisters—their "Somewhere"—where they get as close to a wedding as they'll ever get.

There's a pungent irony when the Jets and Sharks meet to establish the terms of their rumble. They meet in an abandoned warehouse that has an iron grate; it takes two to lift it, and the two are Tony and Chino. They're both unaware that this inadvertent teamwork will lead to both of their destructions.

In Kushner's most daring move, Tony is a convicted criminal who has served a year in jail. He neither keeps this from Maria nor sugarcoats it; he explains his mistake in getting into a brawl where he severely injured his opponent. The look on his face after he murders Bernardo shows that what he most wanted to avoid has turned into history repeating itself on a more dire level.

Kushner added another powerful scene in which Anita must go to the morgue to identify Bernardo's body. That the police first lift a sheet and reveal Riff gives her a glimmer of hope, for it's not Bernardo. That's extinguished when the next sheet is lifted.

Unlike the original screenwriter, Ernest Lehman, who repositioned Maria's "I Feel Pretty" before Bernardo's murder, Kushner smartly returned to Arthur Laurents' original intention to employ dramatic irony:

we know that Bernardo is dead and thus feel terrible that her joy will soon come to an abrupt and inconsolable end.

The song takes place in a department store, for Maria is no longer a tailor but a cleaning woman—a much more odious, demanding, and demeaning job. That so many of her co-workers are so much older, reminds us that this may well be her lifelong fate, too.

Bernardo's murder gives Chino more motivation to seek revenge for the man who'd been so good to him. Now it's a crime of passion on two levels, for he's avenging both Maria and her brother.

Adam Stockhausen's production design is thorough. One scene set on a street shows that the cars parked on each side are short and stocky models from the late 1940s and early 1950s. In 1955, designers made automobiles long and lean, but in this neighborhood that often looks dystopian, no one can afford the up-to-date models.

Choreographer Justin Peck's choreography takes "America"—the challenge song between the Sharks and their girlfriends—and moves it from a rooftop to actual Manhattan streets. This would seem to be a mistake, for wouldn't automobile after automobile interrupt their dancing? Spielberg allowed for this and showed frustrated motorists angrily get out of their cars but impotently put their arms akimbo as the dancing will not stop for them.

The casting came across as more authentic. Ansel Elgort (Tony), Rachel Zegler (Maria), David Alvarez (Bernardo), Ariana DeBose (Anita), and Mike Faist (Riff) all seem grittier and more world-weary than their 1961 counterparts. Here too everyone does his and her own singing of the glorious Leonard Bernstein–Stephen Sondheim score, which wasn't the case in 1961.

And then there's Rita Moreno—the 1961 Anita now is Puerto Rican proprietor Valentina. She's the most likely character to have the age and wisdom to dare believe that "There's a place for us" when singing "Somewhere." There certainly was a place for this new and greatly improved *West Side Story*.

Hedwig and the Angry Inch (2001). Playwrights are told early on "Show, don't tell." The original off-Broadway version did a great deal of telling and hardly any showing with Hedwig and back-up singer Yitzhak the only people on stage and in concert.

Real estate representatives are always citing "location, location, location." That's what we get here, as we take a rainbow tour with Hedwig all over the world.

The film was ignored by the Oscars, but it received twenty-nine nominations from various other organizations and won all but seven of them. So its success can be measured in much more than inches.

The Last Five Years (2014). *Beauty and the Beast* isn't the only musical with a "tale as old as time." Just as seasoned is a story of one partner in a relationship succeeding while the other person isn't.

So in *this* version of *A Star Is Born*, Jamie's a novelist who's rising to the top; Cathy's an actress who's barely staying in the middle of the pack. They're married, but not for long. Cathy feels like the fifth wheel on a 1959 Edsel.

Jason Robert Brown's not-at-all veiled musical about his own experiences of early success and his wife's lack thereof was a two-character musical with a unit set when it played its two-month off-Broadway engagement.

Why so short a run? Brown structured his musical in a most atypical way. Jamie tells of the relationship from beginning to end, while Cathy tells her side of the story from the end to beginning. Without helpful projections on the back wall detailing the month and year, theatergoers were confused. Musicals just don't proceed in this fashion, and no change of scenery didn't help.

Ah, but in film, we're used to flashbacks and cuts in time. Helping too is seeing their apartments pre-marriage and the one they shared afterward as well as a tour of New York: Central Park for their wedding, the Staten Island Ferry, bike paths, restaurants, and bars.

There *is* a side trip to a summer stock theater in Ohio where Cathy performs in everything from *L'il Abner* to *Les Miz*. When we see her spinning around in a field of grass, at least we know that she landed Maria in you-know-what.

Or has she? Could she just be preparing her audition—or, worse, expressing wishful thinking after she didn't get the part? Cathy doesn't have a happy ending with Jamie, but we're hoping that that life-changing offer in a new destined-to-be-a-hit musical will occur the next time she checks her emails.

In the twelve years since the original production, one lyric was changed for the film. In 2002, Cathy could tell Jamie "I saw your book in a Borders in Kentucky," but by 2014, Borders had been out of business for three years. Brown chose "a Target in Kentucky," which just may suffice for a few decades.

However, while Brown was at it, he should have changed a line that had also become obsolete in the ensuing years: "Mitchell got a job at the record store in the mall."

***tick, tick . . . BOOM!* (2021).** Jonathan Larson has such angst at reaching the really Big Three-Oh—the first birthday that brings with it some dread. Given that he hadn't made it as a Broadway songwriter by then, shouldn't he give up?

Unlike most of us, Larson was far unluckier at thirty, for his life was actually five-sixths over; his aortic aneurysm was only a half dozen years away, only hours before he was to see the first-ever performance of his musical *Rent*.

Before that, his ambivalence caused him to write "Johnny Can't Decide," in which he lamented, "Johnny has no guide." That didn't turn out to be true. After he played his songs in a workshop, Stephen Sondheim gave him validation and encouragement.

That and a five dollar bill gets you a cup of coffee at Starbucks. Meanwhile, his lifelong friend Michael tried to become a professional actor, then joined the corporate world as a market research executive and became rich and happy. ("Hello to shiny new parquet wooden floors as waxed as a wealthy girl's legs.")

Jonathan's single-mindedness in getting his musical produced is a problem for his devoted girlfriend who has a good job offer 116 miles away. It comes to a head in "Therapy," which could just as easily have been called "The God-Why-Don't-You-*Understand*-Me Blues."

Too much like a Sondheim title? Well, in one of the show's wittiest songs, Jonathan riffs on "Sunday," Sondheim's first-act closer to *Sunday in the Park with George*. Jonathan describes his Sunday, enduring his day job at the Moondance Diner that became a morning-and-night job, too.

And what did the workshop of Jonathan's latest musical yield? "We're intrigued by your talent," his agent said in a phone call that he'd hoped would include the information "Nine producers are fighting for the rights." Nope: "intrigued by your talent" was the best Jonathan would get—in 1990.

No, art isn't easy, as Sondheim wrote—and this from a man who's won seven Tony awards, an Oscar, a Pulitzer, and a Kennedy Center honor. But little did Larson know that *Rent* would win the same award that Sondheim won for *Sunday*—the Pulitzer Prize—while winning the award denied *Sunday*—the Best Musical Tony.

Author's Choice: *Cabaret* (1972). As stated earlier, the original creators of *Cabaret* felt that Sally Bowles wasn't much of a singer. In Bob Fosse's film, he let us know from the outset that she wasn't a headliner when he had the Emcee introduce her in the middle of announcing everyone else who was performing at the Kit Kat Klub.

So many musical films that have night club settings (such as *Can-Can*) had its cinematographer point the camera at the stage and let the number unfold. You'd never see a waiter pass by and obscure a clear view of the stage. Fosse, who began as a nightclub performer in less-than-high-class venues, knew the hustle and bustle of such a place and put that on screen.

He also ordered close-ups of the cabaret's customers, which reiterated what a seedy place it was. Other movie musicals were content to offer faraway anonymous shots of a crowd, revealing no distinctive personalities.

Cabaret on stage had the songs sung in the Kit Kat Klub comment on what was happening in the outside world: "Life is a cabaret, ol' chum." The film added to the concept. As one of those Tyrolean slap-your-knees-and-chest numbers was being performed onstage, outside the Nazis were doing more than just slapping the club's manager who'd ejected one of their own some nights before.

As the Emcee sang about sex with "Two Ladies," Sally became involved with two men: Brian and Maximilian. Sally thought she'd astonish Brian by being brutally but unapologetically frank when she told him that she was sleeping with Maximilian; instead, he shocked her when trumping her ace with "So do I."

Audiences were shocked, too. Cliff, as he was called in the stage show, was drawn as heterosexual; Brian was bisexual. This was quite a leap from 1966—fewer than six years earlier.

Fosse also carefully calibrated the way the Emcee's songs and sketches moved from spoofing the Nazis to mocking the Jews in if-you-can't-lick-'em-join-'em fashion. The Emcee, who had as many scruples as *Casablanca*'s Captain Renault, sang "She wouldn't look Jewish at all," referring to the gorilla with whom he had just danced.

This was the original lyric when *Cabaret* played its pre-Broadway tryout in Boston. Many thought it too severe, and to original Emcee Joel Grey's chagrin, the lyric became "She isn't a meeskite at all."

Some explanation: Herr Schultz, a character in the stage show, told a story at his engagement party about a meeskite—someone "ugly, funny-looking," as he translated from the Yiddish. Because Schultz and the song were cut from the film, the term couldn't have been used, anyway.

Essentially excised from the movie was Fraulein Schneider, to whom Herr Schultz was engaged. Seeing two seniors in love was endearing, and watching her eventually end the engagement because he was Jewish was heartbreaking. We had to admit, though, that her doing so was smart and prescient: Schneider feared the increasingly powerful Nazis.

The film instead offered a different couple: Natalia and Fritz, decades younger; here, she was the Jew and he the Christian—except that he wasn't; Fritz was a Jew who was trying to pass until he finally admitted the truth to his fiancée. They married, and film audiences feared for their future, while playgoers "only" had to worry about Schultz.

In the stage show, Sally worked hard at being eccentric and was overly pretentious when she was in the company of someone more important than she. The would-be star was still "self-centered and inconsiderate," as she fully admitted to Brian.

Screenwriter Jay Presson Allen retained all that, but also made Sally natively *nice*. When she saw that new neighbor Cliff needed help, she willingly dispensed it. Sally even got him work as a teacher and translator (and didn't charge him 10 percent). After the Nazis mercilessly beat him, she ministered to his wounds. She accepted him on his own bisexual terms, too.

The film relegated four songs from the Tony-winning score to background music. It added one old Kander and Ebb song ("Maybe This Time") and two new ones ("Mein Herr," "Money, Money"). And while Jill Haworth suffered at the pens of critics, Liza Minnelli is as of this writing the only Best Actress Oscar winner for a musical in which she didn't originate the role on stage.

This *Cabaret* played so fast and loose with the original property that it could be better termed a revisal.

WHAT FILM DID THE GREATEST DISSERVICE TO A BROADWAY MUSICAL?

On Broadway, *A Chorus Line* became Broadway's longest-running production until surpassed by *Cats*, which in turn was superseded by *The Phantom of the Opera*.

Yet as films, each was an artistic and financial disappointment.

For that matter, the longest-running off-Broadway show—*The Fantasticks*—wasn't a success on film, either.

Does that automatically put these four on the all-time worst list?

Not when we consider musical films from the early twentieth century. Back then, Hollywood dropped Broadway's songs as routinely as trees discard leaves in autumn.

Lady, Be Good (1941) retained only three songs; *Strike up the Band* (1940) and *Something for the Boys* (1944) kept merely the title tunes. As Denny Martin Flinn wrote in his 1997 book *Musicals! A Grand Tour*, "The Hollywood studios owned music publishing companies and could make more money by inserting their own songs. Thus Broadway scores often got dumped for financial, not artistic, reasons."

This practice turned around in the 1950s. Since then, a film of a musical has, for the most part, been basically faithful to the original stage production. The ones that turned out atrociously during that era and beyond are the ones we'll cite.

Bye Bye Birdie (1963). Screenwriter Irving Brecher played fast and loose with Michael Stewart's plot, turning Albert Peterson from a successful songwriter and would-be English teacher to an unsuccessful songwriter and budding biochemist.

Albert has concocted a super-amphetamine that can make a turtle speed across a room and into the night. (And if you believe that, I've got some Montana Chem stock I'd like to sell you . . .)

Brecher did make the film cinematic, for Albert's drug results in a Russian ballet troupe's dancing at breakneck speed so that *The Ed Sullivan Show* can give superstar Conrad Birdie time to give Kim McAfee one last kiss before he heads into the army.

The teen-friendly movie became the year's twelfth highest grossing film. It was a summer hit that gave adolescents their last bit of carefree innocence before the world crashed down upon them five months later with the assassination of John F. Kennedy.

The film critic for *Time* magazine said of Ann-Margret, "She doesn't convincingly play a fifteen-year-old. But she doesn't even try." True, Ann-Margret had already reached the age where she could drink in every state in the union. Yet she was so mesmerizing that many a fine, upstanding, patriotic, healthy normal American boy (and some girls) didn't care.

In 1995, *Bye Bye Birdie* became a television movie with Jason Alexander and Vanessa Williams. It was far more (if not totally) faithful to the original musical by restoring five songs that the film had excised. This is the one to see for an idea of what the musical was originally like.

Or drop by your local high school this weekend.

Annie. It's been filmed three times, and each iteration has done enough damage to make this list.

The 1982 attempt erred early on by filling the screen with too many orphans whom we couldn't possibly get to know. Better to have a mere seven as the stage show had.

The second blundered by having Kathy Bates' Miss Hannigan later pretend to be Annie's mother in order to collect the reward. Hadn't the mistaken identity ruse been done to violent death long before 1999? Annie's a smart kid, and she would see through Hannigan's not-very-obfuscating disguise.

As for the 2014 urban-centered remake, it works well enough on its own terms. But it's not *Annie*.

The King and I (1999). To all Yul Brynner and Deborah Kerr fans: calm down; notice the date. This is the animated film made at the turn of the century that turned many stomachs.

It's one thing to sing "I Whistle a Happy Tune" when danger could perhaps rear its head. But here, Anna had to sing it while a sea monster reared his.

The film made the Kralahome the villain who wanted to usurp the throne. That the king wasn't aware of this didn't speak well of his observational powers.

The Kralahome did have an advantage of a magic mirror, as the Evil Queen did in *Snow White*, as well as a sidekick who sounded like Ricky Ricardo. The poor soul seemingly endured as many painful accidents as the original production had Broadway performances (1,246). Kids were therefore taught that violence and pain are funny.

You know Rodgers and Hammerstein with their secondary couples. Here Tuptim, bound to service the king, is sought by a much older Prince Chulalongkorn. So now the threatened whipping happens when the king finds out that she's interested in his son. All right, but the line "This girl has hurt your vanity, not your heart" doesn't have the same meaning or power that it had in the original.

Because it was aimed at kids, there was no mention of polygamy—and no need to handle the musical this way.

Cats (2019). Tim Hooper's film has received an orchard's worth of rotten tomatoes. As of this writing, it has a 2.7 rating (out of ten) on imdb.com. (Even *A Chorus Line* more than doubles it at 6.2.)

One can understand Hooper's decision to cast stars. But *Cats* wisely had mostly unknowns in its cast during its eighteen-year Broadway run. Some knew Betty Buckley, yes, but most others had been in flop (*Don't Step on My Olive Branch*) after flop (*The Little Prince and the Aviator*) after flop (*Marlowe*). They'd played such roles as Conceited Man, Neighbor, and Passenger. Chances are that no theatergoer saw Rene Clemente and said "Oh! There's the guy we loved so much when he portrayed Jerome in *Play Me a Country Song!*"

So the comparative anonymity of the twenty-six on the Winter Garden stage helped to make these strangers in cat outfits and makeup look intriguing. Film audiences entered the theater knowing what James Corden, Judi Dench, Jennifer Hudson, Ian McKellen, and Taylor Swift looked like from hairline to chin. Thus as cats they appeared to have faces victimized by some horrifying nuclear accident that had also caused long, thin growths to spurt from their behinds.

On Broadway, John Napier's unit set amused with its oversized junkyard. The film's six designers instead give us an accurate London with an especially detailed Piccadilly Circus and Trafalgar Square. Seeing creatures we'd never seen roam around those familiar areas was jarring.

Yet another problem was that *Cats* takes place almost exclusively at night; most musicals, by their very nature, are sunny. The stage show compensated by having spotlights illuminate those who were singing and dancing. The film's lighting was constantly dark, almost as if London was anticipating the Blitz. The doom and gloom sapped the joy.

And there *is* joy in much of Andrew Lloyd Webber's music and T. S. Eliot's "lyrics." Once *Cats* survived less-than-love letters from the Broadway critics and still became a blazingly hot ticket, the envious backlash soon began. *Saturday Night Live* made "It's better than *Cats*" into a cliché that people still semi-sarcastically say when giving something faint praise. When one takes the film into consideration, almost everything is better than *Cats*.

Author's Choice: *Fanny* (1961), *Mexican Hayride* (1948), and *Lock up Your Daughters* (1969) in a three-way tie. They all dropped their stage scores and ceased being musicals. The best that audiences could hope for was an occasional melody as background music.

Dishonorable Mention goes to *Irma La Douce* (1963), for which director and co-writer Billy Wilder preserved only one song for Shirley MacLaine. The picture won one Oscar—for "Best Music, Scoring of Music, Adaptation or Treatment" of many of the songs from the musical that were used as background music. Doesn't that suggest that they were worth keeping in toto?

WHAT REVILED FILM VERSIONS OF MUSICALS DID AT LEAST HAVE ONE SAVING GRACE?

The Boys from Syracuse (1940). On stage, this musical version of Shakespeare's *The Comedy of Errors* had a disillusioned wife realize that her "Falling in Love with Love" has resulted in a terribly disappointing marriage.

In the film, a man who's finally found the ideal woman sings the song. Then why does he sing to his beloved "Falling in love with love is falling for make believe . . . playing the fool . . . juvenile fancy . . . I was unwise with eyes unable to see"?

Screenwriter Charles Grayson also took the much-too-easy way out by using more anachronisms than Chad Beguelin did in *Aladdin*. The king's palace is mistaken for the Palace Theatre. A war hero is shown singing autographs. Such colloquialisms as "ain't," "oomph," and "wacky" are included as are "chocolate malted" and "pinochle." Then-famous gossip columnist Walter Winchell's opening catchphrase "Good evening, Mr. and Mrs. America from border to border and coast to coast and all the ships at sea" was part of the mix, too.

A woman involved in a chariot race sticks out her left arm before making a left turn. It's what automobile drivers did before directional signals were invented, but the practice was not in place in BC—"Before Cars."

Its saving grace: Despite missing too many Rodgers and Hart songs, it did take advantage of film's ability to split a screen. Because the plot involves not one but two sets of identical twins, Allan Jones could be cast as both leads and Joe Penner as both sidekicks. No stage show could ever find actors so close in appearance that the other characters would genuinely mistake one for the other.

My Sister Eileen (1955). *Wonderful Town*, the Tony-winning musical version of *My Sister Eileen* was never made into a film—only a TV special. There is a musical film of *My Sister Eileen* called *My Sister Eileen*, but it has a completely different score.

Harry Cohn, the head of Columbia Pictures, wanted to bring *Wonderful Town* to the screen as a vehicle for Judy Holliday. The money that producer Robert Fryer demanded struck Cohn as exorbitant.

Because Columbia had produced the original 1942 film, Cohn had the right to musicalize the original play. He hired *Gentlemen Prefer Blondes*' composer Jule Styne and lyricist Leo Robin, who had a fascinating and formidable task ahead of them. A lawyer was hired to ensure that they didn't impinge on what Leonard Bernstein, Betty Comden, and Adolph Green had provided for their hit. Styne and Robin were actually forbidden to write songs in the same spots that *Wonderful Town* had already taken.

Its saving grace: The Styne-Robin songs are very good, too. In this era where musicals have less dialogue and more songs, how about a revival that includes *both* scores?

Jacques Brel Is Alive and Well and Living in Paris (1975). The description on imdb.com makes one wary: "Three attendees at a puppet theater don various roles in order to sing a variety of songs by Jacques Brel, all while hippies and other eccentrics cavort about them."

Sounds somewhere between awful and crazy, no? Director Denis Heroux even had a scene where original cast member Elly Stone sang "Sons" in front of three men hanging on crosses, in "tribute" (?) to Jesus Christ and the two thieves.

Its saving grace: Those who didn't see *Jacques Brel* on stage and only knew its original cast album missed the magnificent song "The Statue."

A bronze sculpture of a soldier in uniform comes to life and sets us straight on who he was when he was alive. He corrects the inscriptions on the base starting with "He lived all his life between honor and virtue" to admit that he "screwed all my friends," "cheated every mistress," and "lied with each caress."

As for the inscription "God calls back the ones He loves and he was the one God loved the most," the statue admits he "only prayed to God when my teeth were killing me."

Finally the statue addresses "He died like a hero; he was a soldier brave and true" by rebutting that "he went off to war to make it with the German broads." That statement is now politically incorrect, but otherwise the reality of what the statue is saying is often correct.

Rent **(2005).** This was greatly criticized for filming much of the original Broadway cast eight long years after they'd debuted the Pulitzer Prize–winning musical.

All those twentysomethings—Taye Diggs (Benny), Wilson Jermaine Heredia (Angel), Jesse L. Martin (Tom), Adam Pascal (Angel), and Anthony Rapp (Mark)—were now thirtysomethings.

Of course, one could look at the situation another way. Those who live hardscrabble lives in the East Village age fast.

The show that cried "No day but today" may well have had its day. Many millennials now criticize these characters who believe they shouldn't be required to pay rent, that they can just take over a restaurant and have no concern for the waiter conscripted to serve them.

Even Dolores Dante would rebel.

Its saving grace: Mark's mother, heard on many answering machine messages in the stage show, seemed silly and clueless. That seemed wrong for a Baby Boomer who'd undoubtedly been annoyed and frustrated by her own mother and father; presumably, she wouldn't make the same mistakes.

Luckily, these messages were kept to a bare minimum in the film.

Author's Choice: *A Chorus Line* **(1985).** Denny Martin Flinn in his 1997 book *Musicals! A Grand Tour* called this "the worst film of a great Broadway musical. Ever."

Director Richard Attenborough's imperative to open it up instead opened a can of worms. In his need to show exterior shots of the theater as well as cast members picking up boater hats from a box and other irrelevancies, songs were shortened. Particularly eviscerated was "Hello Twelve, Hello Thirteen, Hello Love," reduced to a very few lines.

Its saving grace: Arnold Schulman did address an issue that made us say, "Hey, why didn't Michael Bennett, James Kirkwood, or even Nicholas Dante think of that?"

In the stage show, Cassie is immediately seen as one of many dancers who's auditioning. Considering that at this point Zach truly believes he'd never hire her, why did he allow her to even step on stage?

Schulman instead has Cassie arrive late to the audition. When Zach sees her, he makes clear he doesn't want her. Luckily, Cassie has an ally in ol' friend Larry, who's Zach's assistant. He'll see what he can do to ameliorate matters. Larry does, and that more convincing scenario gives Cassie her chance.

WHAT'S THE BEST SONG ADDED TO THE FILM VERSION OF A BROADWAY MUSICAL?

"Bye Bye Birdie" (*Bye Bye Birdie*, **1963).** Who can ever forget Ann-Margret confidently walking toward the camera and delivering this pre-Beatles rock tune to a most appreciative audience?

She even made us not notice the inherently silly lyric "Your super-duper class." No, "super-duper" isn't an adjective one associates with "class."

The song is such great fun, however, that it's been interpolated in one way or another in every revival as well as the 1995 Jason Alexander–Vanessa Williams television movie.

"Something Good" (*The Sound of Music*, **1965).** "Three Blind Mice" would be better than "An Ordinary Couple," easily the most dreary song that Rodgers and Hammerstein ever wrote.

"Money, Money" (*Cabaret*, **1972**). "Sitting Pretty," the original song in this spot, was a good one indeed for the Emcee. This one's better—and not just because of a superior John Kander melody and Fred Ebb lyric, or because Liza Minnelli joins the number.

What seals the deal is the innovative staging that Bob Fosse provided in his almost-Oscar-winning film. Once the song goes into a round, with the Emcee echoing what Sally sang a second before, the repetition doesn't just extend to the music and lyrics, but to the gestures as well.

Sam Mendes and Rob Marshall snatched this one up for their 1998 and 2014 Broadway revivals. No fools they.

"Sign" (*Annie*, **1982**). What a good idea for Miss Hannigan (Carol Burnett) and Daddy Warbucks (Albert Finney) to have a song together. Her ill-advised attempt at seducing the Great Bald Pate doesn't yield the results she wants, but the nifty new Charles Strouse–Martin Charnin song certainly scores.

Author's Choice: "That's Entertainment" (*The Band Wagon*, **1953**). In a way, this one shouldn't count, because film retains little more than the title of the 1931 stage revue. Nevertheless, what a quintessentially wonderful melody and lyric that reiterates that the world is indeed a stage and the stage is indeed a world of entertainment.

Fred Astaire, Nanette Fabray, Jack Buchanan, and Oscar Levant have a great time singing it. Notice, however, that Levant leaves the song once dancing is required.

OF THOSE WHO REPEATED THEIR STAGE PERFORMANCES ON FILM, WHO ADAPTED BEST TO THE SCREEN?
Sad to say, this list can't include Julie Andrews in *My Fair Lady*, Angela Lansbury in *Mame*, or Ethel Merman in *Gypsy*. Less capable performers usurped their iconic stage roles.

Some musical theater performers did get the lucky opportunity to show the nation and the world why they'd received Tonys or sustained applause for creating some memorable musical performances.

In determining the best, let's split them into four categories to give as many performers as possible their due. Yet the lists that follow are hardly comprehensive. Who today can tell us if Fred Astaire was as good on film as he was on stage in (the highly reworked) *The Gay Divorce* or *The Band Wagon?* Ditto Irving Berlin (*This Is the Army*) and Helen Morgan and Charles Winninger (*Show Boat*)?

We know that film welcomed Bert Lahr and Jack Haley in *The Wizard of Oz*, but did they respectively lose anything when replicating their performances in *Follow Thru* and *Flying High?*

As for the others . . .

What Leading Man Best Replicated His Stage Role on Film?

Robert Preston (*The Music Man*, 1962). We always hear that many musicals' stage stars are "too big" for a screen. (Case in point: Lauren Bacall and her disgracefully over-the-*mountain*-top performance in the television version of *Applause*).

By the time Preston did the film of his breakthrough stage hit, he had been a veteran of thirty-two films and three dozen television appearances, so he knew how to work the camera. Those Iowans may have had trouble in River City, but Preston had none at all.

Rex Harrison (*My Fair Lady*, 1964). He'd portrayed Henry Higgins in the original production, won a Tony, and by the time he repeated his role in the film, he'd played the part more than a thousand times. Some critics have said that he looks bored in the film, but enough Oscar voters must have disagreed, for he did win the Academy Award.

(No, it was the 1981 Broadway revival where he seemed utterly bored.)

Tim Curry (*The Rocky Horror Picture Show*, 1975). Here's one of the reasons why so many or those midnight audiences returned and returned and returned (with or without fishnet stockings).

John Cameron Mitchell (*Hedwig and the Angry Inch*, 2001). Every inch of him was angry, not just the damaged part. If you've ever mentored someone who met success, eclipsed yours, and then dumped you, then you will share Hedwig's pain.

Author's Choice: Yul Brynner (*The King and I*, 1957). He was the first musical performer to win both the Tony and the Poor Man's Tony for the same role.

Well, shouldn't the Oscar be called "The Poor Man's Tony"? After all, even IMAX movies only cost a fraction of what a Broadway musical demands.

WHAT LEADING ACTRESS BEST REPLICATED HER STAGE ROLE ON FILM?

Ethel Waters (*Cabin in the Sky*, 1943). Cinemascope wasn't formally introduced to the public until 1953, but you'd think that it was well in place ten years earlier when you see Waters' wide smile.

As Petunia Jackson, she gives it early and often as the type of earth mother who makes Earth a better place. Each time her husband Joe succumbs to gambling and womanizing, she looks to heaven and talks to God. Tevye does, too, but Petunia's sense of devotion suggests that He listens to her more.

Still, matters become bleaker when a younger and svelter Georgia Brown seduces Joe. Petunia must demand of God, "Why do you let me love him so much when he can hurt me so bad?" Waters delivers the line not seeking pity but an explanation.

When the two women meet, Georgia is frank in detailing the reasons why she's the more desirable woman. "I was just speaking my mind," she asserts, to which Petunia answers, "And I ain't heard a sound." Waters shows she knows that underplaying the crack will get a bigger laugh from the audience.

Just when we think that she can "only" act and sing superbly (especially in the title song and the one that became a hit—"Takin' a Chance on Love"), Waters astonishes us with her dancing. That she jitterbugs so easily is one thing; that she can lift her leg so high it's a wonder that she doesn't hit her forehead with it.

But it's not the only wonder in Ethel Waters' performance.

Judy Holliday (*Bells Are Ringing*, 1960). Having one of the best opening numbers ("It's a Perfect Relationship") and one of the best eleven o'clock numbers ("I'm Goin' Back") certainly helps. However, the right performer has to do them—and the right performer did.

Most telling is that Holliday won the Best Actress in a Musical Tony over Julie Andrews in *My Fair Lady*—a musical that would run almost three times as long as Holliday's substantial hit. In the film, Holliday is just as impressive in singing, dancing, and conveying the script's substantial humor.

And yet, the moment that shows her inner beauty comes when she's asked why she cares so much about getting Jeffrey Moss' life back on track. She's so down to earth in her unapologetic explanation: "He needs a mother."

Barbra Streisand (*Funny Girl*, 1968). Sure, she played around with Jule Styne's music, improvising a note here and there, occasionally holding it longer. It was just part and parcel of her confidence, which was extraordinary for a film rookie.

Gwen Verdon (*Damn Yankees*, 1957). She had much more than just a little brains and a little talent. What a thrill to see her in the midst of "Whatever Lola Wants" when she takes that arms-akimbo stance that we've seen on the cover of the cast album and makes it come to life.

Author's Choice: Ellen Greene (*Little Shop of Horrors*, 1986). At the start, Greene made Audrey cartoonish, which was actually a good choice. If she'd been realistic, we couldn't get behind such a self-loathing individual who gives herself to a sadist.

Happily, Audrey begins to respect herself when Seymour names his plant in her honor. She's so overwhelmed that her attempt to say "Thank you" comes out as a squeak. Yet her confidence builds and builds, reaching her apotheosis in "Suddenly Seymour."

But did the authors really need to have her complete suicide?

WHO BEST REPRISED HER ROLE AS BEST SUPPORTING ACTRESS?

Shannon Bolin (*Damn Yankees*, 1957). Now that Meg Boyd has been abandoned by her husband, she takes a shine to her new young border Joe Hardy, unaware that he *is* her husband.

The care and concern that she shows for him makes her as much a mentor as surrogate mother.

Juanita Hall (*Flower Drum Song*, 1962). She shows a great deal of love for her sister's husband and two nephews, even when she doesn't agree with any of them. What pride she takes in attaining citizenship, and what dignity she shows throughout.

Carol Haney (*The Pajama Game*, 1957). Could Shirley MacLaine have possibly done it better?

Kay Medford (*Funny Girl*, 1968). Even with the part whittled down from Broadway, Medford managed an Oscar nomination. Had the film not dropped two stage songs in which she played a prominent part— "Who Taught Her Everything?" and "Find Yourself a Man"—might she have won?

Author's Choice: Bea Arthur (*Mame*, 1974). After Ms. Dennis mentions how she and Vera once appeared in a show's ensemble, Arthur says "I was never in the chorus" *not* with flat-out braying outrage that a lesser actress would have chosen. Instead, Arthur expresses a low-key mixture of calm surprise that Mame could ever make such a mistake.

After Mame ruins Vera's opening night in New Haven, note how Arthur handles the curtain call. She takes center stage, acts as if nothing had gone wrong, bows in dignified you-are-too-kind fashion and pretends that she'd just had an unparalleled triumph.

WHO BEST REPRISED HIS ROLE AS BEST SUPPORTING ACTOR?

Paul Lynde (*Bye Bye Birdie*, 1963). His facial expressions, ranging from outrage to maniacal, could be more appreciated via close-ups on the screen than from the balcony of the Martin Beck.

Stanley Holloway (*My Fair Lady*, 1964). His Alfred P. Doolittle is especially funny when he explodes with laughter right in Professor Higgins' face, unaware that his breath might not be the sweetest.

Jack Gilford (*A Funny Thing Happened on the Way to the Forum*, 1966). After Philia, resident of the best little whorehouse in Rome, states that she's a virgin, how supercilious Gilford is with both his smile and delivery of "Of course . . ."

Howard DaSilva (*1776*, 1972). We didn't hear him on the cast album, because he was hospitalized on the day of the recording. Getting the chance to hear—and see—what he did on stage was a treat.

Author's Choice: Joel Grey (*Cabaret*, 1972). Yet another Tony winner who followed it with a Poor Man's Tony. Some stage actors look uneasy when the camera is on them; not Grey.

ON THE OTHER HAND, WHO REPLACED A STAGE PERFORMED ON FILM AND YET SCORED MIGHTILY?

We're not saying that all listed here eclipsed the Broadway originals; some did, some didn't. But these performers were damn good.

WHO WAS THE BEST ACTOR TO ASSUME A ROLE?

Fred Astaire (*Silk Stockings*, 1957). Thank you, MGM and Arthur Freed, for not taking Don Ameche's phone calls. The way Astaire croons "Paris Loves Lovers" and suavely contributes to "Stereophonic Sound" seals the deal. He makes this the only soundtrack album that's better than the original cast album.

Dean Martin (*Bells Are Ringing*, 1960). The singer was infamous for doing one take and one take alone. If that was the case on this film, he didn't need more than one.

Martin portrayed a playwright who'd had success in partnership that had recently ended. In his real own life, only three years earlier Martin and Lewis—as in Jerry—dissolved their partnership most acrimoniously. Because Lewis got all the punch lines and laughs, straight man Martin was considered the lesser talent of the two.

Under these circumstances, Martin's willingness to say the line "What's the use? I'll never make it alone" was remarkable.

James Shigeta (*Flower Drum Song*). Different people are different people to different people. Shigeta showed us that he was at once sensitive and smart in helping immigrant Mei Lei, and a clueless little boy when dealing with the ultra-sophisticated Linda Low, who could make him do almost anything.

Author's Choice: Victor Garber (*Godspell*, 1973). As Jesus Christ, he radiated a serenity and spirituality that many would expect from Him. For many of us, it was the first time we saw this actor who'd we'd see for more than forty years in what might have even been forty roles.

WHO WAS THE BEST ACTRESS TO ASSUME A LEADING ROLE?

Marilyn Monroe (*Gentlemen Prefer Blondes*, 1953). One can understand why Gus Edmond would be more entranced with this Lorelei Lee than with Carol Channing's . . .

Doris Day (*The Pajama Game*, 1957). To paraphrase a Sondheim lyric, 101 minutes of Doris Day. She bettered Janis Paige, whose performance on the original cast album reveals vocal difficulties.

Petula Clark (*Finian's Rainbow*, 1968). Here was a breath of fresh air compared to Broadway's Ella Logan, who had a most mannered and phony "Aren't-I-special?" one-trick-jackass delivery.

Susan Sarandon (*The Rocky Horror Picture Show*, 1975). Considering that all five of her Oscar nominations (and one win) were the result of dramatic roles, we might assume that Sarandon might not have done her own singing.

Indeed she did, in a much better performance than the one delivered onstage by Abigale Haness. (Who?)

Author's Choice: Liza Minnelli (*Cabaret*, 1972). You've heard that Sally wasn't supposed to be a good entertainer. Well, this Sally was, and certainly the Oscar voters didn't mind.

WHO WAS THE BEST ACTOR TO ASSUME A SUPPORTING ROLE?

Sammy Davis, Jr. (*Sweet Charity*, 1969). "The Rhythm of Life," about a jazz-infused evangelist, benefits from his soulful presence. His vocalizing and scatting near the end makes it no contest compared to the original Broadway performer.

Davis also profited from Peter Stone's new lines when he addressed his congregation: "Thou shalt dig thou neighbor as thou should have him dig you . . . thou shalt not put down thy mammas and pappas . . . thou shalt not swing with another cat's chick."

Or to put it another way, the more things change, the more that a rose by any other name stays the same.

John Cullum (*1776*, 1972). Edward Rutledge, the delegate from South Carolina at the Continental Congress, for most of the show agrees with John Dickinson, the delegate of Pennsylvania. Both believe there should not be a United States of America, but for different reasons. Dickinson wants to be loyal to the crown; Rutledge wants to maintain slavery, and substantiates it through the galvanizing "Molasses to Rum." Here all Cullum's experience on stage as a singer and actor served him well.

Barry Bostwick (*The Rocky Horror Picture Show*, 1975). There's always the temptation to playing a naïve character as merely stupid. Bostwick's Brad Majors is simply a small-town guy who hasn't got out much. That'll change, that'll change . . .

Michael Jackson (*The Wiz*, 1978). The charming young teen showed a sense of wonder in creating a tender Scarecrow some years before he began his rendezvous with propofol, benzodiazepine, and alleged questionable behavior.

Author's Choice: Donald O'Connor (*Call Me Madam*, 1953). After he astonishes in a dazzling dance with Vera-Ellen, he tops it with the second-greatest solo number of his career. Only his "Make 'Em Laugh" in *Singin' in the Rain* betters "What Chance Have I with Love?" To see him dance around a balloon-filled stage and, thanks to spikes embedded in his shoes, pop thirty-six of them in thirty-nine seconds is utterly amazing.

Who Was the Best Actress to Assume a Supporting Role?
Rita Moreno (*West Side Story*, 1961). This is the film that set her on the way to getting a TOGE.

What's a TOGE, you ask? It's an acronym that acknowledges winning at least one Tony, Oscar, Grammy, and Emmy.

(Some people call it an EGOT. But why should the Tony be listed last?)

Chita Rivera (*Sweet Charity*, 1969). Needless to say, we first and foremost think of her as a dancer. But here she gets her greatest screen opportunity to show her comic skills. For after she's led to believe that Charity has become engaged ("Honey, all the luck in the world!") and is told the so-called beau threw her in the lake and stole her money, she easily makes the adjustment to bray "He wasn't for you."

Diana Rigg (*A Little Night Music*, 1977). This movie takes more heat than could be found in Mrs. Lovett's oven, but Rigg's a marvel as Countess Charlotte Malcolm. She knows her husband is cheating on her—yes, that much seems clear, for he's blatant about it—but she holds onto her dignity by laughing—no, chuckling—at the situation. Hence, she only lets a lock of her hair down when singing "Every Day a Little Death" while trying to survive.

Queen Latifah (*Chicago*, 2002). She's Matron Mama Morton, The Keeper of the Keys, the Countess of the Clink, and The Mistress of Murderers Row. Latifah makes her sweet as sugar when she speaks while letting us know she's not even dispensing saccharine. What a decided smirk she gives when Roxie asks her if where she'll be incarcerated will be a little nicer.

And fifty dollars for a phone call? That's $809 in today's money. And yet, Latifah makes her demand seem more like a reasonable request—all from a character whose heart is as black as Bette Davis' red dress in *Jezebel*.

Author's Choice: Catherine Zeta-Jones (*Chicago*, 2002). Too bad that Bob Fosse didn't live to see her Velma Kelly. He would have enjoyed seeing her arms move like legs and her legs move like arms. In the "Hot Honey Rag" finale, he, just like us, would probably watch her more than Renee Zellweger.

Zeta-Jones acts the part, too, initially imperious with Roxie, holding her cigarette in the air as if it were a scepter. After Roxie says "I hate you," what a delicious delivery she gives to Bill Condon's excellent line: "There's only one business in the world where that's no problem at all."

WHO WAS THE MOST MISCAST IN A FILM VERSION OF A BROADWAY MUSICAL?

Douglas MacPhail (*Babes in Arms*, 1939). Teenagers who were sent to a work farm because their parents were touring in vaudeville took matters into their own hands. "They call us babes in arms," went the Lorenz Hart lyric. "But we are babes in armor."

The most logical performer to sing this sentiment would be Mickey Rooney, then eighteen, or Judy Garland, a year younger. No: twenty-five-year-old MacPhail, clad in a very adult suit, tie, and vest (and the tallest of the dozens of "babes" seen marching through town), sings it. And for a babe, his voice is pretty deep.

Frank Sinatra (*Can-Can*, 1960). Ol' Blue Eyes as a nineteenth-century French lawyer? He looked ridiculous in court, clad in a period-appropriate long robe and wearing one of those *bonnets carrés* on his head.

Moreover, Sinatra's adding his then-famous catchphrase of "Ring-a-ding-ding" didn't suggest Montmartre.

During the filming of *Can-Can*, then–Soviet Union premier Nikita Khrushchev visited the set. He was said to have been infuriated at the decadence shown when male dancers dove under the female can-can dancers' skirts and emerged with their panties in hand.

Perhaps Khrushchev was actually enraged by what he saw of Sinatra.

Barbra Streisand (*Hello, Dolly!*, 1969). Dolly Levi should have walks-around-the-block age on her, so we can feel her urgency of having one last chance at marriage (and even love). That poignancy was lost with a Dolly who hadn't even reached thirty.

In a way, casting Streisand may have been worth it, for the soundtrack album lets us forget that she's too young and instead allows us to enjoy a major star's distinctive take on Jerry Herman's marvelous songs.

Lucille Ball (*Mame*, 1974). When Jerry Herman first saw the film and noted that Ball had often been photographed after Vaseline had been slathered on the camera lens, he may well have rethought a lyric that he'd written for *Hello, Dolly!*

"Things look almost twice as well when they're slightly blurry."

Diana Ross (*The Wiz*, 1978). Mentor Berry Gordy wanted Stephanie Mills, that four-foot-nine-inch bundle of dynamite, to re-create her Broadway Dorothy. After all, she'd only aged from sixteen to eighteen.

Ross, despite being a third-of-a-century old, wanted the part. Gordy refused. So Call-Her-Miss-Ross went to Rob Cohen, an executive at Universal. She promised that he could produce the film on the condition that he green-light her as the green-skinned witch's foe.

Cohen agreed, which caused the opposite problem that had plagued *Hello, Dolly!* A young Dorothy would be scared by much of what she sees in Oz, yes, but she would also have a sense of wonder that would somewhat ameliorate it.

An older person has become more aware of the dangers in life. So Ross's Dorothy was well within her rights to whimper and shed tears of fear when encountering strange Ozian creatures.

Screenwriter Joel Schumacher does get credit, though, for setting *The Wiz* in New York; it is, after all, the Emerald City to many. The downside was a scene in a subway where a rat ran across a platform.

Or so it seemed. A closer examination revealed that it was Toto.

Author's Choice: Vic Damone (*Kismet*, 1955). Giving a pop singer the chance to act in a musical movie has its dangers. Damone couldn't shed his Brooklyn background when pretending to be Baghdad royalty.

He was as wooden as the walls of a suburban basement (or as Ed Sullivan in *Bye Bye Birdie*). If Carlotta Campion had been on the set during filming, she undoubtedly would have said to Damone, "You should have gone to an acting school—that seems clear."

WHAT MOVIE OF A MUSICAL DO YOU MOST WISH COULD HAVE BEEN MADE?

St. Louis Woman. In 1953, MGM musical legend Arthur Freed planned to bring the 1946 Harold Arlen–Johnny Mercer score to the screen.

Freed did not, however, invite original bookwriters Arna Bontemps and Countee Cullen to write the screenplay. Instead he turned to Fred F. Finklehoffe, who'd co-authored the smash hit comedy *Brother Rat* and followed it with a modest musical success, the generically titled *Show Time.*

He did three separate drafts of *St. Louis Woman* at the same time when he was entertaining the notion of returning as a Broadway librettist with *Ankles Aweigh*, which he'd co-produce as well.

St. Louis Woman didn't happen, and *Ankles Aweigh* never should have. On the back cover of its cast album, the liner notes start "Things happen so fast in *Ankles Aweigh*—plot, music and lyrics are so rapidly paced and tightly integrated—that a synopsis is difficult."

Translation: sound and fury signifying nothing.

"Anyone who goes to a show with a name like that has been suf-ficiently warned" (Watts, *New York Post*). Brooks Atkinson of the *New York Times* employed such adjectives as *destitute, mechanical, foolish*, and *hackneyed* as well as the phrase *no talent*.

Finklehoffe was married to Ella (*Finian's Rainbow*) Logan when he started working on *Ankles Aweigh*, but they were divorced by the time it opened in 1955. Could this musical have been a bone of contention that led to the split?

No Strings. Diahann Carroll, who tied with Anna Maria (*Carnival*) Alberghetti for the 1962 Best Actress in a Musical Tony, was livid when she heard that Warner Brothers wanted to give her role to Nancy Kwan, fresh off *Flower Drum Song*.

Carroll felt that the show made a potent statement about racism and civil rights at a time when those issues were vital. Indeed, the Richard Rodgers–Samuel Taylor musical centered on Barbara, a Black, and David, a Caucasian; their relationship didn't cause problems for them or anyone else while they were living in progressive Paris.

However, when David wanted to marry and return to his home state of Maine, Barbara knew that she wouldn't be welcomed there. She decided that they'd best separate with no strings attached.

Actually, at the time, any kind of interracial relationship in such a conservative state would have made the same statement. So an Asian woman would have equally suited the script's purpose. Yet it wasn't Car-roll's ire (often called considerable) that scuttled the picture; the studio simply lost interest in a musical that had only been a soft hit.

Had they proceeded with the leading man they were seeking, we would have heard William Holden sing. Or would we have? Bill Lee, often called "The Male Marni Nixon," might have been pressed into service.

Follies. If we had a buck for every time this one's been bandied about, we could buy premium seats for *Hamilton*.

Sunset Boulevard. If we all live long enough, we just might see this. It could have already happened if people had just let Streisand do it when she first wanted to instead of wasting time arguing whether she was too old. Now she certainly is.

Author's Choice: *She Loves Me.* Wouldn't you think that after Julie Andrews and Dick Van Dyke showed such chemistry, star power, and box office pull in *Mary Poppins* that MGM would have made this happen?

In 1967, Hal Prince, who'd staged the 1963 musical on Broadway, was signed to direct. By 1969, Blake Edwards was named to succeed him.

That he was now Andrews' husband might be a reason why.

Alas, at the time, MGM's fortunes weren't fortunate, so new president Kirk Kerkorian limited production to a mere five films a year. With all those late 1960s musical films failing, *She Loves Me* wasn't high on Kerkorian's list. But couldn't he see that a musical with Julie Andrews could have turned the tide?

Kerkorian's face eventually wound up on an Armenian postage stamp. For not green-lighting *She Loves Me*, let's make sure that he's never on one of ours.

What Was the Best Song to Be Cut from the Musical's Film Version?

"A Bushel and a Peck" (*Guys and Dolls*, 1955). By the time that the film was released, Frank Loesser's song had seen two recordings of it make the top twenty.

So why drop such a popular song, one that could have been another drawing card for the picture? Its replacement, "Pet Me, Poppa" certainly didn't help.

"Guess Who I Saw Today?" (*New Faces*, 1954). In fact, the woman singing this song "saw two people at the bar who were so much in love that even I could spot it clear across the room."

One was her husband.

This was the one and only song from *New Faces of 1952* that received a multitude of recordings. We can't guess why it was dropped.

"We Beseech Thee" (*Godspell*, **1973**). Of the many joyous songs in Stephen Schwartz's debut musical, this was arguably the best. Perhaps the fact that there *were* so many joyous songs, the inclination was to go plaintive.

So in came "Beautiful City," with the positive sentiment: "Out of the ruins and rubble, out of the smoke, out of our night of struggle, can we see a ray of hope?"

Luckily for audiences, virtually all revivals of *Godspell* now use *both* songs. It's not a case of an embarrassment of riches but a feast instead.

"To Break in a Glove" (*Dear Evan Hansen*, **2016**). Now that his son Connor has completed suicide, Mr. Murphy wants Evan to have his "best friend's" baseball glove. It went unused when Connor was alive, so it needs some seasoning to get it in shape.

"You might not think it's worth it," sings Mr. Murphy. "You might begin to doubt. But you can't take any shortcuts; you gotta stick it out. And it's the hard way, but it's the right way."

They're words that serve as a metaphor on how Evan might get through the mess that he's inadvertently caused.

Author's Choice: "The Music That Makes Me Dance" (*Funny Girl*, **1968**). Finally all those people who said, "How can you do a musical about Fanny Brice and not include 'My Man'?!?!" got what they wanted.

Some of it, anyway. Brice's famous 1921 trademark song wasn't performed as it had been done originally. Here the unfortunate lyric "He beats me, too" was wisely omitted.

If they'd use the superior song from the stage show, they wouldn't have to make the cut.

What Musical Endured the Most Unnecessary Censorship by Hollywood?

"Stereophonic Sound" (*Silk Stockings*, **1957**). Janice Dayton is telling how this new technological marvel has taken over films—that sound has become more important than the pictures seen on the screen: "If Ava

Gardner played Godiva riding on a mare," she sang, "the people wouldn't pay a cent to see her in the bare."

The line was reassigned to Fred Astaire in the film, who had to sing "the people wouldn't pay a cent; they wouldn't even care."

Where it came to Hollywood, Cole Porter was too darn hot.

"I'm Not at All in Love" (*The Pajama Game*, **1957**). Babe, responding to her co-workers accusations that she's taken with the new foreman, originally sang, "All you gotta do is be polite to him, and they got you spending the night with him."

But film audiences would hear Babe sing, "All you gotta do, it seems, is work for him, and they've got you going berserk for him."

Let's turn to "There Once Was a Man," which had Babe insist that she loved Sid "more than a dope fiend loves his dope." That was in the stage show and *that* stayed in the film. Hollywood apparently had no problem in mentioning drugs, but citing sex was out of the question.

"Quintet" (*West Side Story*, **1961**). Anita is looking forward to her night with Bernardo. On stage, Chita Rivera sang, "He'll walk in hot and tired. So what? Don't matter if he's tired—as long as he's hot."

In the film, Rita Moreno sang, "He'll walk in hot and tired—poor dear. Don't matter if he's tired—as long as he's here."

What a loss for filmgoers to be denied Sondheim's clever use of the word "hot" in two completely different contexts. Anita first meant "hot" as "sweaty" and later "hot" meant "sexually charged."

To the censors, we give a hearty "Krup you!"

Stop the World—I Want to Get Off (**1966**). Once Evie told Littlechap that she was with child, he felt he had to marry her. Given that history, years later when his daughter told him that she was getting married, Littlechap sincerely said, "Really? I didn't even know you were pregnant."

That got a hearty laugh from the audience. That same moment wouldn't receive the same response from filmgoers who heard, "Really? I didn't even know you were engaged."

Author's Choice: "Too Darn Hot" (*Kiss Me, Kate*, 1953). Cole Porter had to change "According to the Kinsey Report" to "According to the *latest* report." Otherwise, the moviegoing public in the Eisenhower Era would have been reminded that homosexuality existed.

WHAT FILM OFFERS THE MOST UNEXPECTED REFERENCE TO BROADWAY MUSICALS?

How to Murder Your Wife **(1965).** Terry-Thomas stands on a roof garden on 54th Street and Sixth Avenue telling us about the perils of marriage. In the background, the Ziegfeld Theatre—not the 1969–2016 movie palace, but the actual showplace that Florenz Ziegfeld built in 1927—is behind him to his right.

And what's playing there? Nothing, of course. And because that was too often the case, the theater was razed in 1966.

The Manchurian Candidate **(1962).** When Frank Sinatra rushes out of Jilly's (his favorite New York restaurant) on West 52nd Street, the Alvin Theatre's marquee shows *New Faces of 1962*.

Given that Leonard Sillman's penultimate Broadway revue was in residence for only the month of February, we can almost pinpoint the day of this filming.

Pat and Mike **(1952).** That we see the marquee of *Two on the Aisle*, the Comden-Green-Styne revue at the Mark Hellinger Theatre, is reward enough. But there's an extra bonus here.

The marquee is on Broadway. Back then, the Hellinger had a lobby entrance there in addition to the one we know at 237 West 51st Street. The office building atop the Broadway entrance eventually appropriated it.

And we all know who appropriated the Hellinger itself . . .

The Producers **(1968).** Among the doctored and defaced window cards festooned in Max Bialystock's office are three musicals from 1964—*Café Crown, Foxy,* and *Something More!*—and one from 1965: *La Grosse Valise*.

And yet, what's the one that says *Alice with Kisses*?

It was a musical version of *Alice in Wonderland* that played at the 41st Street Theatre for a week or so of previews in 1964, but never opened.

The director was Joseph L. Blankenship.

The choreographer was Joseph L. Blankenship.

The book and lyrics were by Joseph L. Blankenship.

One of the two composers was Joseph L. Blankenship.

One of the two producers was Joseph L. Blankenship.

Who did this guy think he was? Peter Allen?

Author's Choice: *The Graduate* (1967). Despite the obscurity of those discussed, the all-time champ is found in this classic.

After Benjamin has humiliated Mrs. Robinson's daughter Elaine by taking her into a tawdry strip club, she runs out to rid herself of this woefully insensitive creep. Benjamin now feels guilty and chases and catches up with her.

As he tries to apologize and soothe her, behind them is a three-sheet advertising *Mouche*—the French word for *Fly* and, inexplicably, the name chosen for the Paris production of *Carnival*.

Those who have a Blu-ray copy of the film will be able to see bookwriter Michael Stewart and songwriter Bob Merrill's names on the poster.

Where did they *ever* find *this*?

CHAPTER SEVEN

Two Last Questions

WHOSE FOUR FACES WOULD YOU PUT ON A MUSICAL THEATER MOUNT RUSHMORE?

Indeed, who *are* musical theater's George Washington, Thomas Jefferson, Theodore Roosevelt, and Abraham Lincoln?

In the early 1920s, Gutzon Borglum only had thirty presidents from which to choose for his artwork on the Black Hills of South Dakota. We have hundreds, especially if we include the comparatively new kids on the Broadway block: Laura Benanti, Jason Robert Brown, Thomas Kail, Idina Menzel, Lin-Manuel Miranda, Audra McDonald, Donna Murphy, Ashley Park, Susan Stroman, and Jeanine Tesori, among others. Should they be considered?

The Baseball Writers' Association of America provides some guidance. This august body anoints the players that it will grant membership in Baseball's Hall of Fame (which, as any musical theater enthusiast can tell you from its mention on the cast album of *Damn Yankees*, is located in Cooperstown).

The association long ago decreed that a retired player is not immediately eligible for the hall. Five long years must pass before he can be considered. If this rule were not in place, even the hardest-bitten sportswriter could become sentimental after seeing a player weep copiously when announcing his retirement at his final press conference.

We won't be that strict, but we will honor seniority. In the years to come, other mountain ranges can honor some of today's great stars, writers, and stagers if they continue to produce in the worthwhile fashion to which we're becoming accustomed.

In the meantime, in alphabetical order, *Author's Choices:*

Oscar Hammerstein II. In the operetta era, Hammerstein had big hits with *Rose-Marie, The Desert Song,* and *The New Moon.* Then he reinvented the musical with *Show Boat* before going on to further refine it with *Oklahoma!*

What made that achievement extra impressive was that Hammerstein was supposedly all washed up by the time Richard Rodgers was smart enough to seek his talents. Both could have assumed that time had passed him by.

Hammerstein could have retired; he didn't really need the money. But he returned to work, and by the end of 1943, he had not one but two smashes on Broadway: *Oklahoma!* followed by *Carmen Jones* eight months later. Each of which was a far-from-safe commercial choice.

Resiliency was just one of Hammerstein's many all-American qualities. The talent that brought to the books of *Carousel, South Pacific,* and *The King and I* couldn't be denied.

Some say that Hammerstein mocked Blacks. They point to the language he chose for *Carmen Jones:* "Dat's Love," "Dere's a Café on de Corner," and "Dis Flower."

There's an explanation here. Dialects fascinated Hammerstein. Hence "I Cain't Say No" in *Oklahoma!* and "Geraniums in the Winder" in *Carousel,* both sung by white-breads.

A better way of proving just who Oscar Hammerstein was is the song that starts "You've got to be taught to hate and fear." That he wouldn't drop it when many of the era urged him to is better proof still.

Last but hardly least, we wouldn't have Stephen Sondheim without Hammerstein. How lucky for Little Stevie to have Hammerstein as a neighbor and mentor. As Sondheim has said on more than one occasion, "If he'd been a geologist, I would have been a geologist, too."

Geology's loss has been our eternal gain, no small thanks to Oscar Hammerstein II.

Ethel Merman. Did any star so dominate the musical theater scene as the woman chummily known as "The Merm"?

For forty years, Merman starred in an inordinate number of famous vehicles where she introduced, by way of a solo or a duet, many household name hits.

Girl Crazy: "I Got Rhythm." *George White Scandals of 1931*: "Life Is Just a Bowl of Cherries." *Anything Goes*: "I Get a Kick out of You." *Red, Hot and Blue*: "It's Delovely." *DuBarry Was a Lady*: "Friendship." *Annie Get Your Gun*: "I Got the Sun in the Morning." *Call Me Madam*: "You're Just in Love." *Gypsy*: "Everything's Coming up Roses."

No, in *Annie Get Your Gun* she wasn't the first voice heard in "There's No Business Like Show Business," but she did join the song midway. And when you think of this anthem, who pops into your head: Merman or William O'Neal, Marty May, and Ray Middleton, a.k.a. the men who started it.

Merman didn't originate Dolly Levi in *Hello, Dolly!* but she could have, for she was offered it first. Give her credit for coming in and steering it right to the end of its record-breaking Broadway run.

Fans will note that this is only a partial listing of her accomplishments, which further proves that there should be a Merman on the Mount.

Harold Prince. Yes, he won more Tonys as a producer, but here's betting that Prince himself would first and foremost want to be remembered for directing. After all, he abandoned producing but never stopped directing.

Prince, in his 1974 memoir *Contradictions*, stated of his production of *Fiddler*, "I don't think a show will run longer than its 3,242 performances." Little did he know that a dozen years later *The Phantom of the Opera* would begin a run that would last (at least) four times as long. Its director: Harold Prince.

Stephen Sondheim. First, the flashy lyrics: "Someone who in fetching you your slipper will be winsome as a whippoorwill" . . . "Shub's a boob and you belong to me" . . . "Exclusive you, elusive you. Will any person ever get the juice of you?" . . . "Each in her style a Delilah reborn" . . . "And be hopelessly shattered by *Saturd*ay night" . . . "If the tea the Shogun drank will serve to keep the Shogun tranquil" . . . And what about the more than four dozen clever rhymes in "A Little Priest"?

If deft rhymes were the only requirement for Mount Musical, Sondheim would deserve to be carved and commemorated in stone. But his words also carry so much perception and emotion: "Sorry/grateful" . . . "Children can only grow from something you love to something you lose."

And really, for all the talk of the lack of melody, were any of those lyrics ones you didn't hear the melody when you read them?

In *Bounce*, he set "You're still the best thing that ever has happened to me" to a most beautiful melody. Was Sondheim getting sentimental on us? Note the woman's response to equally beautiful music: "Bullshit!"

It's certainly no bullshit that Stephen Sondheim is still the best thing that has ever happened to musical theater.

Let's add one from films: "More" from *Dick Tracy* states "Something is better than nothing, but nothing is better than more," making for two completely different meanings of "nothing" (which is really something).

Now one from television: *The Fabulous Fifties*, a 1960 special, invited Sondheim to submit a song. With Burt Shevelove, he co-wrote "Ten Years Old," which catalogued what had been introduced in that decade. It was set to the melody of "London Bridge (is falling down)."

"Who had heard of Salk Vaccine? Dexadrine? Mr. Clean? Who had heard of Fulton Sheen or *My Fair Lady*?"

What makes it wondrous is that the original "London Bridge" has the words "My fair lady" in the same spot.

And wouldn't you know that the damn fools in charge of the show didn't use it?

FINALLY, WHAT LITTLE THING INVOLVING MUSICALS BOTHERS YOU THE MOST?

Cast shrinkage. Here's a Tale of Two *Little Women*. The 2005 musical version that played in Broadway's 1,228-seat Virginia Theatre had a cast of ten.

A 1964 musical version, named *Jo* for its main character, that played in off-Broadway's 347-seat Orpheum Theatre, had a cast of nineteen.

(And while we're at it, orchestras have shrunk in size, too.)

Mandatory responses. At the start of the second act of *Lysistrata Jones* (2011), Liz Mikel entered and said, "Welcome back, everybody!" Everyone took it as a genuine welcome, but Mikel had more on her mind.

She stared at the crowd and snarled "I *SAID* 'Welcome back, everybody!'" This rebuke to the audience for not loudly acknowledging her resulted in everyone dutifully applauding.

Soon after Mikel started her song, she walked to the lip of the stage, raised her hands high over her head, started clapping in rhythm, and gave us a curt nod of the head—the universal symbol for "Now you must clap in rhythm, too."

In their opening night reviews of *The Music Man*, critics noted that the audience clapped in rhythm midway through "76 Trombones." Fine—but Robert Preston did *not* walk to the lip of the stage, raise his hands high over his head, start clapping in rhythm, and give a curt nod of the head for everyone to obey him.

"My Favorite Things" as a Christmas song. How did this happen? Has anyone ever hoped that under the tree there'd be raindrops on roses, whiskers on kittens, or bright copper kettles? Sure, warm woolen mittens would be welcome on that cold winter night, but brown paper packages tied up with strings only hit the spot if something good is inside them.

An original cast album is not a soundtrack album. Films have soundtracks, for each has a *track* of *sound*. Albums made from Broadway musicals are cast albums—original cast albums, revival cast albums, and studio cast albums—but *not* soundtracks.

"Since the musical opened, it hasn't played to an empty seat." While press agents must let the world know that a show is a sellout hit, they can't say for sure that there hasn't been an *empty* seat. Certainly somewhere in the run, at least one person became too sick (or dead) to attend.

A more accurate description would be "Since the musical opened, it hasn't played to an *unsold* seat." That we'll buy.

"The Tony-winning musical . . ." A show wins in one category that is *not* Best Musical, and yet ads are suddenly trumpeting it as "The Tony-winning musical."

Well, yes, all right, it is, in a manner of speaking. But when the unknowing public sees "The Tony-winning musical," it infers that the show won Best Musical.

Not always . . . and these days, not often.

Author's Choice: The term "critic." If you were given a diamond and wanted to learn whether it was good or bad, valuable or worthless, the person you'd take it to for a judgment is an appraiser.

So why is a person who makes judgments on plays, saying whether they're good or bad, valuable or worthless, called a critic?

Let's change the term *critic* to *appraiser*. It's nicer—and it even includes the word *praise*.

INDEX

Page numbers for photographs are italicized

Washington Post, 137
Waters, Ethel, 291–292, *315*
Watling, Dylis, 196
Watson, Susan, 47–48
Watt, Douglas, 81
Watts, Jr., Richard, 30, 171, 301
Wayne, David, 23, 134
Webb, Jimmy, 138
Webster, Noah, 120
Wechsler, Walter, 204
The Wedding Singer, 154
Weidman, Jerome, 200, 269
Weidman, John, 12, 65
Weill, Kurt, 9, 257, 269
Weinstock, Jack, 18–19
Weissenbach, James, 94–95
Weitzenhoffer, Max, 163
Welch, Raquel, 158
Welcome to the Club, 125
Welles, Orson, 3
Westergaard, Louise, 191
West Side Story (1961 film), 273–274, 297, 304
West Side Story (2021 film), 274–276
West Side Story (stage), 21, 51, 92, 103, 107, 109, 111, 113, 114, 140, 188, 199, 202, 213
What Makes Sammy Run?, 178
What's New, Pussycat?, 75
Wheeler, Hugh, 17, 42, 259
When Pigs Fly, 36
When the Boys Meet the Girls, 217
Where's Charley?, 174, 201
White, Onna, 213

White, Stanford, 13
White, Theodore H., 50
Whitty, Jeff, 60–61, 130
Whoop-De-Doo, 129
Who's Afraid of Virginia Woolf?, 77, 120
The Who's Tommy, 110, 200
Whyte, Jerome, 158
Wicked, 10, 38, 93, 103, 123, 147, 208, 229
Wilbur, Richard, 43
Wilde, Oscar, 62, 111
Wilder, Billy, 12, 285
Wilder, Thornton, 271
Wildflower, 62
Wildhorn, Frank, 209, 264
The Wild Party (LaChiusa), 207
The Wild Party (Lippa), 161
Williams, Andy, 254
Williams, Tennessee, 252
Williams, Vanessa, 268, 282, 288
Willis, Ailee, 208
The Will Rogers Follies, 216
Willson, Meredith, 77, 107, 127–128, 249–250, 255–256, 264
Wilson, Dooley, *315*
Wilson, John C., 187
Wilson, Patrick, 269
Winchell, Walter, 285
Windust, Bretaigne, 187
Winter Garden Theatre, 139, 284
Wish You Were Here, 70, 187, 202
Winninger, Charles, 290